The Movie World of ROGER CORMAN

The Movie World of ROGER CORMAN

J. Philip di Franco
Editor

Karyn G. Browne
Associate Editor

Peter Davis
Designer

1979
CHELSEA HOUSE PUBLISHERS
New York/London

To Jesse, Dylan, Peter, Diane and Joe
—and to all those who dream dreams
and are ready to pay the price
to make them come true.

ACKNOWLEDGMENTS

This book was a labor of love. As a creative venture, it was overwhelming for us to produce. I thank Harold Steinberg for conning me into doing the book and for his inspired vision to dream it up. For her editing of the manuscript and constant support I thank Karyn G. Browne and wish her best of luck with her new Leo baby. I thank Susan Lusk for her dynamite creativity as managing editor and for lending me her understanding ear over creative problems. For tunneling through the mountain of material and artwork and for his super design, I thank Peter Davis. My thanks also to Grace Corso and Anita Hildenbrand for their careful typing of the manuscript. For their superhuman ability to hear and transcribe almost inaudible tapes, I thank everyone at National Secretarial Service in Los Angeles, especially Cathy and Lloyd. For being so helpful at New World Pictures, I thank Caren Singer, Mary Ann Fisher, Frances Kimbrough and Gail Hurd-McGrath. Special thanks to my dear lady Anne Dyer for her friendship and help when needed most. To Elaine Church, special thanks . . .
The first shall be last: My love and thanks to Diane Belmonte, without whose support, love, friendship and amazing creative talent this book would not have been possible. To Peter Meyer, my deepest gratitude for his being with me at the bottom-line at all times. Super-special thanks to Roger Corman for being him, for accomplishing what he did and for helping me so much with this book.

J. Philip di Franco

Managing Editor, Art Direction:
Susan Lusk

Assistant Editor:
Joy Johannessen

Library of Congress Cataloging in Publication Data

Di Franco, J. Philip.
The movie world of Roger Corman.

Filmography: p.236
1. Corman, Roger, 1926- I. Corman, Roger,
1926- II. Browne, Karyn G. III. Title.
PN1998.A3C7864 791.43'0233'0924 [B] 78-56948
ISBN 0-87754-050-0

CHELSEA HOUSE PUBLISHERS
Harold Steinberg, Chairman and Publisher
Andrew E. Norman, President
Susan Lusk, Vice President

A Division of Chelsea House Educational Communications, Inc.
70 West 40th Street, New York, N.Y. 10018

CONTENTS

The meaning of anything is just other words for the same thing.
— CHARLIE CHAPLIN in *Limelight*

If you were to run all Roger's movies back to back, you'd understand the man. If you could take all zillion of them . . . you'd start seeing something that's right there, really right in front of you.
— TALIA SHIRE

From the commercial standpoint, producing is running the show. From the artistic standpoint, it depends upon the particular picture. Sometimes it's the director, the writer, or an actor, and sometimes the producer. The producer's original creative vision is the thing that starts everything rolling. And so, on that basis, his creativity is the cornerstone of the entire edifice.
— ROGER CORMAN

PREFACE

A book on Roger Corman? Impossible. Just impossible! Roger Corman is impossible—he's on the run, he's in, he's out, he's in the air, everywhere, making movies. He'd never sit still to do a book. ("A book on me? Why? Sure, go ahead, it's okay. Why not? If you think so, it's all right with me.") His films are impossible—he's made so many, he's produced so many, he's distributed so many. ("Just how many, Roger?" "Oh, I don't know, maybe a hundred fifty or so.") The many Roger Corman "alumni"—Bogdanovich, Scorsese, Coppola, et. al. —are impossible to reach, to talk to. Material on the films? Impossible. There couldn't be anything anywhere—all thrown away. Roger doesn't save anything!

I went ahead anyway. Producing this book had to be like making a Roger Corman movie—at once fast, furious, delightful, grueling, intoxicating, full of commitment, overwhelming. Tight production deadlines, tight budgets—just impossible. But the book is done.

Before proceeding, let us establish some working **definitions.**

PARADOX: a person with seemingly contradictory qualities.
ENIGMA: an inscrutable or mysterious person.
PHENOMENON: an exceptional, unusual or abnormal person.
ROGER CORMAN: paradox, enigma, phenomenon.

Roger Corman is generous, cheap, liberal, conservative, charming, perverse, respectable, iconoclastic, engaging, standoffish, radical, bourgeois, honest, deceptive, an artistic genius, a brilliant businessman, all of these, none of these, all at the same time. Not an ordinary man.

Now, you may be saying to yourself that this is just impossible. If so, you are getting the idea of the book. You're catching on.

When Chelsea House asked me to produce this book, I was intrigued with the Roger Corman who is a legend in his own time, one of Hollywood's most interesting and dynamic personalities. I was also impressed by his staggering credits as a director and producer, by his amazing success with New World Pictures, by the unbelievable roster of Corman protégés, by the mystique of Corman as "The Patron Saint of Young Filmmakers," and when I met him, by Roger Corman the person. Roger had always existed for me as some vague notion of a director who helped young filmmakers get a start. I've never understood why I didn't go to him myself in connection with my own career—until I met him to do this book. I knew then that my destiny with Roger Corman was of a different, more interesting and rewarding nature.

Thus inspired, I began my research into Roger Corman's career, which spans about twenty-five years and encompasses about one hundred sixty-five films.

I think Roger could be, if he really wanted, a really great director — if he had the patience.

— SAM ARKOFF

Roger has no patience, and that is his great strength.

— ROBERT TOWNE

The actual film is never as good as the film I have in my mind. In my mind the visions are always beautiful . . . actors are always beautiful . . . sets are great . . . music is the best.

— ROGER CORMAN

We live in a compromised society, and I would think of myself as something of a compromised artist.

— ROGER CORMAN

After months and months of tortuous digging and delving, we came up with a huge mountain of fabulous material—photos, posters, press books, one-sheets, and much more. This was when I knew we had a monster on our hands. Now our concern would be what to exclude. Roger Corman is prolific indeed. Then came months of interviews with Roger, with his family and friends, the people who worked for and with him—all of whom responded enthusiastically with strong feelings of affection, admiration, and respect for this man. They also presented us with exasperating contradictions and beguiling inconsistencies—and many of them were completely aware of this. Somehow the more I found out about the phenomenon of Roger, the less I understood; the more I got to know him, the deeper the paradox grew; and the more information I collected, the more perplexing the enigma became.

Roger Corman as a phenomenon represents more than just a great success, and perhaps in some ways, especially to Roger himself, he is not such a great success. He makes money like crazy, and he makes movies he likes to make. He is into everything, and everything he's into makes money. Is Roger fulfilled? Only he can answer. While this book was in progress, Roger was offered the presidency of a major studio. Although he was, I think, intrigued and flattered, as if he had won some kind of victory, he made the conditions of the contract impossible for the studio to accept. He really didn't want the job, and being able to turn it down on his terms was another kind of victory.

Yet Roger remains a paradox. His career is a paradigm of the tug-of-war between art and money in the picture business, and this constant collision of forces runs through all his work. It is fascinating to speculate about what would have happened if Roger had been guided solely by "artistic considerations" rather than allowing "financial considerations" to dominate, as was evidently the case. What if *The Intruder had* been a box-office success? What kinds of movies would we have had from this potentially great director? Then again, what would Roger have become? Would he have made all his other great contributions to the world of film?

Roger has done films in almost every conceivable genre: western, gangster, horror, science-fiction, motorcycle, drama, comedy, black, nurse-teacher-stewardess, women-in-prison, and sex-role reversal. *But* he has not made that one really great movie everyone wants him to make, the one without budget restrictions, without tight production deadlines, and without pressure of any kind—except *artistic*—the one that Roger himself wants to do out of a compelling creative drive to say something.

Still, Roger's achievements are undeniable, and what is amazing is that he did all this in a system that by its very nature stands almost in contradiction to his world. Roger takes risks when everyone else plays it safe; Roger is original when everyone else copies; Roger is straightforward and definite in the Hollywood land of "maybe"; Roger keeps his word in a world of made-to-be-broken contracts, and Roger is real in the world of make-believe. He has not only survived the system, he has beaten it—on his own terms, apparently. There is bitter irony in the fact that three top directors who have gone on to great success and who got their first big boosts by working with Roger (Bogdanovich, Scorsese, and Coppola) have all expressed a desire to return to the way they made movies with him. The excitement, the need for invention, the tight budgets, the free spirit—all are gone up there on the multimillion-dollar pictures.

To a great extent, Roger Corman's career in filmmaking in the 1950s and 1960s represents a bygone era. Hollywood is different today —dominated by the powerful attraction of big television money, overrun by agents and "packagers," and ruled not really by movie people but by corporate executives. Independent movie producers are the last heroes who really care about *making movies* and not about statistical profit projections. Yes, they care about money, but they also care about the actual craft of filmmaking. They are struggling desperately to survive in this age of computerized corporate decisions. The world of filmmaking is different now—for most people—but Roger Corman is still making movies with great success.

The idea behind this book has been to present The Movie World of Roger Corman, to present the movies he directed, produced, and distributed, to present a multifaceted view of Roger through the eyes of his associates, family, and friends, to present Roger Corman the creative artist, the consummate businessman, and the person—for everyone to experience and enjoy. Of course, this is merely a glimpse, for it is impossible to get it all in.

It is for you to decide about the paradox, the enigma, the phenomenon of Roger Corman as you discover his world. Draw your own conclusions based upon your perceptions. Read the book and see all his movies, and maybe then you'll understand certain things about him. Maybe then you'll start seeing something that's right there, really right in front of you.

As for Roger Corman, right now, at this very moment—he is making a movie, he is keeping his eye out for a great art film to distribute, he is watching for a new business to try out, he is putting deals together, he is guiding a writer through a script, he is hiring a hot young filmmaker, he is editing the rushes of a new release, he is figuring out the profit pattern of his restaurant venture, he is playing with his three kids, and he is loving his wife, Julie. Roger Corman is enjoying his world, and welcome to it.

J. Philip di Franco,
Hollywood, September 1978

Roger is a very enchanting tyrant. Instead of using swords or poison to obtain what he wants, he uses a very peculiar smile.

— RAF VALLONE

Paul Bartel told me once that he watched Roger's eyes turn from blue to black and back to blue again. Somehow I can believe that, ya' know, because there is something supernatural about Roger.

— DAVID CARRADINE

When I took LSD before The Trip, *one of the ideas I had was that if I were to lie flat on the ground and form the image of a film or any other art form in my mind, the image would go from my body to the earth; anybody who wanted to view the film would only have to touch the earth, and the image would come to them.*

— ROGER CORMAN

STARRING
SUSAN CABOT · FRED EISLEY · BARBOURA MORRIS
Produced and Directed by ROGER CORMAN · Written by LEO GORDON

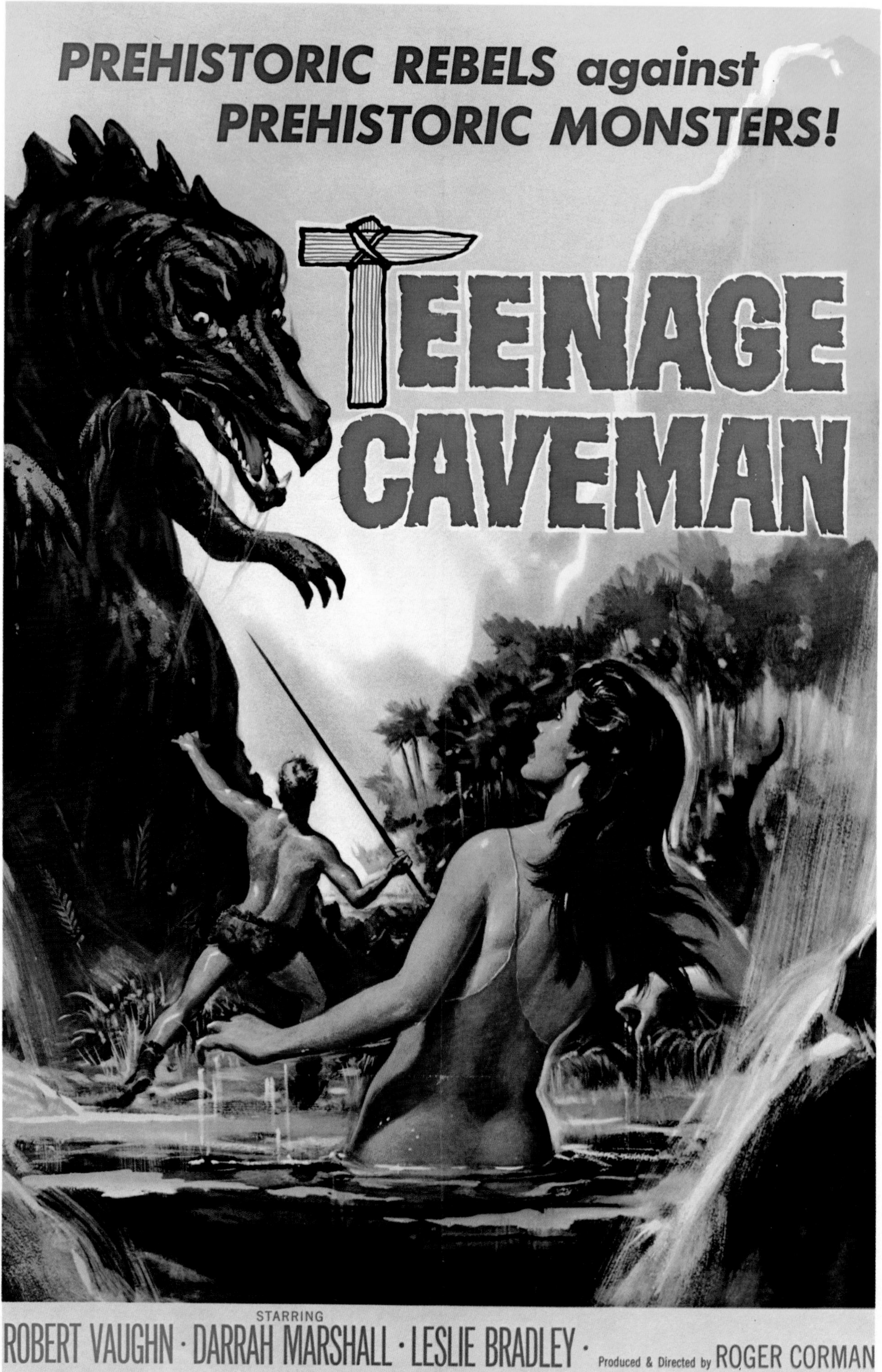
PREHISTORIC REBELS against
PREHISTORIC MONSTERS!
TEENAGE
CAVEMAN
STARRING
ROBERT VAUGHN · DARRAH MARSHALL · LESLIE BRADLEY ·
Produced & Directed by ROGER CORMAN
Screenplay by R. WRIGHT CAMPBELL · A JAMES H. NICHOLSON and SAMUEL Z. ARKOFF Production · An AMERICAN-INTERNATIONAL Picture

TEMPTATION
and TERROR...
in a savage land
of wild desire!
RICHARD DENNING
in
THUNDER OVER HAWAII
(FORMERLY...NAKED PARADISE)
co-starring
BEVERLY GARLAND • LISA MONTELL • LESLIE BRADLEY with Dick Miller • Jonathan Haze
Produced and Directed by ROGER CORMAN • Executive Producer JAMES H. NICHOLSON • Screenplay by CHARLES B. GRIFFITH and MARK HANNA • A Sunset Production • AN AMERICAN-INTERNATIONAL ENCORE HIT
WIDE VISION COLOR

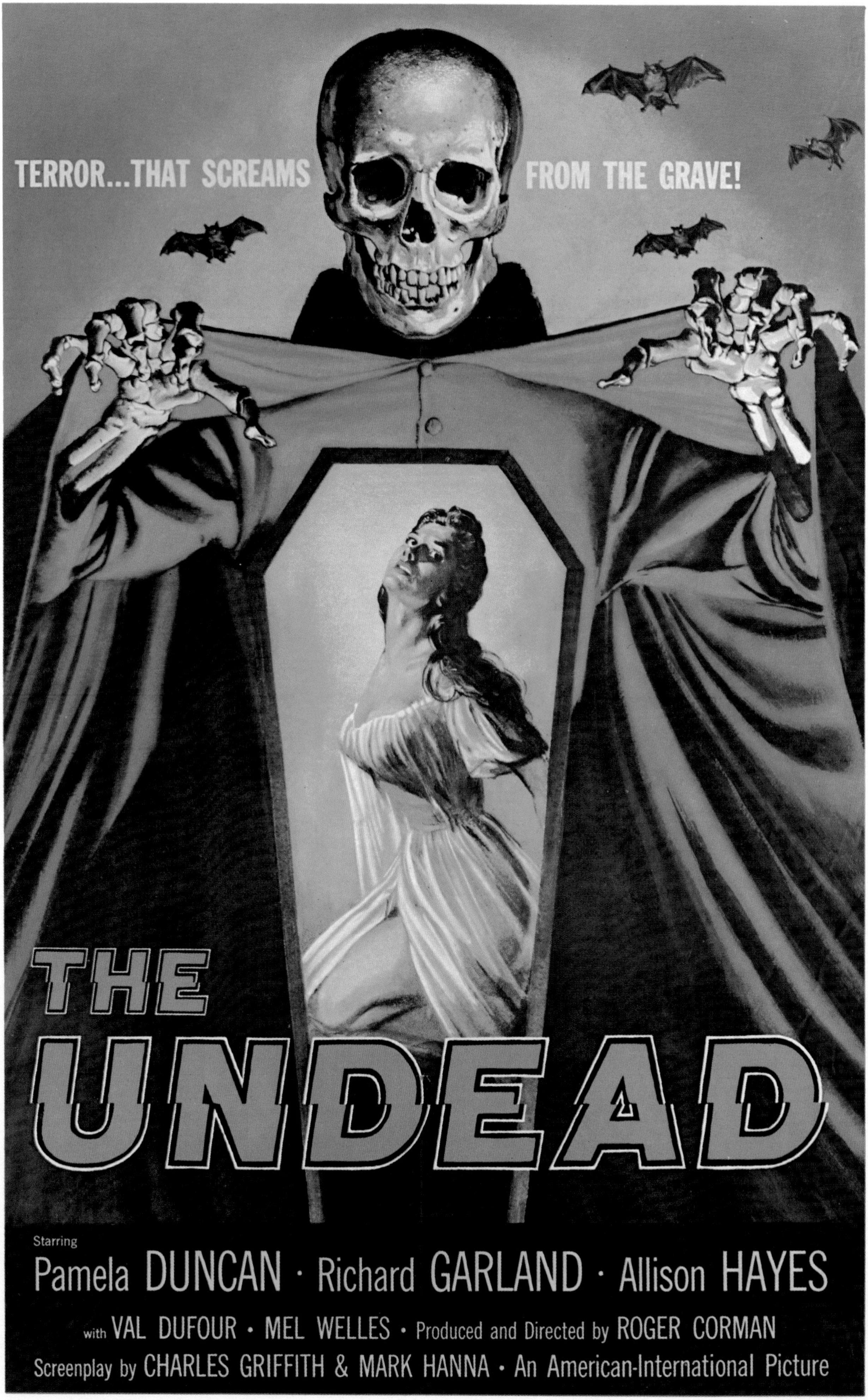
TERROR...THAT SCREAMS
FROM THE GRAVE!
THE
UNDEAD
Starring
Pamela DUNCAN · Richard GARLAND · Allison HAYES
with VAL DUFOUR · MEL WELLES · Produced and Directed by ROGER CORMAN
Screenplay by CHARLES GRIFFITH & MARK HANNA · An American-International Picture

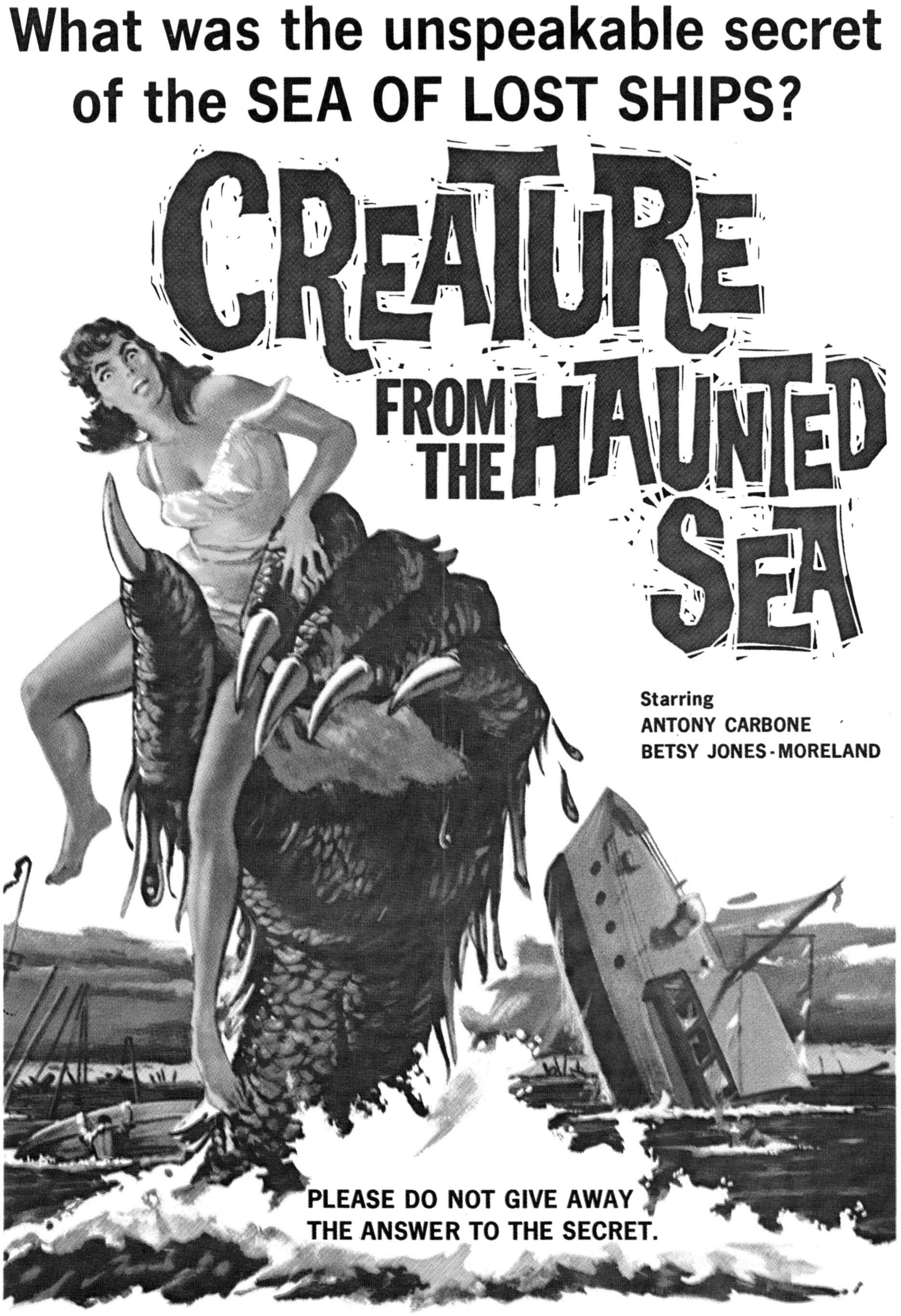
What was the unspeakable secret
of the SEA OF LOST SHIPS?
CREATURE
FROM THE HAUNTED
SEA
Starring
ANTONY CARBONE
BETSY JONES-MORELAND
PLEASE DO NOT GIVE AWAY
THE ANSWER TO THE SECRET.
Produced and Directed by
ROGER CORMAN
A FILMGROUP
PRESENTATION

"Evil things,
in robes
of sorrow,
assailed the
monarch's
high estate."
—POE
What was the terrifying thing in the PIT that wanted women?
AMERICAN INTERNATIONAL presents
EDGAR ALLAN POE'S
THE Haunted PALACE
in PATHECOLOR AND PANAVISION
STARRING
VINCENT PRICE · DEBRA PAGET · LON CHANEY
Produced and Directed by ROGER CORMAN · Screenplay by CHARLES BEAUMONT
Executive Producers: JAMES H. NICHOLSON and SAMUEL Z. ARKOFF · AN AMERICAN INTERNATIONAL PICTURE

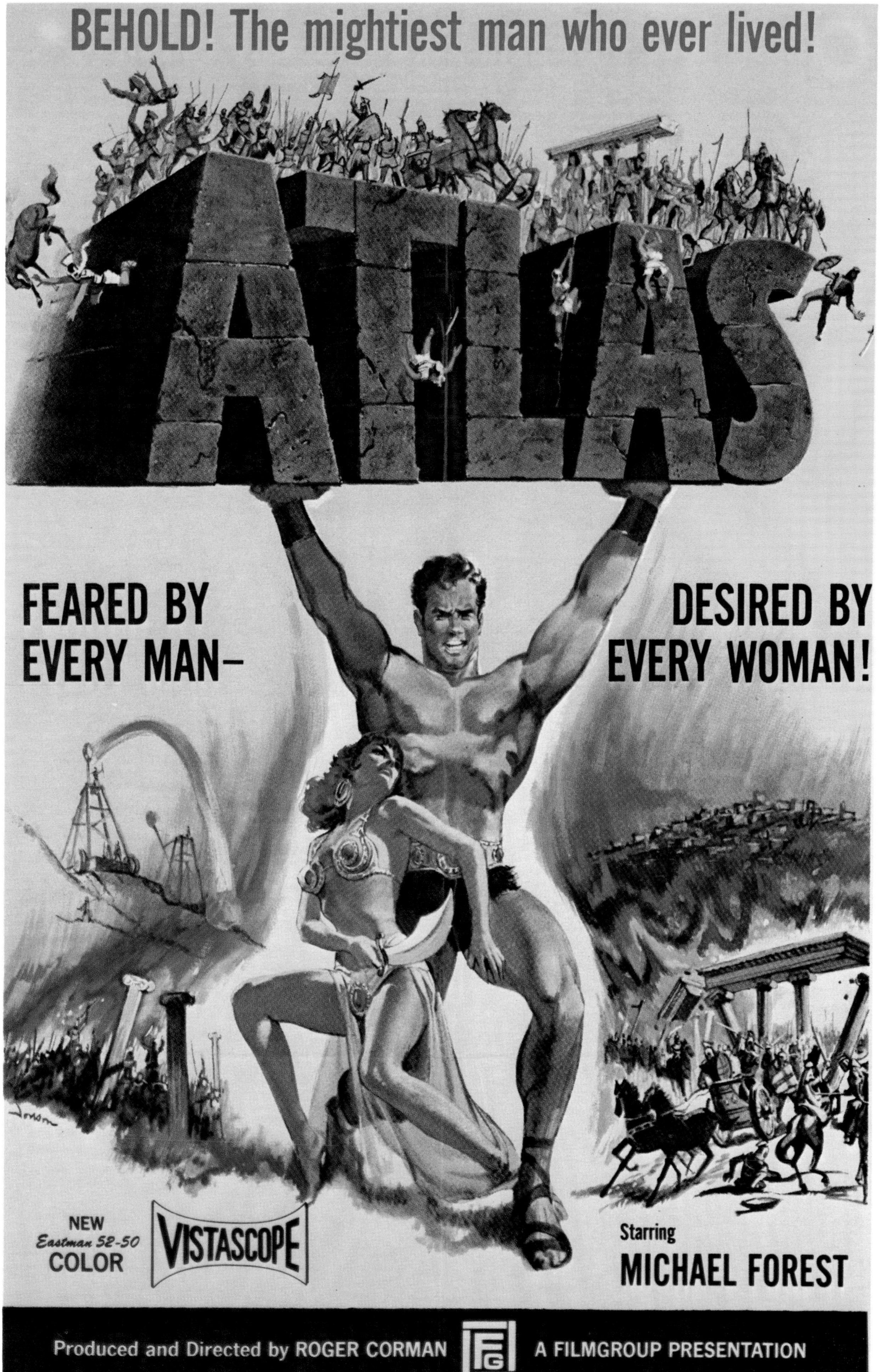
BEHOLD! The mightiest man who ever lived!
ATLAS
FEARED BY EVERY MAN–
DESIRED BY EVERY WOMAN!
NEW Eastman 52-50 COLOR
VISTASCOPE
Starring
MICHAEL FOREST
Produced and Directed by ROGER CORMAN
A FILMGROUP PRESENTATION

YESTERDAY a Teenage Rebel...
TODAY a mad-dog slayer!
CRY BABY KiLLER
HEAR Dick Kallman sing "CRY, BABY CRY"
Starring
HARRY LAUTER · JACK NICHOLSON · CAROLYN MITCHELL
Executive Producer ROGER CORMAN · Produced by DAVID KRAMARSKY and DAVID MARCH
Directed by JUS ADDISS · Screenplay by LEO GORDON and MELVIN LEVY · An ALLIED ARTISTS Picture

SOMEWHERE
IN
THIS
WORLD
STALKS
A
THING
THAT
IS...
NOT OF THIS EARTH
Starring
Paul BIRCH · Beverly GARLAND · Morgan JONES
A ROGER CORMAN PRODUCTION · Screenplay by CHARLES B. GRIFFITH and MARK HANNA
Produced and Directed by ROGER CORMAN · An ALLIED ARTISTS PICTURE

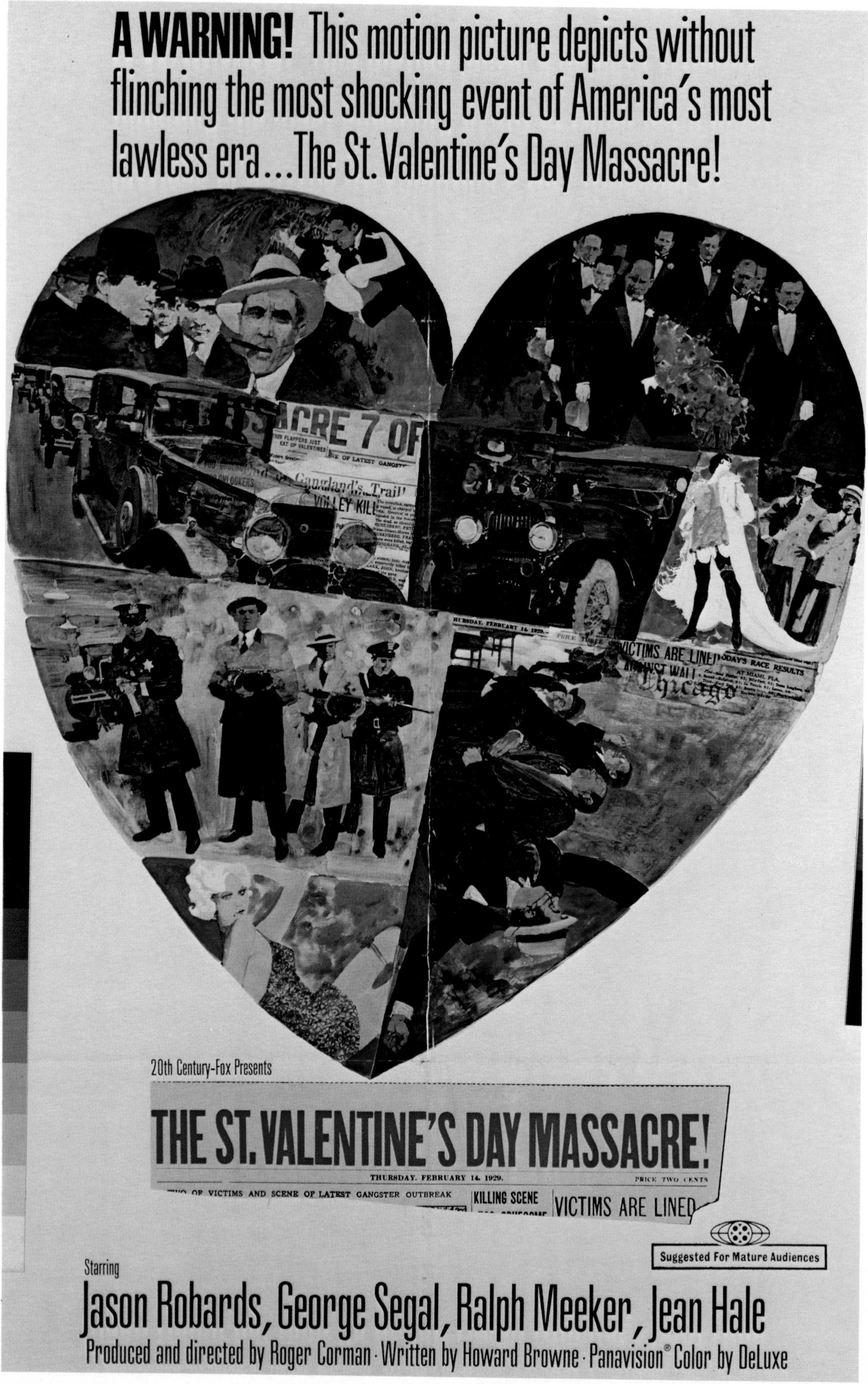
A WARNING! This motion picture depicts without flinching the most shocking event of America's most lawless era...The St. Valentine's Day Massacre!
20th Century-Fox Presents
THE ST. VALENTINE'S DAY MASSACRE!
THURSDAY, FEBRUARY 14, 1929.
PRICE TWO CENTS
KILLING SCENE
VICTIMS ARE LINED
Suggested For Mature Audiences
Starring
Jason Robards, George Segal, Ralph Meeker, Jean Hale
Produced and directed by Roger Corman · Written by Howard Browne · Panavision® Color by DeLuxe

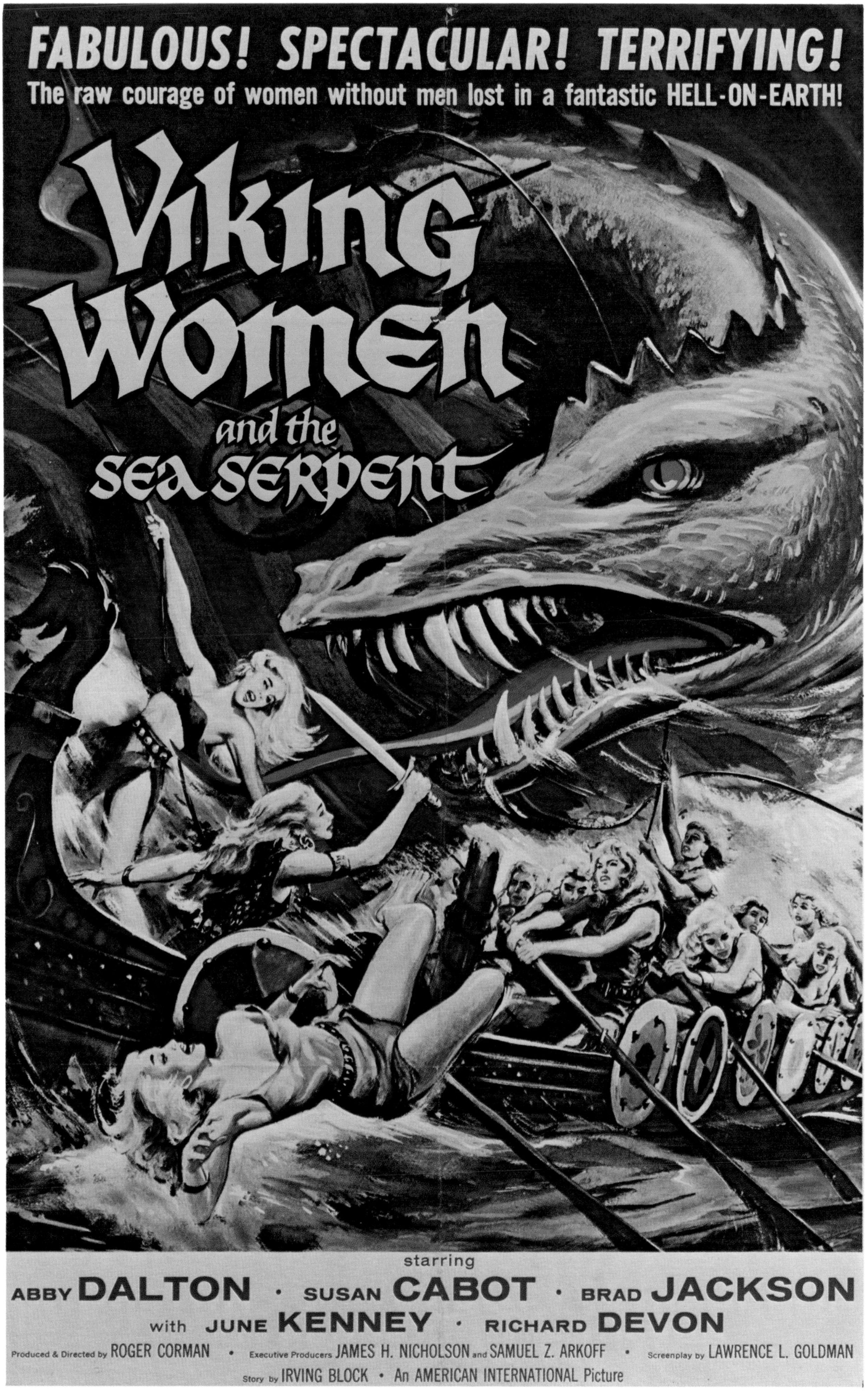
FABULOUS! SPECTACULAR! TERRIFYING!
The raw courage of women without men lost in a fantastic HELL-ON-EARTH!
Viking Women
and the
SEA SERPENT
starring
ABBY DALTON · SUSAN CABOT · BRAD JACKSON
with JUNE KENNEY · RICHARD DEVON
Produced & Directed by ROGER CORMAN · Executive Producers JAMES H. NICHOLSON and SAMUEL Z. ARKOFF · Screenplay by LAWRENCE L. GOLDMAN
Story by IRVING BLOCK · An AMERICAN INTERNATIONAL Picture

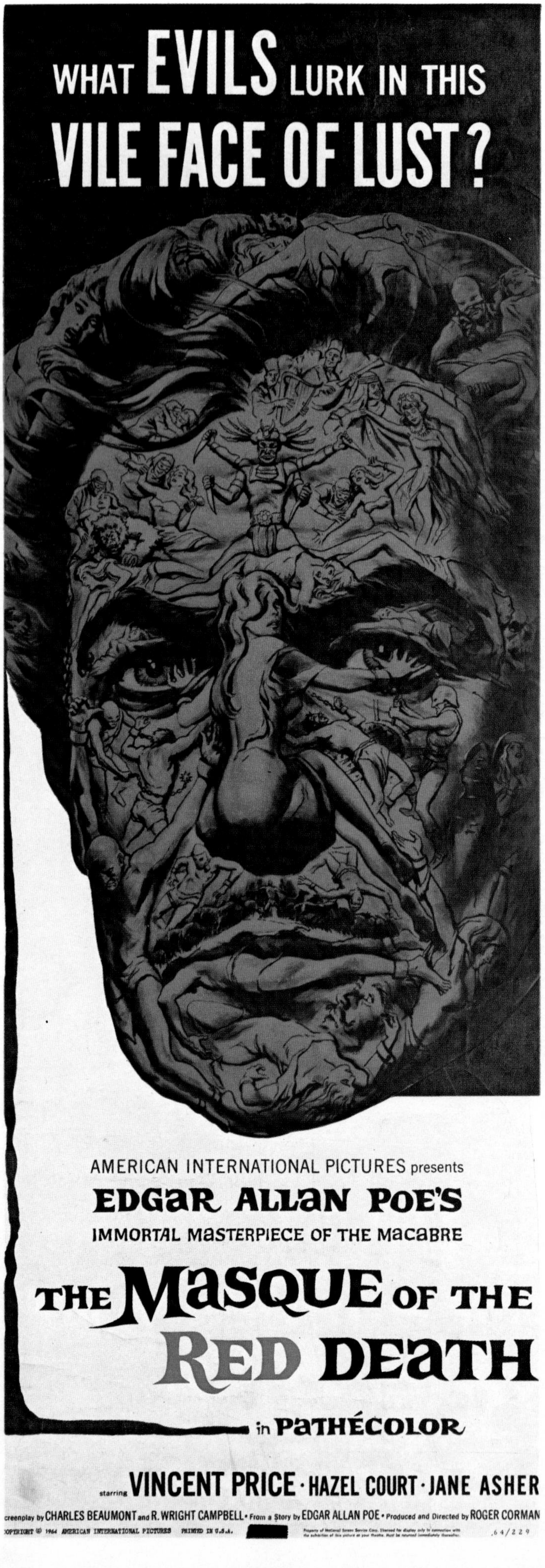
WHAT EVILS LURK IN THIS
VILE FACE OF LUST?
AMERICAN INTERNATIONAL PICTURES presents
EDGAR ALLAN POE'S
IMMORTAL MASTERPIECE OF THE MACABRE
THE MASQUE OF THE
RED DEATH
in PATHÉCOLOR
starring VINCENT PRICE · HAZEL COURT · JANE ASHER
creenplay by CHARLES BEAUMONT and R. WRIGHT CAMPBELL · From a Story by EDGAR ALLAN POE · Produced and Directed by ROGER CORMAN
OPYRIGHT © 1964 AMERICAN INTERNATIONAL PICTURES PRINTED IN U.S.A. [redacted]
64/229

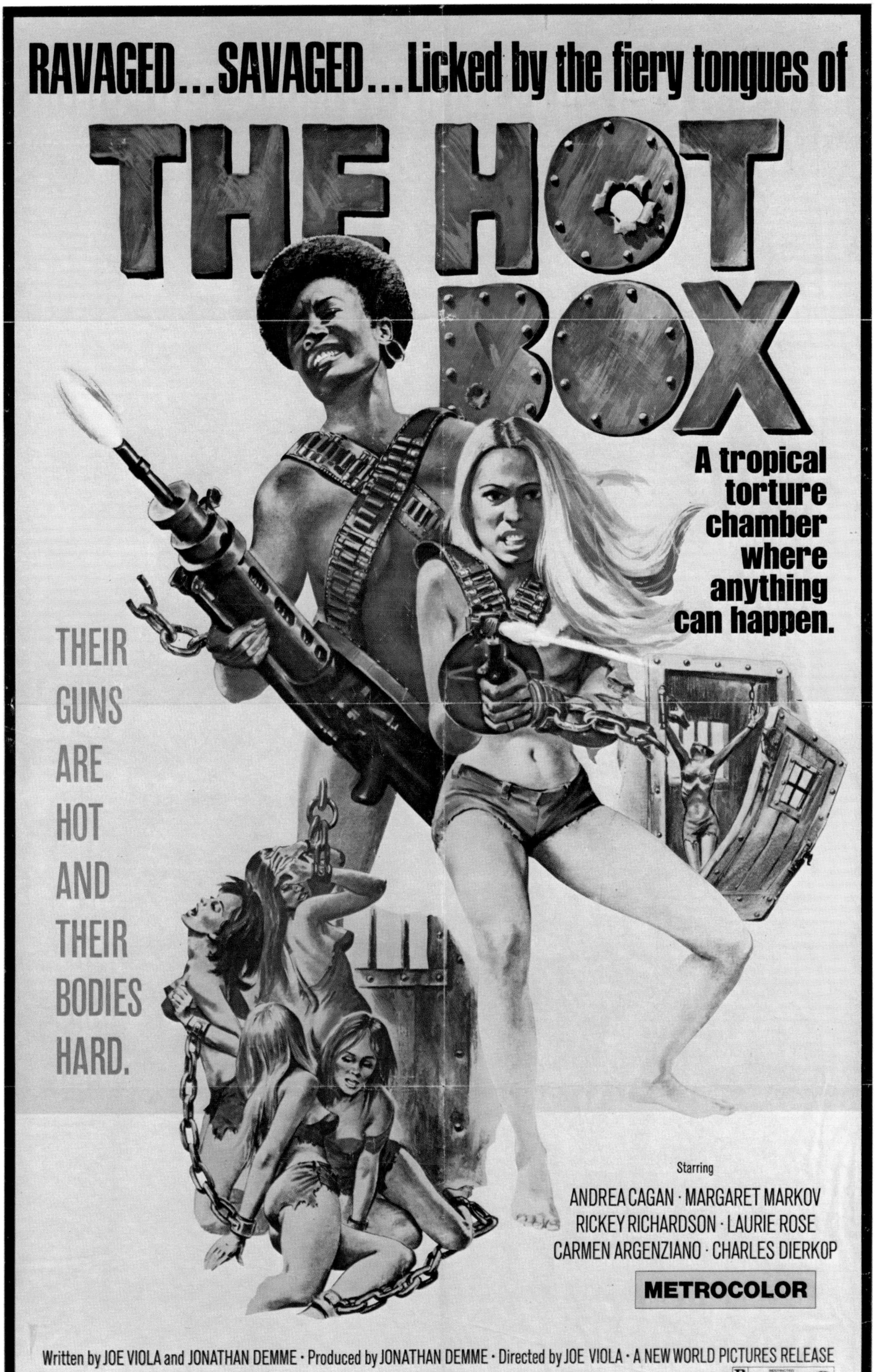
RAVAGED... SAVAGED... Licked by the fiery tongues of
THE HOT BOX
A tropical torture chamber where anything can happen.
THEIR GUNS ARE HOT AND THEIR BODIES HARD.
Starring
ANDREA CAGAN · MARGARET MARKOV
RICKEY RICHARDSON · LAURIE ROSE
CARMEN ARGENZIANO · CHARLES DIERKOP
METROCOLOR
Written by JOE VIOLA and JONATHAN DEMME · Produced by JONATHAN DEMME · Directed by JOE VIOLA · A NEW WORLD PICTURES RELEASE
R

ONLY THE MONSTER SHE MADE COULD SATISFY HER STRANGE DESIRES!
Lady FRANKENSTEIN
R
Starring JOSEPH COTTEN · SARAH BAY · Mickey Hargitay · Paul Muller
Produced by Harry Cushing · Directed by Mel Wells · METROCOLOR A New World Pictures Release

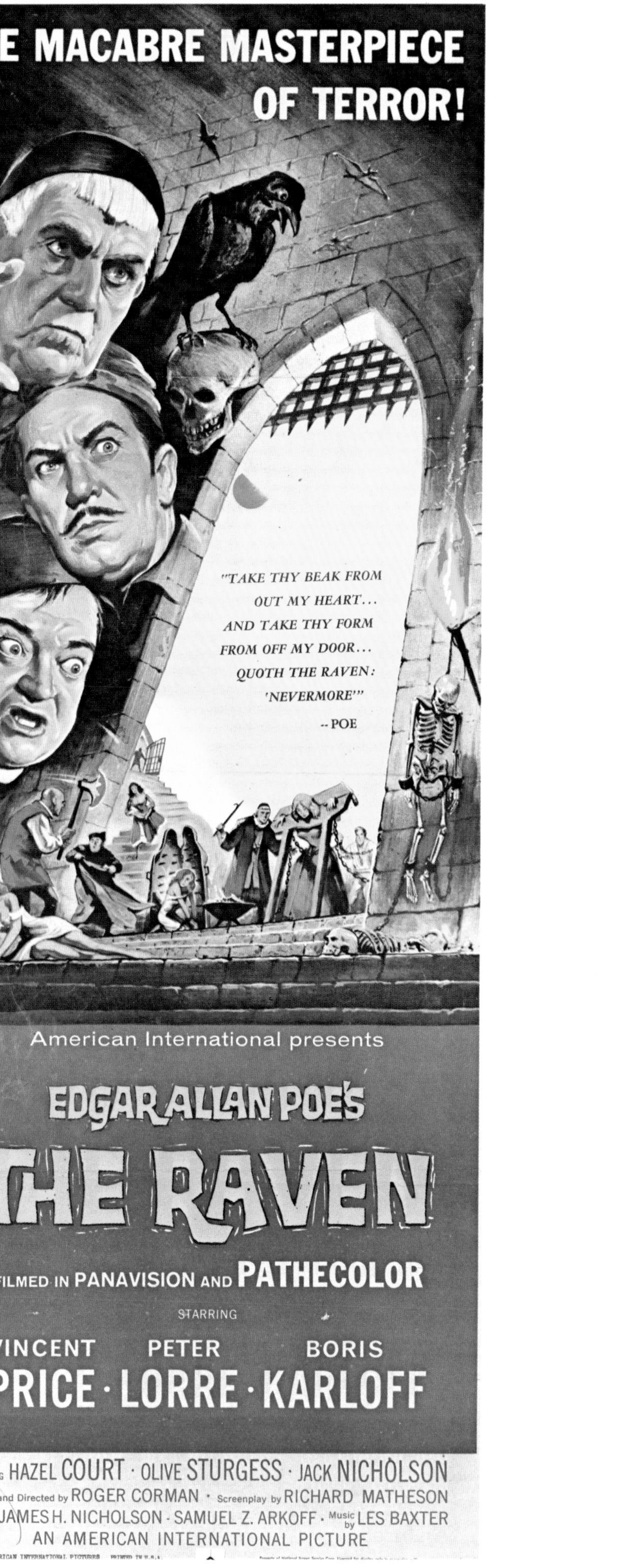
THE MACABRE MASTERPIECE OF TERROR!
"TAKE THY BEAK FROM OUT MY HEART... AND TAKE THY FORM FROM OFF MY DOOR... QUOTH THE RAVEN: 'NEVERMORE'"
--POE
American International presents
EDGAR ALLAN POE'S
THE RAVEN
FILMED IN PANAVISION AND PATHECOLOR
STARRING
VINCENT PRICE · PETER LORRE · BORIS KARLOFF
CO-STARRING HAZEL COURT · OLIVE STURGESS · JACK NICHOLSON
Produced and Directed by ROGER CORMAN · Screenplay by RICHARD MATHESON
Executive Producers JAMES H. NICHOLSON · SAMUEL Z. ARKOFF · Music by LES BAXTER
AN AMERICAN INTERNATIONAL PICTURE

A few years ago in Dunwich
a half-witted girl bore illegitimate twins.
One of them was almost human!
The Dunwich Horror
H. P. LOVECRAFT'S CLASSIC TALE OF TERROR AND THE SUPERNATURAL!
M Suggested for MATURE audiences (parental discretion advised)
COLOR by MOVIELAB
STARRING
SANDRA DEE · DEAN STOCKWELL · ED BEGLEY · LLOYD BOCHNER
CO-STARRING DONNA BACCALA AND JOANNA MOORE JORDAN
SAM JAFFE
PRODUCED BY JAMES H. NICHOLSON and SAMUEL Z. ARKOFF · SCREENPLAY BY CURTIS LEE HANSON, HENRY ROSENBAUM & RONALD SILKOSKY
EXECUTIVE PRODUCER ROGER CORMAN · DIRECTED BY DANIEL HALLER · Based on a story by H. P. LOVECRAFT · AN AMERICAN INTERNATIONAL PICTURE
0 American International Pictures, Inc.
70

SPINE SHATTERING BONE BLASTING
SHE'S A ONE MAMA MASSACRE SQUAD!
TNT
JEANNE BELL WINNER OF THE EBONY FIST AWARD!
METROCOLOR
TNT Jackson
SHE'LL PUT YOU IN TRACTION.
R RESTRICTED Under 17 requires accompanying Parent or Adult Guardian
Jeanne BELL as TNT • Stan SHAW • Pat ANDERSON
WRITTEN BY DICK MILLER and KEN METCALF
PRODUCED AND DIRECTED BY CIRIO H. SANTIAGO
A NEW WORLD PICTURES RELEASE

SHE'S A VERY PRIVATE DETECTIVE!
STACEY ALWAYS SCORES!
TAKE A RIDE ON THE WILD SIDE WITH STACEY. SHE'S FAST!
STACEY!
66
METROCOLOR
R RESTRICTED
starring
ANNE RANDALL • MARJORIE BENNETT • ANITRA FORD • ALAN LANDERS
Screenplay by WILLIAM EDGAR • Produced by LEON MIRELL • Directed by ANDY SIDARIS
PENN-PACIFIC CORP. Presents A film by THE SIDARIS COMPANY • A NEW WORLD PICTURES RELEASE

THEY LIVE HARD...THEY LOVE HARD...
"ANGELS DIE
HARD!"
IN COLOR
CHOPPER OUTLAWS!.. riding their hot throbbing machines to a brutal climax of violence!
THEIR BATTLE CRY- "KILL THE PIGS!"
STARRING
TOM BAKER · WILLIAM SMITH
R

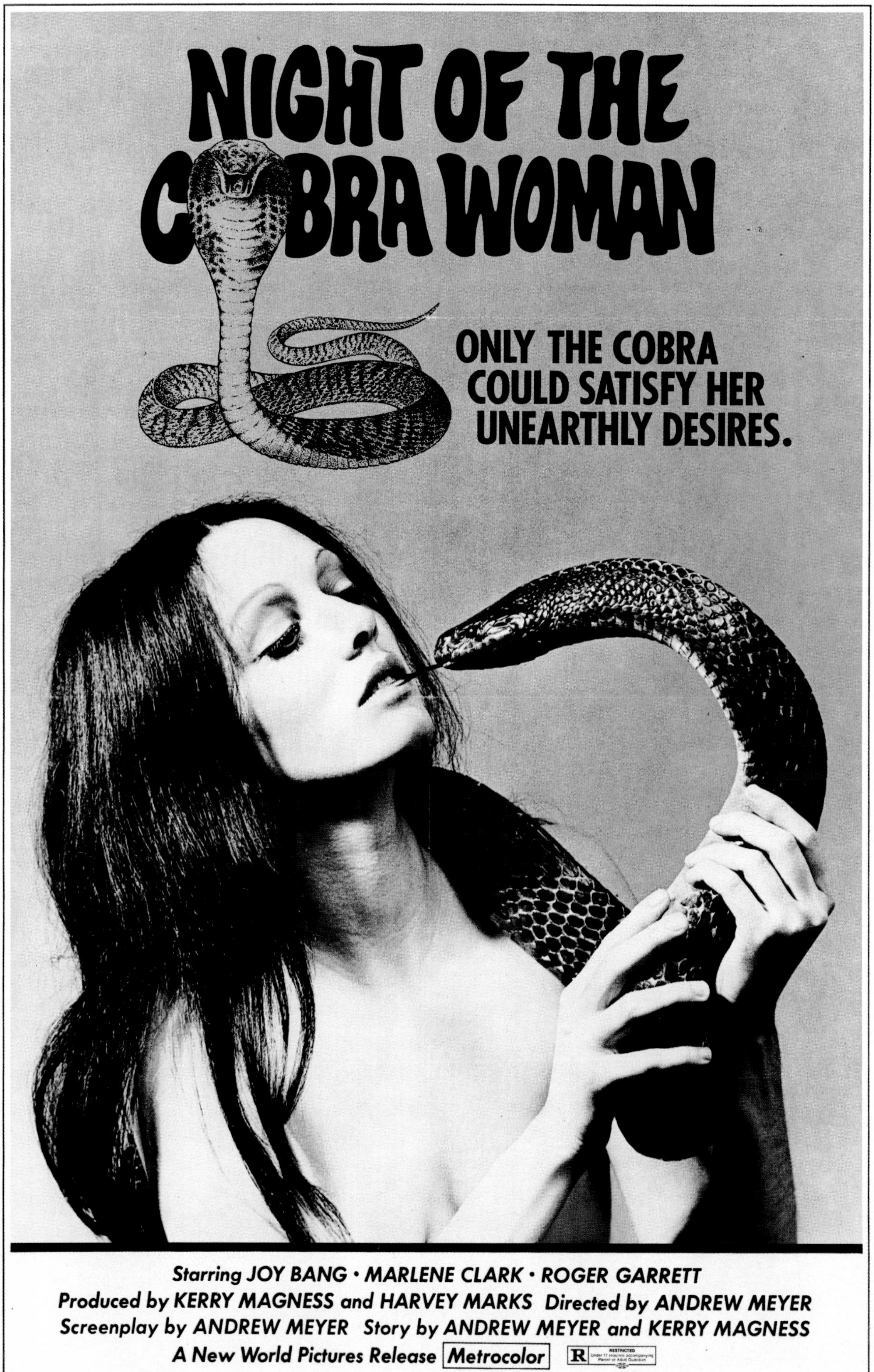
NIGHT OF THE COBRA WOMAN
ONLY THE COBRA COULD SATISFY HER UNEARTHLY DESIRES.
Starring JOY BANG • MARLENE CLARK • ROGER GARRETT
Produced by KERRY MAGNESS and HARVEY MARKS Directed by ANDREW MEYER
Screenplay by ANDREW MEYER Story by ANDREW MEYER and KERRY MAGNESS
A New World Pictures Release
Metrocolor
R

YOU GOTTA' BELIEVE... YOU GOTTA' HAVE FAITH...
BUT FIRST, YOU GOTTA' GET RID OF THE WITNESSES!
JAMES H. NICHOLSON AND SAMUEL Z. ARKOFF PRESENT
SHELLEY WINTERS
AS
"BLOODY MAMA"
STARRING
PAT HINGLE · DON STROUD · DIANE VARSI
CO-STARRING
BRUCE DERN · CLINT KIMBROUGH · ROBERT DeNIRO · ROBERT WALDEN
R RESTRICTED
PRODUCED & DIRECTED BY ROGER CORMAN EXECUTIVE PRODUCERS SAMUEL Z. ARKOFF & JAMES H. NICHOLSON CO-PRODUCER NORMAN T. HERMAN
SCREENPLAY BY ROBERT THOM STORY BY ROBERT THOM AND DON PETERS COLOR BY MOVIELAB AN AMERICAN INTERNATIONAL PICTURE
Original Sound Track Album available on AMERICAN INTERNATIONAL RECORDS

RON HOWARD
pops the clutch and tells the world
EAT MY DUST!
The wildest car chase ever filmed -
see cars, boats, buildings destroyed!
A Very Funny Car
PG PARENTAL GUIDANCE SUGGESTED
Some material may not be suitable for pre-teenagers
CHRISTOPHER NORRIS · WARREN KEMMERLING · DAVE MADDEN
JESSICA POTTER · CHARLES HOWERTON · KATHY O'DARE
WRITTEN AND DIRECTED BY
CHARLES GRIFFITH
PRODUCED BY
ROGER CORMAN
MUSIC BY
DAVID GRISMAN
A NEW WORLD PICTURE
PRODUCTION SERVICES BY TBC PRODUCTIONS—I
METROCOLOR
RIGHT ©1976 NEW WORLD PICTURES, INC.

"EAT MY

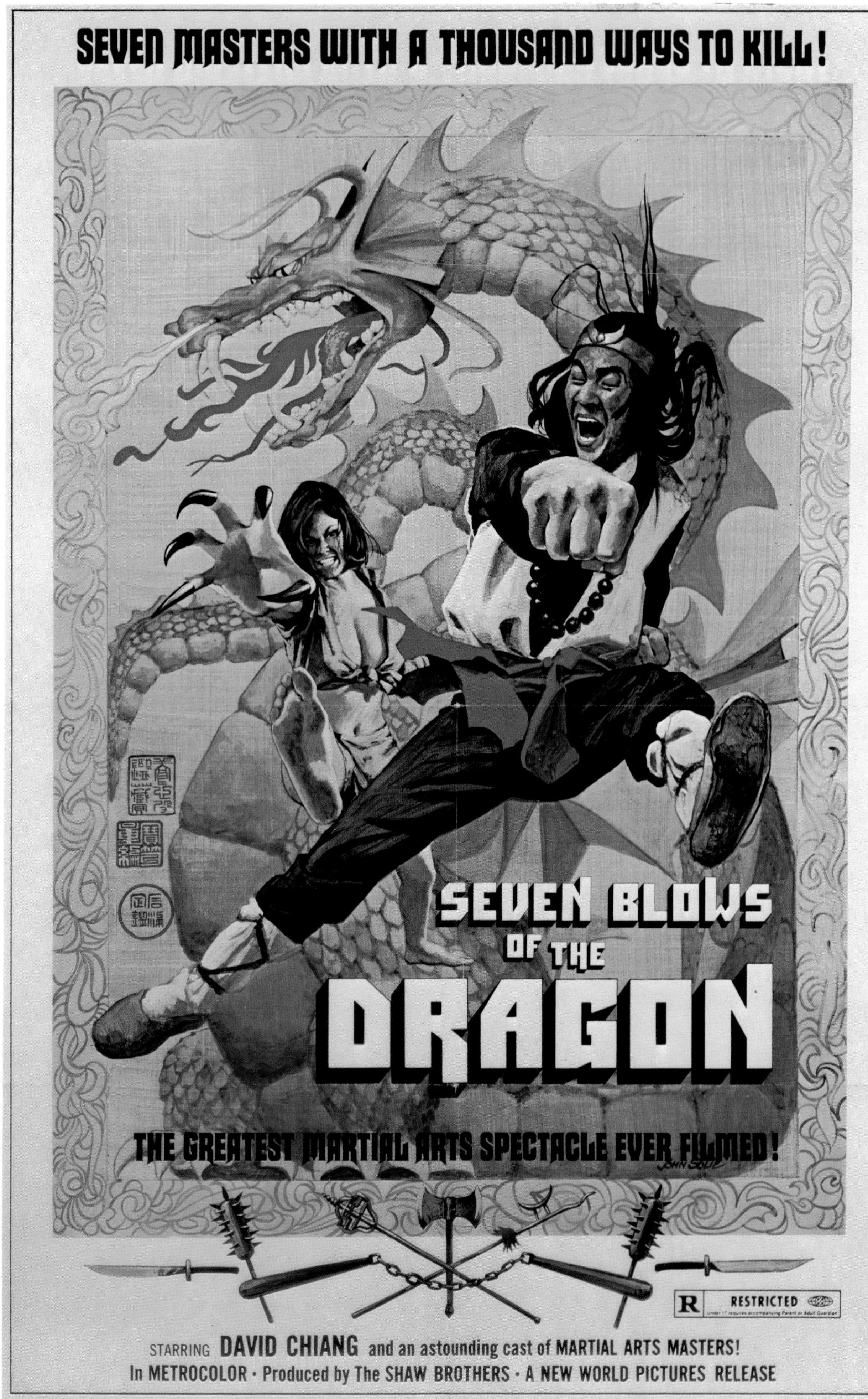
SEVEN MASTERS WITH A THOUSAND WAYS TO KILL!
SEVEN BLOWS OF THE DRAGON
THE GREATEST MARTIAL ARTS SPECTACLE EVER FILMED!
JOHN SOLIE
R RESTRICTED
Under 17 requires accompanying Parent or Adult Guardian
STARRING DAVID CHIANG and an astounding cast of MARTIAL ARTS MASTERS!
In METROCOLOR · Produced by The SHAW BROTHERS · A NEW WORLD PICTURES RELEASE

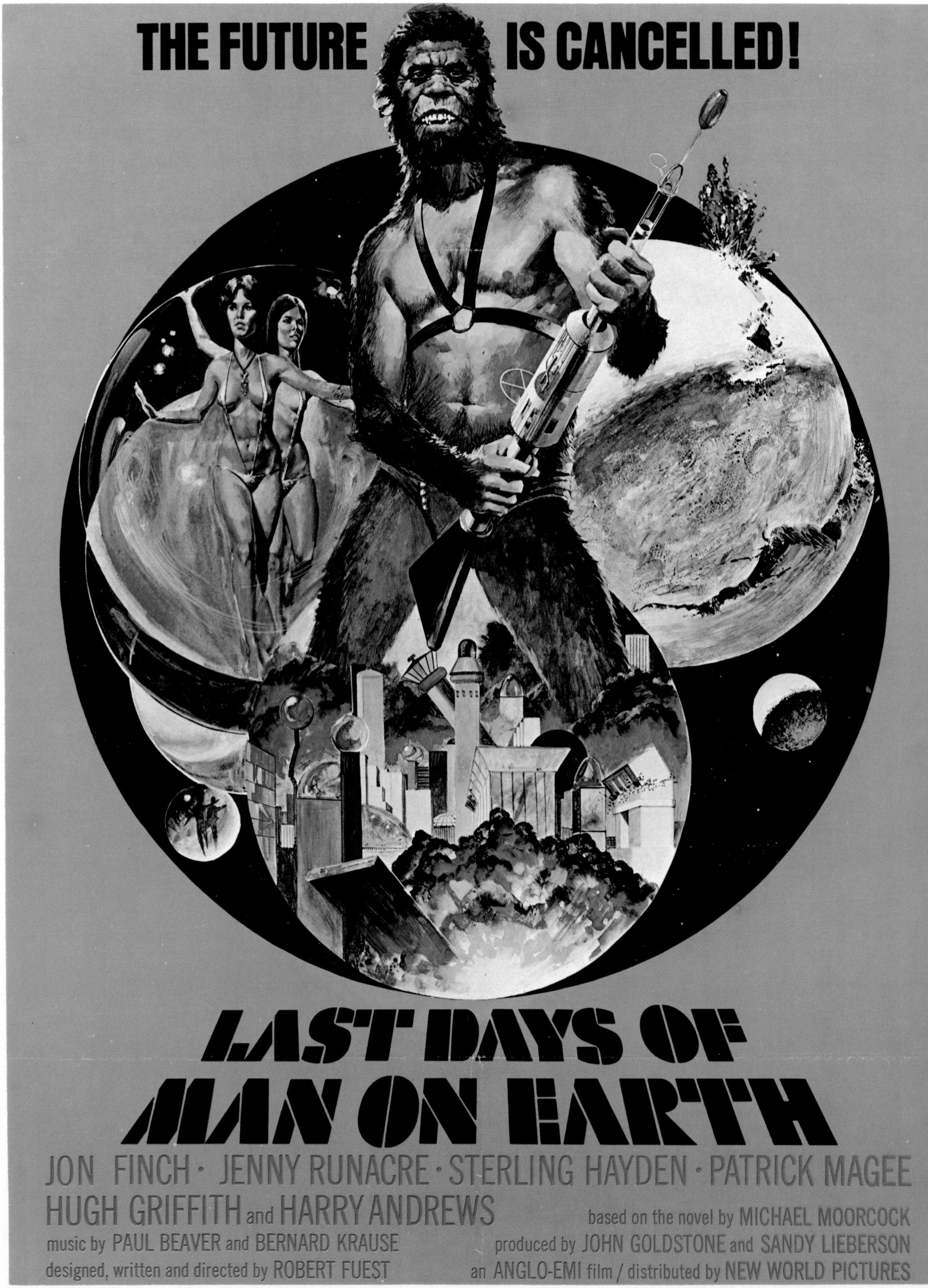
THE FUTURE IS CANCELLED!
LAST DAYS OF MAN ON EARTH
JON FINCH · JENNY RUNACRE · STERLING HAYDEN · PATRICK MAGEE
HUGH GRIFFITH and HARRY ANDREWS
based on the novel by MICHAEL MOORCOCK
music by PAUL BEAVER and BERNARD KRAUSE
produced by JOHN GOLDSTONE and SANDY LIEBERSON
designed, written and directed by ROBERT FUEST
an ANGLO-EMI film / distributed by NEW WORLD PICTURES

AN INTERVIEW WITH ROGER CORMAN AND HIS "ALUMNI"

CHAPTER ONE

BEGINNINGS

I started in films as a writer. I had previously held all kinds of jobs, including messenger at Twentieth Century–Fox, stagehand at a television studio, and literary agent. But I had grown somewhat discouraged with my lack of progress and gone to Europe and studied at Oxford University in England. Eventually I sold a script to Allied Artists, called *The House in the City*; they changed the title to *Highway Dragnet* (1953) because *Dragnet* was a popular television series at the time. They also changed the picture somewhat.

The picture was written from the climax back. On vacation, I'd been down to the Salt'n' Sea, which is a large saltwater body in Southern California. I was struck by the flooding of beach houses that had been built on the shores of the sea in the early part of the twentieth century. I thought of a wild nighttime chase between a killer and a man and a girl in one of these flooded houses, with flashlights being dropped in the water and people falling from the second floor into the water on the first floor, and worked out a chase across the desert climaxing in the hunt in the flooded house. When the time to do it came, however, the producers decided to shoot in a studio. They created a metal basin around a one-room set. The water was a couple of inches deep, and the most dangerous thing that happened was if somebody splashed, they wet their socks.

I was a little bit discouraged by this. However—thinking ahead—in selling the script I had negotiated an associate producer credit which enabled me to set myself up as a producer, and I then produced independently my own first Roger Corman Production, as such. It was a low-budget science-fiction picture, shot in six days on a budget of twelve thousand dollars, which was all the money I could raise, and I called it *It Stalked the Ocean Floor*. (The distributors thought that title was too arty and changed it to *The Monster from the Ocean Floor* [1954], and the picture did rather well.)

As I think back, both these pictures started with a visual concept, which is really the key to my work. Technically, if there's been any thread, it's been the fact that I consider film to be a visual medium and I think primarily in terms of the images, then the dialogue. *Highway Dragnet* started with the flooded house. *The Monster from the Ocean Floor* originated with an article I'd seen in the *Los Angeles Times* about a midget one-man submarine developed by Aerojet General. I called them up, claiming to be a producer, and said I'd like to use it in a picture. I couldn't pay them for its use, but they would get some publicity. They were delighted and said yes immediately.

Richard Conte in *Highway Dragnet*, 1953

I then rented an office over the Cock 'n' Bull Restaurant on Sunset Strip for twenty-five dollars a month. Actually, it wasn't really an office. It was the reception room of somebody who was in the process of going broke and couldn't afford both an office and a reception room. One of the first actresses I interviewed was a little surprised because during the interview people were constantly walking through the reception room to get to the office in back. After I hired her for the *Monster* picture, she told me she was convinced that of all the pictures she'd been interviewed for, this was the least likely to be made.

When Roger interviewed me, he looked me right in the eye with this twinkle and this smile and said, "Look, I'm gonna pay you scale, you'll bring your own costumes, your own jewelry, you'll drive your own car, you'll do all your own stunts, you won't get fed, you'll work overtime—do you want the job?"

—LYNN BERNAY, *actress in many Corman films*

The Monster from the Ocean Floor made money, but I could see that if I financed a film and waited for it to pay off so I could plow the profits back into the next film, I was going to make a picture only once a year or once every eighteen months. My next picture—*The Fast and the Furious* (1954), starring John Ireland and Dorothy Malone—developed from my interest in sports car racing. It was made for about fifty thousand dollars and shot on a ten-day schedule. Republic and Columbia offered to distribute it, but I saw before me the trap that would tie up my money until the film proved successful.

Monster from the Ocean Floor, 1954

Meanwhile, Jim Nicholson, who was the sales manager for a little production company called Real Art, approached me with the idea of starting his own company and using my picture to inaugurate it. I was willing—Jim was a friend of mine—but I wanted money up front so I would not have to wait for the picture to be released, and I wanted a commitment for financing two more films. Jim and his partner, Sam Arkoff, raised a very small amount of money, something like a thousand dollars, and Jim and I flew all around the country with the print of *The Fast and the Furious*, which we showed franchise distributors in key areas. We explained that this was going to be the first picture for Jim's new company and I would be producing two more films; we wanted them to put up money for *The Fast and the Furious* immediately, and to commit more money for the next two pictures as they came along.

It worked. That is how American International Pictures (AIP) started, and how I started making films on a more regular basis.

There's a little bit of rogue and scoundrel in almost everybody in this game, including Roger. Roger is an honorable man. He has a twinkle in his eye. He can talk out with the best of them and yet there's a twinkle at the same time. Roger is all things to all men. He can take on colorations. Overall he's fundamentally a very nice man. There are some people about whom you can say only *that they are very nice, and generally that form of niceness has to do with weakness. Roger is* not *a weak man. He is a fundamentally kind man, too. He does get upset now and then, but he has some qualities that I haven't found in anybody else.*

He was a hard worker from the very beginning, and he didn't have much money to work with. He almost had to *direct and produce to be able to get on the screen in a short period of time with the amount of money available. If he hadn't been his own director, he couldn't possibly have made them so fast. If he hadn't been his own producer, he wouldn't have known what he as the director wanted. There aren't too many people who can really carry that off successfully, and Roger is one of the few who can.*

—SAM ARKOFF, president and co-founder of American International Pictures

Other writers, producers, and directors of low-budget films would often put down the film they were making, saying it was just something to make money with. I never felt that. If I took the assignment, I'd give it my best shot. . . . the ones who said, "It's just a crummy little picture, I'm doing it for the money, I'll do something better later on," failed and are no longer working in films.

I did four westerns, all distributed by AIP. Two of them were my ideas and two of them were AIP's ideas—the titles alone will tell you which were which. The two that were my ideas were *Five Guns West* and *Gunslinger* (1956). The two that were AIP's ideas were *Apache Woman* (1955) and *The Oklahoma Woman* (1955). The ideas and story lines were from Lou Roussof, who was a writer under contract at AIP, with some work by me on the script.

The Day the World Ended (1955) was my first science-fiction film, and is notable primarily because it was AIP's first real financial success. They had made money with all of these other films, but this was the first time you would go to a theater on a Friday night and not be able to get into an AIP picture—there'd be a line around the block. Needless to say, we were all very happy about that.

With The Beast with a Million Eyes *[1955] Roger*

Lori Nelson in *Day the World Ended*, 1955

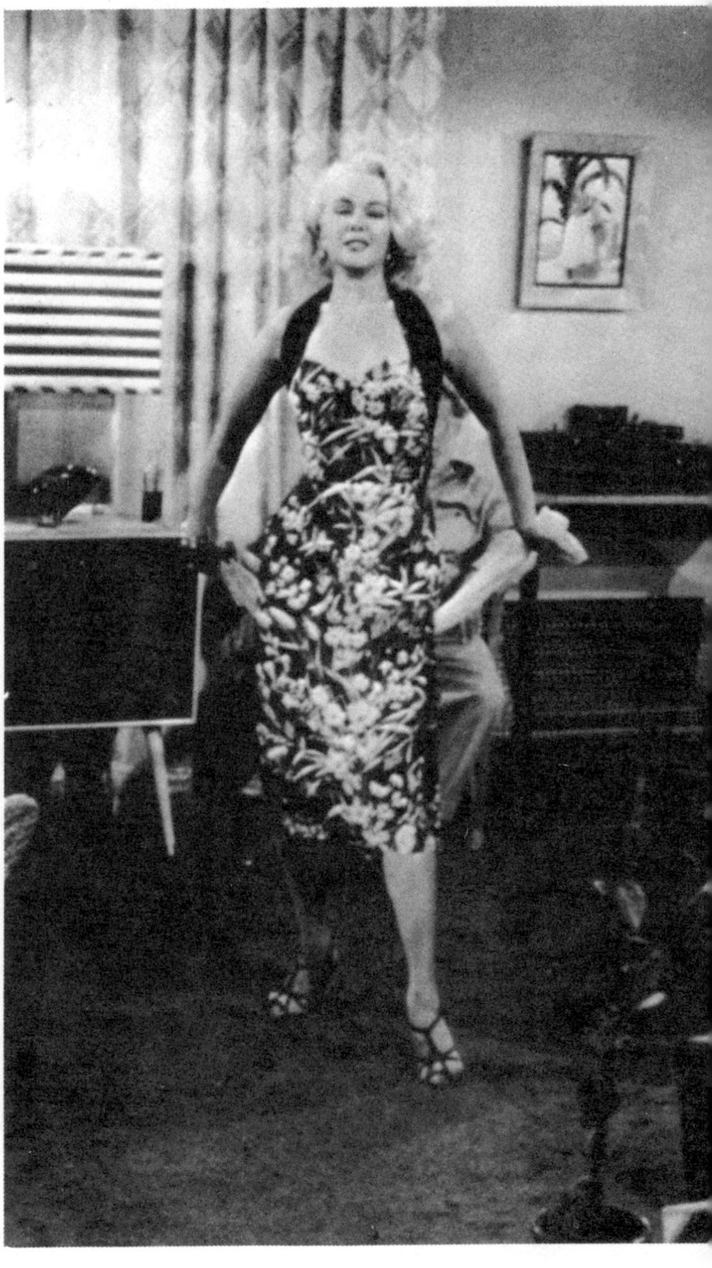

was very sparse on the money because he'd actually spent more than he wanted to on Five Guns West. *So he wanted to make an inexpensive picture. We decided to make a little horror picture in the Palm Springs area. I think the whole picture had a budget of something less than thirty thousand dollars, so Roger went non-union, and hot on his trail were those watchdogs from Screen Actors Guild and IATSE. They would run into Roger and he would dart off the other way into the desert. It was a kind of continual chase. The picture, of course, didn't take very long to make. Its budget didn't allow for more than two weeks. So now we get the picture together. Jim Nicholson, who is very good on titles, called it* The Beast with a Million Eyes. *Terrific title. We sent out a glossy to all our franchise holders. We didn't use stars. The usual stars were Luke McGluke and Susie Glutz. Anyway, Joe Levine was our franchise holder in Boston, and he loved that title. He said he could make a terrific campaign. He really got the hots for it. When the whole thing was put together, we sat and looked at it, this little black-and-white picture with very little money in it. And you know, the monster, the beast with a million eyes, really looked like a teakettle. It would exhale steam. No, really! It looked like a teakettle. I think it* was *a tea kettle!*

—SAM ARKOFF, president and co-founder of American International Pictures

According to Roger Corman, he did not actually make The Beast with a Million Eyes *himself. It was produced by David Kramarsky, who was fulfilling one of his commitments with AIP.*

—Editor

After writing and producing my third film, I decided I wanted to direct in order to have more control. *Five Guns West* was a western that I wrote with Bob Campbell; it starred John Lund and Dorothy Malone, and was shot in color on a nine-or ten-day schedule. And it did well.

*I worked on one of Roger's first pictures—*Monster from the Ocean Floor *—it was the only picture I saw made without any direction at all*

—FLOYD CROSBY, cameraman

I just kept going from then on—I was never really out of work. In fact, if I have any regrets, it is that I wasn't ever out of work. I would generally be stacked up with assignments; while doing one picture, I would already have commitments for two more to come. There was little time to sit back and reflect. I think if I had been unemployed longer between films, I could have sat and thought a little bit about what I was doing, but I was just going as

Mike "Touch" Connors in *The Oklahoma Woman*, 1955

fast as I could from one picture to another. I took most of the assignments that were offered me, just to keep working. The only films I turned down were the ones I could clearly see were hopeless. I mean, people would come up with an idea that was just terrible and I would say, "I can't do anything like that." But with any idea that seemed at all reasonable, I always felt there would be some way I could work with it, something I could do. So I did all manner of films: horror, science fiction, gangster, teenage, racing, adventure—whatever there was. I'd say fifty percent of them were my own ideas, fifty percent were ideas given to me. But I tried to bring something of myself to each one. Despite the low budgets, I have no excuses. I tried to do my best on every film.

It Conquered the World followed in 1956 for AIP; then I did *Not of this Earth* (1956) and *Attack of the Crab Monsters* (1956) with Allied Artists. They had the same basic formula as AIP, which was to do two black-and-white science-fiction horror films and send them out as a double bill. Although I thought *Not of This Earth* was the better film—it had a slightly more interesting story line and some nice performances in it, and I used a great deal of natural locations—*Attack of the Crab Monsters* was probably the one that made the combination sell, primarily because of the title.

Chuck Griffith wrote both pictures. I told Chuck I would like to have every single scene end either on a note of horror or with the suggestion or expectation of horror. When you're working in horror (and particularly in science fiction), so much exposition has to be shown that you can get stuck with some really dull scenes where people are essentially just holding the plot. A horror film has got to have something in every single scene so the audience never has a chance to sit back for more than a moment. These films are constructed very carefully—you do have to give people a few moments to relax and then come back into it. My main goal in *Crab Monsters* was to integrate tension into each scene, leading to the horror conclusion.

The picture was very successful. The film rental was over ten times the negative gross of the film. I remember the giant crab which we built for twelve hundred dollars; Ed Nelson, who had a nice career and one of the leads on *Peyton Place*, made his film debut inside the crab.

While I was writing Attack of the Crab Monsters *in 1956, I happened to see Jacques Cousteau's* Silent World *and became enamored of underwater photography, so I wrote a lot of underwater into the script. I said to Roger, "I'll direct the underwater for you for a hundred dollars," and he*

Not of This Earth, 1956

jumped at the bargain. If I had said, "Look, I'll do it for nothing," he'd have suspected that I didn't know how. Anyway, he agreed to that and then it was all forgotten. Months later, when we were going to make the picture, I got a phone call from Roger, who said, "The actors will be there in half an hour for you to teach them aqua-lung diving,"—and I had no idea how to do that. Jonathan Haze, one of the actors in the film, was bringing over the equipment, and I got him to bring it over early, so that he had five minutes to check me *out on the stuff before the cast arrived for me to teach them. And everything went well. Of course, the scene was incredible—all these strange people walking around with diving outfits at my apartment-house pool, all the neighbors peering out through the venetian blinds to watch. The next day they were shooting in a tank three stories deep in Marineland, and breaking every rule. It was mayhem—Floyd Crosby, the cameraman, would be motioning through the glass in one direction, while I was motioning everyone in another direction.*

—*CHUCK GRIFFITH, scriptwriter*

Swamp Women (1955) was a little picture that was really a lot of fun. It was financed by some theater owners in Louisiana, and again we shot on a typical ten-day schedule, in the bayous of Louisiana. It was with this film that I developed a crew that became known as "the Corman Crew": Floyd Crosby, the cameraman; Chuck Anawalt, the key grip; Dick Rubin, the soundman, and a number of other people who worked with me on picture after picture. We all got along together. One of the reasons I was able to make so many pictures so inexpensively and so quickly is that we all worked very well together, so much so that when I would not be shooting, people would hire my entire crew. Its composition changed a little bit over the years, but we probably stayed together ten years.

Roger is fascinating to work for—he is both reckless and conservative. He comes up with a "what if" sort of idea and passes his enthusiasm on to others. Then his fears that the money is being wasted—that the idea being tried is too far out—creep in, and he cuts back. You get an unusual *heavily flavored film. And this is a repeated process. Roger has a lifetime of near misses.*

—*CHUCK GRIFFITH, scriptwriter*

It Conquered the World was the successor to a certain extent to *The Day the World Ended* (1955), AIP's most successful picture to that point. They wanted another science-fiction picture. I did it on a

The Undead, 1956

ten-day schedule and for a fair amount under a hundred thousand dollars.

The main thing I remember about *It Conquered the World* was that the creature had come from a planet larger than earth, such as Jupiter. Since I had majored in engineering with a minor in physics, I thought I would try to be accurate in designing the creature. A planet that large would obviously have a very heavy gravity—much heavier than earth's—so the creature would be very low slung to the ground and very massive.

The first day we were shooting, I took the creature out. Beverly Garland, the leading lady, went over and looked at the creature. Standing *over* it, she said, "So you've come to conquer the world, eh? Take that!" and she kicked it. I realized that what was right from the standpoint of physics was absolutely wrong for the picture. The creature had to be bigger than man. I reworked the schedule so we wouldn't shoot the creature until the second day and I sent it back to the shop. We took the creature and used it as the head and built a whole framework down.

The Undead (1956) started with the title *The Reincarnation of Diana Love.* It was a story of reincarnation, which at that time was very popular—everyone was talking about it. I developed the script, but before shooting I had a feeling that reincarnation was losing its appeal. The book that had been Number One on the best-seller list was starting to slip, but I still liked the script even though the reincarnation interest was fading. I thought I'd just make a horror film and make a few changes that were strictly about reincarnation. This was an extremely low-budget film, and it still had a ten-day schedule, but I must have filmed it for under sixty thousand dollars.

Rock All Night (1956) was a picture that I personally have always liked, and I shot it in six days on a set that was leftover from another film. It was a little bit strange from the standpoint of the music because the group I had was The Platters and they were available for one day, but it wasn't the day I was shooting. They were on tour and weren't going to be in town when we were shooting—we had written the script around them. I had to revise the script and rewrite the opening. I shot the picture when I was supposed to, and then I shot the opening sequence with The Platters and put the two together. The picture is a little distorted from this standpoint because it says, "starring The Platters," and The Platters were in and out of the film in the first ten minutes and then you never see them again. We had some other groups that were good, though. This was the first picture that Abby Dalton did, and she did

Rock All Night, 1956

several for me. I met her through a friend of mine, and I thought she was tremendously pretty. Abby introduced me to Jeff Corey, who I studied with for acting. I was always very pleased with her work. Dick Miller played the leading man. The whole film takes place on two sets, and there isn't much you can do with it cinematically, but it is a personal favorite of mine.

Sorority Girl (1957) was AIP's idea, and they had developed the script. For most of the pictures I worked on, I had developed the script myself. I didn't like theirs, and I rewrote it very hurriedly, and though the film turned out well, it was done in some haste. At the time, almost all films were shot in studios—there was very little location work other than for exteriors—and I questioned some of the construction costs because I was a partner in the film with AIP. But they kept the bill, and I felt the construction costs were wrong. So I rented a great house and used it for the sorority house, and as I remember it, two things happened: one, I got more of a feeling or knack for making the picture, and two, there was a major saving of money. We were among the first of the modern-day filmmakers to shoot on natural locations. At the beginning of my film career I shot on natural locations, and then for a long time I did shoot in the studios, but I went back to natural locations. And I think that is a trademark, in a way.

Susan Cabot in *Sorority Girl*, 1957

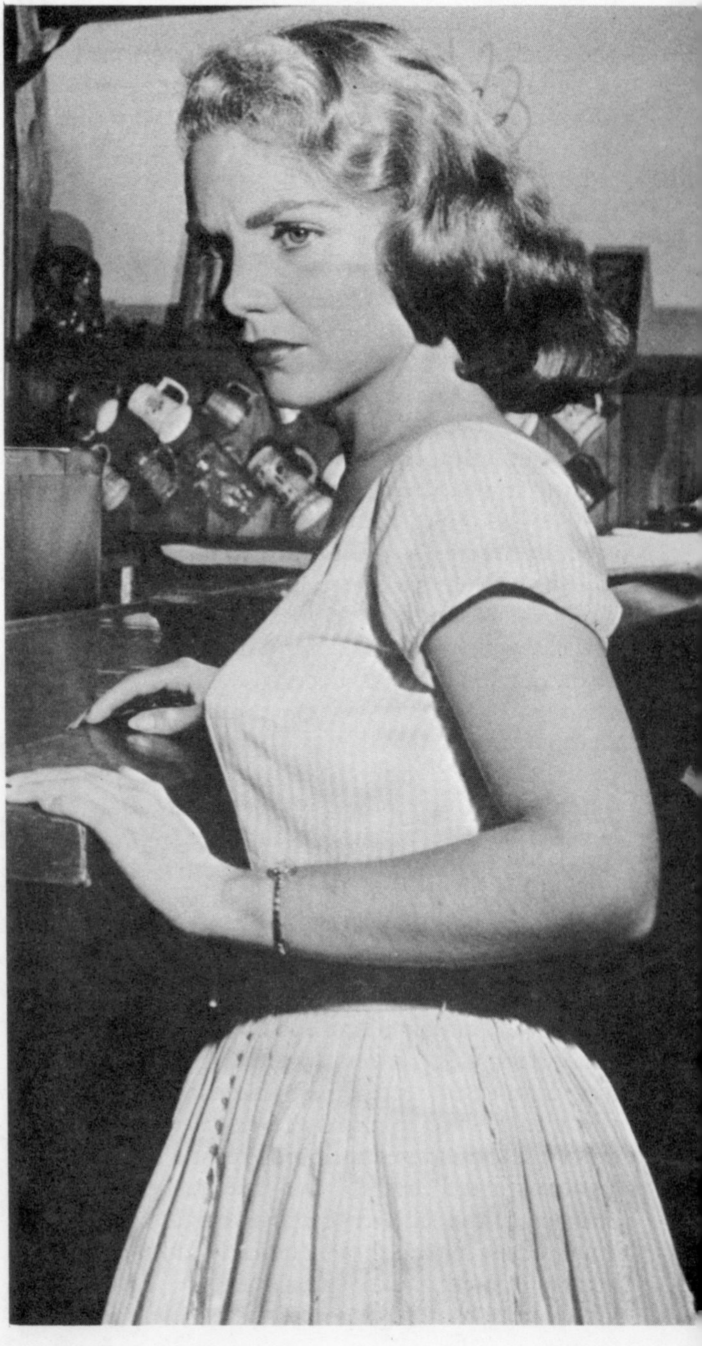

The Viking Women and the Sea Serpent (1957) taught me a great deal, because although we had a ten-day schedule and a budget of about a hundred thousand dollars, the picture was obviously too big to be made on that budget. As a result, I decided it would be better to do a low-budget film and do it well than to try to do a big picture on a low budget. There were just so many compromises, and the special effects didn't turn out right.
It taught me one other lesson. Some good friends of mine designed the special effects, created the script, and made large drawings of the scenes with the sea serpent climbing out of the water and the Viking women in the big boat. They guaranteed that they could do all the special effects for twenty thousand dollars and a piece of the picture. I thought, "That's terrific!" When I took all this to AIP, they were amazed, too. They thought this would be wonderful. This would be a lot of fun and be a great show in itself. What happened, of course, was that the special effects weren't one percent of those drawings. It was the first time I had been the victim—if "victim" is the right word—of a presentation of the Madison Avenue approach.

I think I had my all-time maximum in setups—seventy-eight shots in one day. That's the most I've ever gotten, and in those days we worked with only one camera. It should have been a million-dollar film and *not* ten days at a hundred thousand dollars. As I got into it I realized that I was in a total trap. I felt relieved when I finished it, because I knew by the middle of filming that I was not going to pull it off. It was also one of the first times I'd worked with boats in rough seas, and I had a lot of trouble shooting them.

Roger fits all the bills of a Selznick or Goldwyn, because he's both well versed in the economic aspects and a good solid businessman. Artistically he is good. He's creative. He's hard-nosed, and at the same time he is able to talk to sensitive people on their own level. I think Roger could, if he really wanted to, be a really great *director. He is a terrific guy. If he had the* patience, *and it's the only thing I would accuse him of not having, he could have, and he really hasn't, been a director. He's had terrific success.*

—SAM ARKOFF, president and co-founder of American International Pictures

AIP wanted to do a gangster film based upon a real gangster, and I came up with *Machine Gun Kelly* (1958), mostly because I liked the name. When I did the research for the picture, I found that although Kelly was Number One on the FBI's Most Wanted list, and had pulled many, many bank robberies, he was really a coward. I keyed the picture to his statement when he was captured. He had pulled a kidnapping and was surrounded in a wooded area by the FBI and the local police. They called out through megaphones, "Come out, Kelly, or we'll open fire. Throw down your gun" —whatever. He threw down his gun and came out. When they put the handcuffs on him the local head of the FBI said, "You must be the toughest man in the country, Kelly, we never thought you'd come out. Why did you do it?" He said, "I knew if I didn't do it you'd kill me." Completely logical statement. I worked back from there.

I was very fortunate in having a young actor doing his first lead part play Kelly—Charlie Bronson. Bronson was just brilliant—he did an amazing performance considering the role and the circumstances of low-budget filming. For instance, it means that a director is probably working with a small crew, and with the limited schedule, he isn't able to have very many elaborate shots. He isn't going to get very much coverage. He may have to leave a scene covered with one or two shots where he would have liked to have broken it up and gotten into individuals. The action scenes are probably going to be a little thin. You can't do too much in action.

From the actor's standpoint, there is very little

Charles Bronson and Morey Amsterdam in *Machine Gun Kelly*, 1958

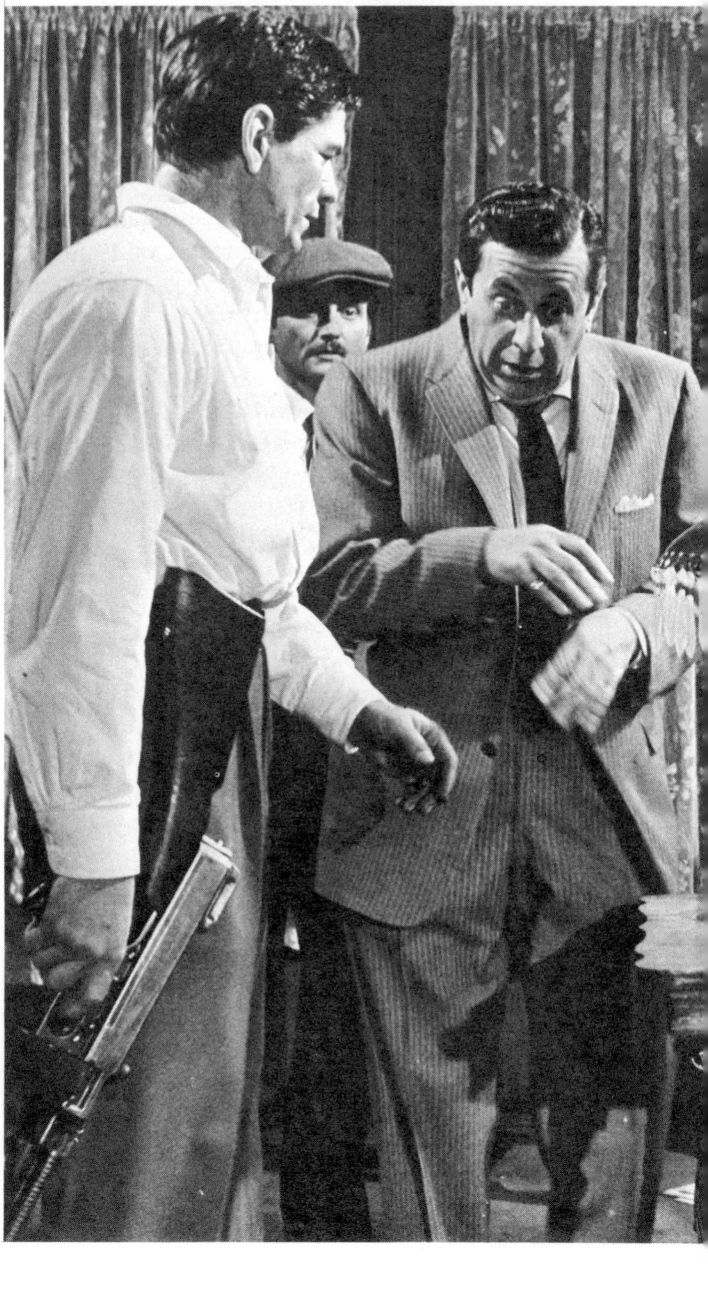

time, and you're printing, if not the first take, no more than the second or third take. No matter how much I was pressed, I made a point of trying not to have to print the first take unless it was good. If it wasn't good, I would really find the time to go for a second or third take. But we very seldom went beyond a second or third take. You heard Willie Wyler went for sixty takes to get a particular performance, and so when I say Charlie Bronson and Susan Cabot, who played his girl friend, were both excellent in the film, you have to know that they were acting in a film in which they had almost no rehearsal time and in which we were printing the first, second, or third take almost every single time. Considering the circumstances, I've nothing but admiration for the performances of most of the actors in my films. I was working generally with unknown actors, and I could pay only about union scale or maybe ten percent over union scale.

Charlie and I got along very well on the picture. He was a fairly young actor and he had a reputation as a troublemaker on the set, but I had no trouble with him whatsoever. While one set was being lighted, Charlie and I were sparring on the side, just fooling around, and I just kind of put out my left hand and he knocked on my left hand very lightly, must have put twenty blows into my stomach, just touching my stomach, in ten seconds, or five seconds. He didn't hurt me, he was just fooling around. That was when I learned he'd been a professional boxer in his youth. He was also instrumental in attracting critical attention to my films in Europe and particularly in Paris. *Machine Gun Kelly* was picked up by the French critics and went to a number of film festivals and got really a very nice critical response.

One of the constant little debates with Roger is everyone's attempt to get him to upgrade his product. I think everyone at one time has tried to do that—tried to talk him into moving into a higher category. So in 1956 we had a discussion in the Hamburger Hamlet about "I want to do comedy" and he said, "No, no, we can't do comedy or drama—because you have to be good. . ." Therefore we could only do action pictures, which didn't "have to be good."

—*CHUCK GRIFFITH, scriptwriter*

AIP changed my title *Prehistoric World* to *Teenage Cavemen* (1958), but it played in only one or two theaters before the title went back to *Prehistoric World*. AIP had the best titles going, even though there was a fine line between what made their titles interesting and commercial and what pushed it over and made them silly.

In *Prehistoric World* we came up with what I

Robert Vaughn in *Prehistoric World*, 1958

thought was really a nice idea—you follow a prehistoric tribe with very strange customs and unusual culture and a very complicated religion. As a young man growing up in that tribe, you follow his initiation into the religion and its mysteries. Most religions and cultures that are disguised in various areas have practical reasons for their customs. For instance, people in some religions don't eat pork, I think, because pork spoiled in the hot weather. In *Prehistoric World*, a certain area is taboo to this tribe; eventually the young man wanders into it and finds himself in the future after a nuclear holocaust has destroyed the world. He finds a book in the midst of the destruction, and the picture ends with him looking at the book, with the implication that civilization will now start once more. It was a very nice idea, and I think the picture turned out well. Again, a good young actor, Robert Vaughn (later in *The Man from U.N.C.L.E.*), did this as one of his first films.

Again, if the picture suffered, it was for the same reasons as *Viking Women*: we were trying to do too much in ten days, with a budget under one hundred thousand dollars, and the shallowness of the production showed.

I had to make one cut after the sneak preview. In the scene, Vaughan was supposed to kill a deer, and the propman provided a stuffed deer. I protested, "Look, a deer is not a stiff immediately after it's killed. He can't carry a stuffed deer." But it was the end of the day, we were losing light, we weren't coming back to that location, and I couldn't go over AIP's ten-day limit; I shot them on schedule, always. I had to take a shot, so I made it a long shot and put the camera behind some trees and kind of disguised the deer so it couldn't be seen too well. At the sneak preview the picture was really playing well—I mean, the people liked the film. Then that shot came on, and the people laughed as they saw the ridiculous deer. It was the only thing I later cut out of the picture.

As I say again and again, that lesson was brought home to me each time I tried a picture that was really too big for the budget. I would end up making compromises that were more than you really can make on a low-budget film. On almost any film you make some compromises, but these compromises would defeat nice stories with good actors.

There's one story that really is insane and tells you a lot about Roger. I did a film for him called Teenage Caveman *starring Robert Vaughan. I was going to be Roger's assistant and work one week on the film. That was cool. So the first day we're working in this, as they called it, "arboretum," and one of us has to drown by falling into the "sand," as it's called in the script. Well, guess*

Viking Women and the Sea Serpent, 1957

who got to drown in that murky, swampy water? So he kills me off the first day. I figure, cool, I'm already dead, so he can't really attack me again. We move to Bronson Canyon in Hollywood, and I'm sitting in this wagon, and he says, "What are you doing here?" I say, "Well, they're having my funeral!" He says, "Who the hell will recognize you? Get over here immediately." So all of a sudden I'm standing in the front row playing a tom-tom at my own funeral. And here I am, very *recognizable,* very short. *I said, "I don't believe this. I can't believe this is happening—playing a tom-tom at my own funeral."*

*Two days later they bring this mean, scroungy old horse in, and all of a sudden, in the script, a Man from the Burning Plains is supposed to show up. We're waiting for the stunt man to show up—he has to fall off the horse—and all of a sudden I see this idiot outfit, a bearskin, coming toward me. And I say, "What is this?" He says, "*You're *going to play the Man from the Burning Plains." I say, "I'm not a stunt man." He says, "You can fall off the horse as well as anybody else." I say, "I know—and save you fifty dollars!" He says, "Nevertheless, you're the Man from the Burning Plains." I say, "Oh, for Christ sake, Roger, this is insane." Anyway, I look like General Grant when he gets through with me—a great big beard, the bearskin—and I get that horse to come riding in, with me in this ridiculous outfit. I fall off the horse, and I'm thrilled to death that I did it in the first take. And he's real happy, but the cameraman says, "I think I saw his jockey shorts." Roger goes hysterical and screams at me, "How dare you wear jockey shorts?" And of course, the horse is crazy, and we have to do it again, and everyone's throwing rocks at me. So I get the horse going and fall off, and I'm careful to not let my jockey shorts show. They bring in the camera—I wasn't supposed to move—and I look up at the camera, raise one hand, and say, "Peace." So now I had two death scenes on camera.*

Then we go over to Iverson's Ranch a couple of days later, and we're supposed to be waiting for the bear to show up, because we're going to have a big bear hunt and kill the bear. And poor me, when I see that bear suit I say, "This is the end of the world." I was sure they'd strap me in the bear suit. It's a hundred and ten degrees out, and I'm trapped in this bear suit, so I get on all fours and the head goes through my legs, and I can't see anything. And they will not listen to me—I can't explain that when I get on all fours, I'm looking between my legs. So they take me on top of the hill, leave me there, and say, "Okay bear, come down the hill." So I turn around and waddle down, and Roger goes insane. He says, "What are you doing?" I scream, "Now listen to me—I can't

Viking Women and the Sea Serpent, 1957

see." "Oh," he says immediately, "what should we do? What should we do, Beach?" Now, of course, I'm petrified, and I'm dying in this bear suit. I've gotta get out—immediately. So I say, "Look, Roger, put a rope between my legs and I'll follow the rope down the trail," and he says, "Brilliant! Get the rope, boys." So they string the rope down the hill, about a hundred feet! I waddle down, and he screams, "Stand up, bear." So I stand up, and the thirty townspeople are ready to kill the bear in the bear hunt, and he screams, "You're a mean bear—argh!" So I'm growling, and he says, "I don't believe you're a mean bear. You're not mean enough." And so I just get ferocious; I'm growling and snarling. Then I hear this low voice say, "Kill the bear!" and thirty people jump on me and beat the hell out of me. I think this was enough to retire. I was the only person to have three death scenes in one picture. That's the economy of Roger Corman in using people. This is the wonderful training Mr. Corman gave me.

—BEACH DICKERSON, actor

AIP wanted a horror film produced for fifty thousand dollars, and I took it as a challenge. Chuck Griffith and I worked out the story—it was the time of the beatnik movement, and Sunset Strip was the center in Los Angeles. Chuck and I met one evening in a coffeehouse and started talking about it. We decided to do a comic-horror film entitled *Bucket of Blood,* played in a coffeehouse, and drifted up and down the Strip pulling the script together. After *Viking Women* and *Prehistoric World*, where the production problems were so great that they more or less defeated the cost and discouraged me, the five-day schedule was cause for enthusiasm, because at least I didn't have to play with special effects. Essentially I was working the camera and the actors, and I felt it was a challenge to see what I could do in five days. I liked that picture very much. Again, you have to consider it a good picture for a five-day picture.

Roger doesn't feel that his people—or he himself—have "A"-picture material, and therefore there is no point in striving for an "A" picture. He once said, "No one who earns less than fifty thousand dollars could write a good script." That is, anyone who is paid less than fifty thousand dollars is incapable of writing a good script. So that helps him to resist all the ideas.

—CHUCK GRIFFITH, scriptwriter

In *Not of This Earth* Dick Miller played a Fuller Brush salesman trying to sell brushes to a man from outer space who was interested in getting humans for their blood. Miller was trying to get in-

Dick Miller in *Not of This Earth*, 1956

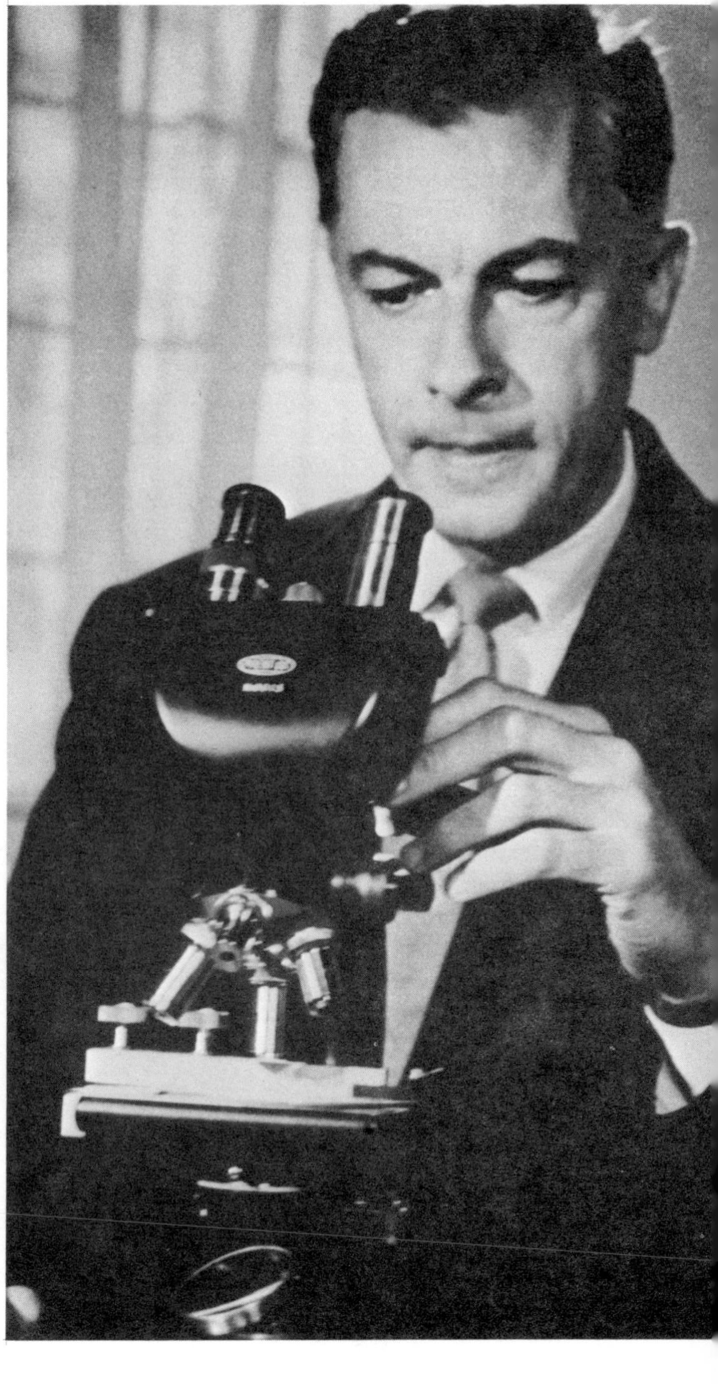

to the house to demonstrate the brushes, and the man from outer space wanted to trick him into the house and get his blood. It was really a very funny scene. It was one of the first times I worked with humor in that vein, and from then on I started putting more and more humor into horror films, because the audiences really loved it. They really broke up.

I think really what was involved is that he has a rather mathematical cast of mind and inevitably he gravitated toward that which he could keep score with best. And so things got translated into "I did this movie in five days," "This movie cost twenty thousand dollars and grossed one hundred thousand dollars." This was a way of measuring your achievement. I think there was a natural tendency to measure things in the way he knew best—instinctively best—which was with numbers. The texture of a scene is less palpable, less easy to define than numbers. "I did this movie in two days. Nobody else in the world could make a movie in two days." There was that tendency to take pride in the skill with which he was able to turn things out so quickly. I think inadvertently he felt that if he didn't do it quick he did it wrong. Even when he knew better, he was measuring himself by two standards—the alacrity with which he was able to do something, and as a man of great intelligence and sensitivity who really wanted to make fine films. I think there was this kind of split in him and so it was exceedingly difficult to take the time to make certain things work a little more carefully. This is just an observation, not a judgmental statement. What he should or should not have done was up to him.

—ROBERT TOWNE, scriptwriter

War of the Satellites (1957) is an example of producing very, very rapidly. The first Russian sputnik had been launched. A friend of mine, knowing I worked very rapidly, called me and said he had within the hour constructed a story line and was I interested. After I heard the story, I called Steve Brady, president of Allied Artists, and I said I could be shooting this picture in ten days and cutting it in three weeks. In roughly two months we could release the first picture about satellites. He said, "Done, we'll do it."

The *Cry Baby Killer* (1957) was the first picture I ever made that did not make money, though it did get its money back off the television sale. And it's weird. I'd been riding a kind of nice success streak, and AIP wanted me to scout a location for them in Australia. I decided to turn it into a trip around the world. As part of my deal with Allied Artists, I was to make one more film. So I thought on this

War of the Satellites, 1957

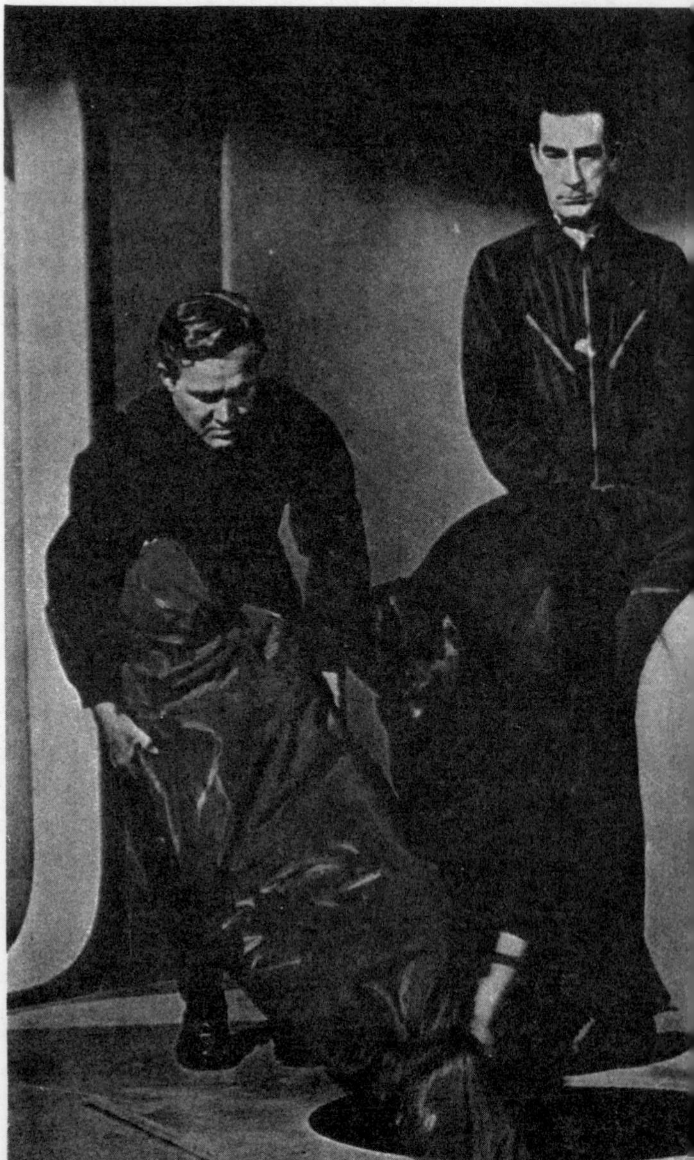

one I would just produce, and assigned a script by Leo Gordon, who's an actor, and turned it over to my assistant to prepare. I was going to be back a couple days before they started shooting.

I started on my two-month trip around the world, and in New Delhi, while I was walking down the street, a Sikh with a white turban came up to me and offered to tell my fortune. I said, "Oh no," and he said, "If I can't tell you your mother's first name, you don't have to pay me." I figured that was fair enough: certainly there was no way he could have known my mother's first name. We wandered over to a little park and sat down on a bench and started talking, and he must have put me under hypnosis, because I don't remember whether he ever told me my mother's first name or whether I paid him. The only thing that I *do* remember is his telling me to beware of business deals with anybody whose initials were "DK." "DK" were the initials of my assistant. I figured, okay. I came back to Hollywood, went in to see my assistant, and said, "How is everything?" He said, "Great, we licked the script." I said, "What do you mean, licked the script? It was a fine script. There was nothing wrong with that script." He said, "It had all kinds of problems. We've rewritten it totally and we solved all those problems." Well, they had wrecked the script, but were to begin shooting in two days. We put back a few things, but it was too late. The only good thing about the film was that Jack Nicholson made his debut in the picture and did a very nice job. But the basic idea of the picture still remained, which was rather good. A teenager pulls up in a drive-in and commits a burglary, and what follows is essentially a suspense story around the drive-in, where he has taken everybody hostage and the police have him ringed and he doesn't know what to do. He's simply stuck. He knows he can't get out. He threatens to kill the people. He knows he isn't going to kill the people, but nobody else does. So it was a suspenseful situation which was somewhat damaged. Leo Gordon, who wrote the original script, had one good line. Playing a bystander, he said, "Teenagers—we never had 'em when I was a kid." I think it was true.

Money always superseded artistic situations with Roger. Art was not germane to our work. He is an excellent gentleman, and I am tickled to death that he is doing exactly what he wants to do.

—*JACK NICHOLSON,* actor

Jack Nicholson in *Cry Baby Killer*, 1957

Attack of the Crab Monster, 1956

CHAPTER TWO

MONSTERS, MONSTERS EVERYWHERE

I made so many horror and science-fiction films in the late 1950s that I decided to make a war picture, and since winter was coming on, I thought I would make it a ski troop picture. It seemed like a nice idea, and I thought I would get some interesting visual things. I shot *Ski Troop Attack* (1960) on a two-week schedule, in Deadwood, South Dakota, because there was a railway near there and certain geography fitted the European area of operations. It was the story of an American ski patrol that got caught behind the German lines with certain information. In other words, it was a straightforward, not particularly original, but workable premise.

A German ski instructor from Sun Valley who had been in the German ski troop was to play the leader of the German ski troop. The day before we started shooting he broke his leg coming down the slopes at Sun Valley one final time. I was stuck at South Dakota; there was no way to replace him. The only thing I could think of was to play the part myself, but I couldn't ski and didn't speak German. It ended up a giant mess, with me kind of faking my way into the close shots on skis and cutting to doubles for long shots. I muttered in barely understandable German. Later, the only guy I could find to dub my voice was a German accountant, and his voice came out as that of minor office worker speaking impeccable German.

It was the first time I remember working with multiple cameras.

It was about 1957 and I was just finishing up at USC in telecommunications, and I went with Roger to South Dakota. We drove in my little VW together—because he didn't want to spring for the air fare. I was Roger's assistant director, the propman, the wardrobe man, and I did all the stunt skiing, and *I played a major role in* Ski Troop Attack. *I think I played about thirty-seven different parts in it, because we had hoods on our faces when we were Germans and goggles on when we were Americans and it was really crazy.*

In all his movies he always seems to want to put in one big scene—kind of the big exploitation scene. So he took two or three hours, which was a colossal amount of time, to let us climb to the top of a mountain that was real virgin snow—a huge, beautiful hill with no trees on it. It took us so long to get up there because the snow was up to our chests. Roger wanted to have this great big wide-angle long shot, and he screamed over the bullhorn—and started an avalanche. The snow started coming down all over the place, which of course made the mountain look all skied over, and Roger started screaming over the bullhorn, "Stop that snow, stop that snow!" I always thought it was funny—even then he thought he would stop that mountain.

—PAUL RAPP, production manager

Ski Troop Attack, 1960

The Little Shop of Horrors (1960) was made as kind of a joking challenge. I was having lunch with the manager of a studio, who showed me this set of a store—not being used then—and asked me if I could use it. I said I didn't have anything but if the set could be left rigged and dressed for a couple of weeks, I would use it for two days. *Bucket of Blood* (1959) had been successful on a five-day schedule, and I thought I would try to shoot a picture in two days just to see what would happen. So I called Chuck Griffith, who had written *Bucket of Blood*, and we went back to the coffeehouse on Sunset Strip for an evening and worked out a new story line which had a little similarity to *Bucket of Blood*. He wrote the script in a week and shifted the scene to a florist's shop. I did shoot in two days (actually, two days and a night).

I've always been struck by the fact that Roger makes more of a claim about how quickly he can do a film than about how well he's done a film.

—ARTHUR KNIGHT, *film critic*

The film got very nice reviews and has become a little bit of a cult film. It continues playing on college campuses and at midnight screenings. I'm generally pleased with it. The surprise to me was there were three of these low-budget comedy-horror films—*Bucket of Blood*, *The Little Shop of Horrors*, and *Creature from the Haunted Sea* (1960)—that were all so audacious; I mean, it's so wild to do films that cheaply and on that short a schedule and with such insane subject matter. It seemed to me I would have either a great success or a colossal failure. It was disappointing that they were all modest successes. And it didn't figure that I could do something so wild and get a little conservative return on the money and the end would be so routine. Bob Towne, a good friend of mine, and I were talking after *The Little Shop of Horrors*, and he said, "Roger, you have to remember, filmmaking is not a track meet. It's not how fast you go." I was thinking roughly the same thing, and I said, "Enough of the two- and five-day pictures." *The Little Shop of Horrors* was the film that in the long run has made me whatever legend I am at this point. It's interesting because that picture has made me more fans and friends and people that I meet all the time who know that picture and who have even memorized parts of it.

If you were a well-known Corman actor, as I was at that time, it was very, very hard to go on to doing big studio pictures, or anything else. Today the people who came out of Corman have made the jump, but at that point it was all people who had either only just started out, were trying to work their way up, or were on the way down—such as Richard Denning and John Ireland—people who

The Little Shop of Horrors, 1960

had had a big career that was slightly on the back side of the power curve and were on their way downhill.

—JONATHAN HAZE, *actor in more than twenty Corman films*

I once shot three pictures in five weeks in Puerto Rico. The first one, directed by Joel Rapp for a film group, was called *The Battle of Blood Alley* (1960), and I put it together with *Ski Troop Attack* in a war picture combination. That film was done in two weeks. Then I did *The Last Woman on Earth* (1960) with the same crew in two weeks. Bob Towne, who later won an Academy Award for the screenplay of *Shampoo*, wrote the script. Bob was a somewhat slow writer, and he didn't have the script finished when we left to shoot in Puerto Rico. I couldn't afford to bring him along just to finish it, so I gave him the second lead in the picture and he made his debut as an actor. He was writing and I was working with him up until the night before we started shooting.

Roger had no patience, and that was his great strength. He has the intelligence and originality of a Fellini or a Truffaut, but let's say you're shooting Lawrence of Arabia *and you have in your mind that you want this figure to emerge out of the desert as just a shadow, as just a mirage—you may have to wait three weeks to get that shot. If you don't have the patience to do that, then there's no point having the discussion. And if Roger can't do that, it's not because of lack of raw talent or intelligence—it's because it's either a character flaw or a virtue, depending on how you look at it. He's someone who just doesn't have the patience—he's gotta do it fast. I really love the man. He's an extraordinary person.*

—ROBERT TOWNE, *scriptwriter*

In Puerto Rico I established a process that later led me to do *Dementia 13* (1962) with Francis Ford Coppola—that is, I had paid to get my people to the location and I could have a second film with everything laid out, so the second film would be very inexpensive. From Puerto Rico, I called Chuck Griffith and said I wanted a comedy-horror film to be shot in Puerto Rico in six days. I told him a rough story line and pointed out how many and what actors I had there, and I said, "It's got to be written for these same actors—I'm not flying anybody in—and I've got to have the script in a week." He said, "Well, that's not enough time." I said, "There's nobody else," and he said, "Why don't you play one of the roles?" I said, "Okay." He hung up and went back to sleep. When he woke up in the morning, he read his notes, decided I hadn't offered him enough money, but

The Last Woman on Earth, 1960

took the assignment anyway. But in order to get me, he made my part the most complex role it was possible for an actor to play— laughing hysterically in one scene, sobbing in another scene, trying to kill somebody in the next scene, even a victim of the killer in the next scene, and so on. It would have taxed the abilities of the finest actor in the world! I was supposed to direct, and he had increased the size of my role. There was a young actor—a high-school actor, not even a professional—named Bobby Beam, who had asked my assistant if we would give him a job on the crew if he got to San Juan on his own. Knowing that we could always use somebody, she had said, "Sure," so he hitchhiked across the United States and arrived in Puerto Rico in time for the second picture. We put him on as the boom man in the sound crew, replacing a Puerto Rican boom man who didn't know English too well and really messed up his cues. I gave Bobby Beam the part I was supposed to play in *Creature from the Haunted Sea.*

Chuck Griffith got conned into writing a rewrite of The Beast from the Haunted Cave, *which was a rewrite of* Naked Paradise. *It would now be called* Creature from the Haunted Sea. *This was the third time he'd written the same script. I think Roger offered him the enormous sum of five hundred dollars to do it. Anyway, Chuck wrote a character for me called Pete, an ex-Vaudevillian who did one birdcall too many and blew his brains out.*

—BEACH DICKERSON, actor

The film had a really weird story line. Chuck had sent us the script on a Thursday. I read it Thursday night, rewrote sections of it between takes on the set Friday, had it duplicated Friday afternoon, passed it out and rehearsed it Friday, Saturday and Sunday, prepared it on the location on Sunday, and started shooting on Monday.

The story line was based on my experiences in Havana the night Castro's men invaded the town. I was sharing a suite at the National Hotel with Woolner Brothers, who were interested in doing some work with a company called Cuban Color Films. In the middle of the night I heard what sounded like a car backfiring and went out on the balcony. The National was in a park and across the park was a string of restaurants and nightclubs, and it was clear there was machine-gun fire going on there. When we came down to breakfast the next morning we asked the maitre d' what had happened, and he said, "Fidel Castro's men came in and they killed the chief of police and a number of other people coming out of a nightclub." As we were driving out to Cuban Color Films that morning, Batista's men were patrolling with machine-guns. We stopped at a pay phone, called the travel bureau back at the hotel, and got on an afternoon flight to New Orleans.

Creature from the Haunted Sea, 1960

Creature from the Haunted Sea revolved around the Castro takeover. Batista's men were trying to get out of the country with a supply of gold, and the only "honest" man the Castro men would trust was a Mafia gangster running a casino, played by Tony Carbone. It was an insane story. They made a deal with Carbone to get on his yacht, and Carbone and his cohorts invent the story of a murderous sea monster and started killing off Batista's men to get the gold. What Carbone and his men didn't know was there really was a sea monster that was crawling up out of the water each night and killing men.

There was one great scene between Carbone and one of his henchmen, a really dumb killer played by Beach Dickerson. Beach was supposed to kill one man this night, but the next morning there were two men dead on the deck. Carbone said, "I told you to kill one." Beach replied, "I thought I did kill only one. I don't understand what's going on here."

Then Roger said to me, "We have to make a monster." "We have to make a monster?" "We have to make a monster that can run on land and swim underwater," Roger said. I said, "You're kidding!" He said, "No, I'm not kidding." I said, "What do you mean, we? Every time you say 'we,' you don't do a thing." He said, "Beach, I know you can do it, so don't worry about it." I said, "How much money are we talking about, Roger?" He said, "Well, for a monster that can run on land and swim underwater, I think a hundred and fifty dollars should be sufficient." "Including materials?" "Of course including materials!"
Well, this kid—Bobby Beam, another actor in this movie—and I made a monster that ran on land and swam underwater, and the thing held up. For one hundred and fifty dollars! And it was a funny monster—we stole army helmets and stacked them to form its face. We draped its body in oilcloth, to give it a sleazy look, and we gave it fangs—we cut out holes and pasted in the teeth. We got two tennis balls and a ping-pong ball and cut them in two—that was the monster's eyes. Then we draped it in steel wool. That monster was seven and a half feet tall—we spent a fortune on steel wool. Those were the good old days.

—BEACH DICKERSON, actor

I decided in this one to have the monster live. The final shot of the picture was of the monster sitting at the bottom of the ocean, with the gold and the skeletons of everybody piled around him, picking his teeth.

The film had a mild success. I couldn't believe you could do such insane stuff on film and get a little tiny profit. As I've said, it should have been a big success or a big failure. I stopped at that point. I'd

Creature from the Haunted Sea, 1960

done three of these. It was time to move on to other things.

Atlas (1960) was my last attempt to do a big picture on a low budget. The picture itself was not as notable as the preparations. This was just after the U-2 spy plane was shot down over Russia. I got the idea to do a picture in Europe mainly because I wanted to go to Europe. With the title of *I Flew a Spy Plane over Russia*, Bob Towne and I worked out a story line. I went to Europe, and Bob was to send me the script. I showed the treatment to the people at EMI in London, and they said, "Yes, we'll make a deal with you." It was a good treatment, and I had previously worked with them on a film I'd done for AIP. I sat in London for a number of weeks and Bob never sent me the script. It was the same thing as when I was in Puerto Rico—he couldn't finish that script. He'd written a picture for me earlier, called *Fraternity Row*, which had taken him a year to write; by then I'd lost interest in the project.

I finally left London because I was beginning to feel very foolish about the whole thing. At that time Joe Levine had had a giant success with the picture *Hercules*. I thought, "Okay, it's quite clear that Bob Towne is never going to finish *I Flew a Spy Plane over Russia*, and here I am sitting in Europe. I've got a little bit of the money for a production. I'll go to Greece and do a picture called *Atlas*."

In Greece I met with a small Greek production company which agreed to put up most of the money; I would put up just a little bit. Again I called Chuck Griffith, who was in Tel Aviv at the time, and broke. He said, "Send me money and I'll be right up there." I said, "You'll have to write the script and you're going to be assistant director and you'll play one of the roles." He said, "Fine." So Chuck came in from Tel Aviv and started writing. I then called home and had a couple of actors come over. Something like three or four days before we were ready to shoot, my partner, Vion Papamichalis, took me to a restaurant called Flocia, which is one of the finest restaurants in Athens. He bought me this wonderful lunch with a lot of wine, and at the end of lunch he started crying and told me that he had not obtained the financing and we would have to cancel the picture. I said, "I've spent what little money I've already invested—actors are coming in from Hollywood—Chuck is here. There's nothing I can do." I was committed to the tune of about twenty thousand. I remembered having done *Gunslinger* in six days and doing other low-budget, action-adventure films, so I thought, rather than lose the twenty thousand, the thing to do was do a

Atlas, 1960

low-budget epic, to at least protect my investment.

Once, we were in Athens to make Atlas, *and we passed a sign outside a nightclub that said, "Floor show at 2:00 A.M." So we came back at 2:00 A.M. and were joined by a couple of hookers, but there was no floor show. So Roger became very angry and refused to pay the bill. The band and the waiters all moved in on us very ominously—the bill was sixty dollars or so for a bottle of champagne. Roger paid the bill and we left. He then discovered he forgot his lighter, and he screwed up his courage and went right back into the lion's den to get it. This was very brave of Roger. That same evening there were pimps all over the streets of Athens, and they gave us a ticket that said we could have a free beer in The Canada Club. We decided it was probably a trap for hookers, but Roger said, "We have a slip here that says we get a free beer. We will get a free beer!" So we went into the place and were immediately surrounded by prostitutes and bouncers. We drank the two beers and left, amid great screaming and hostility—"Come on, cowboy, stick around for awhile." Roger calmly said to them, "No thank you," and left. Great presence of mind!*

—CHUCK GRIFFITH, scriptwriter

I did *Atlas* for about all the money I could scrape up, which was about seventy-five thousand. This picture actually made a little money, but it was the same old story of inefficiently doing a giant film. We had to revise the script—actually, the best thing about the film probably was the revisions we did on the script. We felt when we rewrote the script that it would be a great picture. But we ran into problems in shooting around Greece, because of all the ruins—how to account for them? We had Atlas say to Praximides, "Tell me, Praximides, ah, your country seems to be all ruins. Why is that?" Praximides said, "There's been constant warfare here for six hundred years. We've not had time to rebuild." That took care of that!

I think his main talent is inspiring a search for ideas on the part of people who are working for him. And his main flaw is squelching the same ideas when they come up.

—CHUCK GRIFFITH, scriptwriter

Battle Beyond the Sun (1962) was originally a Russian science-fiction picture. I've forgotten the original title, but it had wonderful special effects and an outrageous story. I bought the English-speaking rights to the film from the Russians with the provision that I could rewrite the story line within the sound track. As I recall, the original story had something to do with space competition

Battle Beyond the Sun, 1962

between the Russians and the Americans. It was so anti-American, I was really surprised; I had not been aware that their propaganda was so frankly outrageous. The Russian spacemen were all good-looking, brave, courageous, while the Americans had twisted faces and short squatty bodies—I think one of them had a huge scar across his face—and were cowards and liars. When the Americans got up into space, their shoddy American equipment malfunctioned and they realized they were going to fall into the sun and die. At this point they began crying and moaning; one man was hitting his head against the wall, another man was sobbing uncontrollably, another was calling hysterically for his mother to come and save him, and the other was drinking. I was amazed that our agents over there had accepted the story.

I had to stay somewhere near the situation, which took place slightly in the future, but obviously I could not release a picture with a story line like that. So I came up with the idea that they were not Americans or Russians; I said, "This is the future and the world has been divided into two new countries—North Hemis and South Hemis. North Hemis is all the countries of the Northern Hemisphere and South Hemis is all the countries of the Southern Hemisphere." I had rights to the picture for the United States, Canada, and England. So the good guys, the former Russians, became North Hemis and the former Americans became South Hemis, and on that basis we were able to make a reasonable film.

This was the first picture Francis Coppola worked on; I had hired him out of the UCLA film school. I gave him the job of editing the picture and writing the American version's dialogue. At one point I wanted a battle between two outer-space creatures, and he was going to shoot the battle, using miniatures made by some friends of his from UCLA. The sequence was going to take only a few seconds. He said, "What kind of outer-space creatures do you want?" I just said casually, "Maybe we can have some phallic concept to this battle, it might be interesting." He said, "Fine." When he came back and showed me what he had shot, it wasn't phallic, it was graphic. I said, "Francis, you know we can't put this in a picture." He said, "Nobody will even know. The only reason it seems raw to you is you know the origin of what it's all about." I said, "This is simply taking two models—a model of a male sex organ and a female sex organ—and having them fight together and eventually join and one defeats the other." He said, "Nobody will ever know." And, weirdly enough, he was right. We never had any complaints about it in the picture. Nobody protested, no censorship problems whatsoever. And the film turned out to be fairly successful.

Battle Beyond the Sun, 1962

The greatest thing about Roger from the point of view of us who were associated with him was that he gave us a chance at a time, considerably at a time, when no one would give anyone a chance. And the fact that he was giving us a chance primarily so he could make money was fine. My feeling is if Roger Corman were running one of the major film studios and specifically gave new people the kind of opportunities to work on films a lot of people would go on to do more ambitious things and would find their own talent. Roger was a one-man talent developer. And he was the only one. And so, as I look back on him, I'm real grateful, because I got my first opportunities in films from him. He's also been a good friend, and he's a nice man.

—FRANCIS FORD COPPOLA, director, writer, producer

Pit Stop (1963) was a very-low-budget black-and-white film written and directed by Jack Hill. It was actually a rather well-made little picture. It was the closest thing in recent times to what used to be called a "B" picture—a film designed as the second half of the bill. Some were quite well made in a workmanlike way. This was really in that vein, although it wasn't designed to be a second half. It was a straightforward action picture of a young stock car driver, the owner of the team, and the wife of the owner. It was notable probably because Ellen Burstyn, then Ellen McRae, played her first lead in the film and was very good. With people like Ellen Burstyn, you know from the beginning that they are good, purely. You may not know they are going to be great stars, but the ability shows. It was clear that she knew what she was doing. She was a good actress and she was an intelligent actress, even in this really very-very-low-budget film, which cost about forty thousand dollars. The only thing I regret about the picture is that we shot it in black-and-white. I wanted to shoot in color, but there were more stock car races in Southern California at night and we didn't have enough exposure at night to shoot the races without lighting —obviously we could not light a stadium. In retrospect, the film made money and did nicely—that is, from a commercial standpoint; I consider it to be just a nice workmanlike film.

I always felt somehow that Roger was slightly intimidated by actors and didn't really want to get into arguments with them, like he thought they knew more about acting than he did."

—PETER BOGDANOVICH, director

I met Roger in the mid-1950s, when he came to my acting classes. He had seen this "new breed" of actors coming from New York. He was intrigued with this new mystique of the Stanislavski method

Ellen Burstyn in *Pit Stop*, 1963

acting—actors who were acting with excessive introversion. He didn't know how to handle that, how to cope with it. He wanted to penetrate the mystique of how actors could be giving and gracious, not grumpy, yet at the same time be creative. *Actors didn't have to be morbid and pathological to act well. "What the hell is this crazy thing that comes from New York?" he asked. I was most admiring of his impulse to come to my classes, where he met many talented people—something bothered him and he wanted to find out about it.*

—JEFF COREY, actor, teacher

Francis Ford Coppola was the soundman on the film *The Young Racers* (1962). Our first work was on the Monte Carlo Grand Prix, and then we came through Paris on our way to the Belgium Grand Prix; I think we stopped in Paris to see the first rushes. Floyd Crosby, the cameraman, commented during the rushes that the sound wasn't too good because you could hear the cameras. Francis, defending himself, said, "Yes, but it's the cameraman, it's not my fault. It's your fault." Obviously, the soundman is supposed to blanket out the camera noise; you can't truly blame that on the cameraman. But it showed me that Francis was thinking fast, even if not correctly, at that early date.

He had me doing everything: I did a little bit of editing, a little bit of writing, I was on a sound stage. Around that time I won a writing prize and shared a golden award. Roger was pleased to have as an assistant someone who did that. He liked that kind of thing. At one point he was going off to make The Young Racers *and asked me if I knew someone who could be the soundman. I immediately said I could do it and went home and took out the tape recorder and read the instruction book.*

I did some second-unit photography; on Roger's films, everyone got to do everything. It was really like an intensive course in the mechanics of putting a film together. Roger always had a pattern—when he made a film he figured that all the costs of getting the people over to Europe or wherever had been paid for by someone else, so he always made a second film for himself. But when The Young Racers *was over he had to go back immediately to do* The Raven, *so I said I'd do it. At that time he was interested in doing some kind of picture like "homicidal." He asked if I would do a picture called* Dementia. *He wanted* that. *He said, "Okay, great." He gave me twenty-two thousand dollars, and I went to Ireland, where the film could be made cheaply. We wrote the script to order.*

—FRANCIS FORD COPPOLA, director, writer, producer

The Young Racers, 1962

CHAPTER THREE

A LOVE AFFAIR WITH EDGAR ALLEN POE

I think that Roger himself would smile a great deal if anybody would talk of him in terms of being an artist. Because he's dealing with those figures every day and how to keep the budget down and things like that. But I would say that over the years he's produced on those low budgets a number of things, like The Masque of the Red Death, *the Vincent Price movie, which are superior in their genre, and perhaps twenty-five years from now someone will look back and say, "Yes, they're works of art." But I think it would be arrogant on his part and possibly arrogant on my part to claim that they are works of art.*

—*ARTHUR KNIGHT, film critic*

The Poe series was never designed as a Poe series. I simply wanted to do *The Fall of the House of Usher.*

I'd always admired the works of Edgar Allen Poe and had read him extensively. When AIP approached me again with the idea of double-bill horror films, I convinced them to make one color film in fifteen days instead of two black-and-white films in ten days each. Up until *House of Usher* (1960) I'd never had a fifteen-day schedule, and AIP had never financed one.

I remember Sam Arkoff saying at our final pre-production meeting, "There's no monster in this story." I really had no retort, but said, "The house—the house is the monster." I don't know if Sam really went along with that, but he agreed to make the picture.

During the filming with Vincent Price, while we were going over lines, Vincent questioned the line "The house lives, the house breathes." I said, "That line is in there so we can make this picture," and then related the story about Sam. Vincent said, "Fine, I'll bring life to that line."

I was really very impressed with Roger. He has sort of a lot of pretensions towards psychoanalysis or whatever you want to call it—all that sort of psychic reasons and psychoanalytical stuff. I think he was a student of that. There was a great deal of talk about Freudian methods, which Boris [Karloff] and Peter [Lorre] and Basil [Rathbone] all kind of joked about, but it was also very helpful, because Roger was trying to get an idea across. There wasn't really very much room for camaraderie, because when you do a picture like that in nineteen days you're working your ass off. I think the waste on other pictures is just ridiculous. Roger had a marvelous knack of getting people together beforehand and kind of conning them, in a way, into a rehearsal—I mean, every actor wants a rehearsal, but of course we're not allowed to do it without being paid, but Roger would get us down and we

Vincent Price in *House of Usher*, 1960

would read it and walk over on the set—well, even that much of it was very helpful.

—*VINCENT PRICE, actor*

When *Usher* did well, AIP asked me to do another Edgar Allen Poe picture, and I chose *The Pit and the Pendulum*, primarily because I felt I could get a very interesting climax to the film. The stories obviously lent themselves to cinema, and this, to a certain extent, has determined the way we did the rest of the Poe films. Most of the short stories were only two or three pages long. They were really fragments—wonderful fragments. The method we adopted on *The Pit and the Pendulum* (1961) was to use the Poe short story as the climax for a third act to the motion picture, because a two-page short story is not about to give you a ninety-minute motion picture. We then constructed the first two acts in what we hoped was a manner faithful to Poe, as his climax would run only a short time on the screen. As a result, a number of critics reviewed the films merely as Corman/Poe, or Poe/Corman, which was a little bit more fitting on the basis that there was some necessary additional work for me. Dick Mathieson, who understood Poe and understood the way I worked, did most of the writing on the first two Poe films, and Bob Towne, for his second screenplay, did *The Tomb of Ligeia* (1964), which was the last of the Poe series.

How I got The Pit and the Pendulum *is a very interesting story. Roger was going with an actress at the time, and I think they had a falling out. Roger called me and said, "Do you want to go to Greece on a big picture?" and I almost dropped the phone. I said, "Yes." He said, "Pack your bags—you leave in two days. You're going to star in a picture in Greece." Obviously, she was to have starred and they had had a fight and he needed an actress. I immediately ran to the doctor to get my shot and bought my luggage, and I had this big Band-aid on my arm with a huge scab underneath it, but when I got to the airport it seemed that he and his friend had made up, and she went on the plane with my ticket. I stood in the airport, crying, going crazy, and ripping the scab off my arm, I was so upset; I still have a little scar there. When Roger came back from Greece, I called him on the phone and said, "How could you do that to me?" He said, "I'm gonna make it up to you, Lynn, I'm very sorry that all happened. How would you like to do* The Pit and the Pendulum? *There are three very small scenes, but I'll carry you for the picture on salary." And he did—and I never forgot him for that. I played the sneaky maid who was lurking behind every bedpost, every corner, every door. The camera would zoom in on my face—and I looked like the one who had just committed the*

Vincent Price in *The Pit and the Pendulum*, 1961

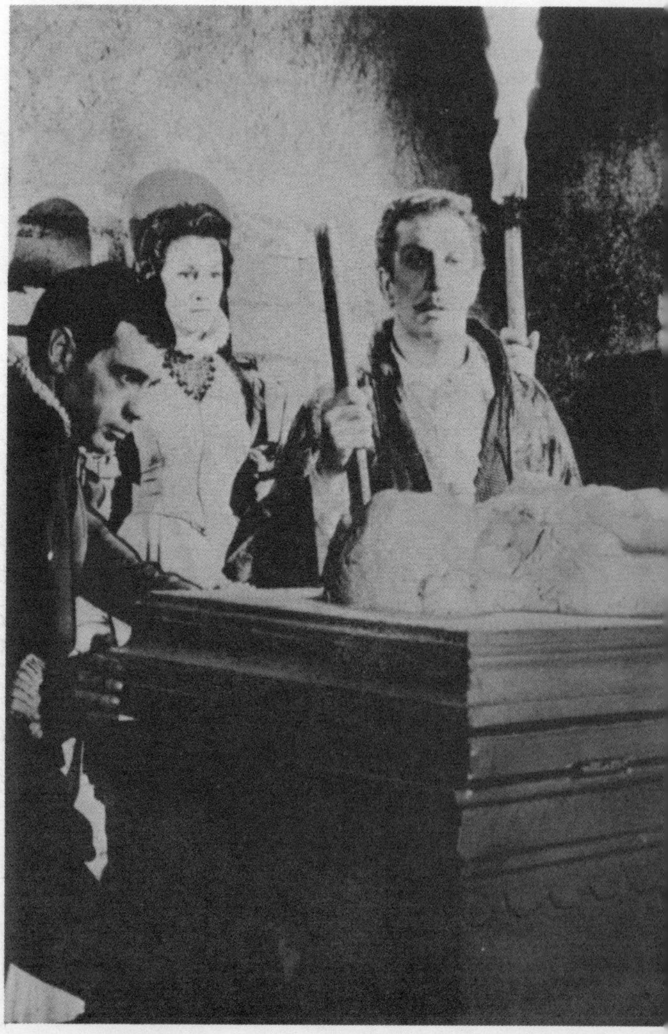

murder, when all I was doing was dusting. Really!
—LYNN BERNAY, actress

The script on *Premature Burial* (1961) was not as strong, I felt, as the previous two Poe films. I made a conscious effort in certain areas to add more horror, probably because I was doing a great deal of reading at the time and had talked with a number of psychologists, including a doctor in Beverly Hills who had written a book called *Beyond Laughter*, in which he discussed the psychological origins of laughter and terror, which he felt were two sides of the same coin. I based some of my work on his theories and on further theories that I developed, coming to the conclusion that terror was really the re-creation of childhood fantasies. The child is sometimes alone in a house or in a room—in a world he only dimly understands. It's possibly a dark night, it's stormy, there's thunder, lightning—forces that are very frightening to him—and he has no way of coping. And they make a very deep imprint on the mind. The parent can later say, "It's only thunder, it's only lightning—these are normal things," but to the child, I think, these explanations are only partially helpful. The unconscious terror of the dark and the strange noises and lights remains. Therefore, the horror film taps that unconscious and takes one back to childhood fears.

I think it's the function of the horror film—and it's a useful function—to expose those fears and show they are baseless. The unconscious minds of most people have common underpinnings. After all, we've all been raised in Western civilization in basically the same ways, so there are similarities among us. I try to reach what I consider the uniform elements of the unconscious by building up a sense of suspense and then cracking through it quickly. The process is much the same as in telling a joke or engaging in the act of sex. There is a similar building of tension in all three. The climax of a horror film and the punch line of a joke and a sexual orgasm are alike in that they all provide a break or release of tension. In a horror film, if it's done correctly, very often you'll get a scream from the audience—for you've affected their unconscious—followed by a little ripple of laughter—which is when the conscious mind takes over again and says to the unconscious, "Okay, you didn't need to scream." And this is why, in my later films, I added humor and made essentially comedy-horror films. These are a lot of fun to make but are also challenging—like a complex piece of music.

The Masque of the Red Death (1964) was the first of the Poe films that I did in England, and it has a

Jane Asher in *The Masque of the Red Death*. 1964

slightly bigger look than the films I did in the United States. The films in the United States were shot in three weeks; the one in England had a five-week schedule (however, English crews work slower than American crews). I also had access to some very beautiful sets left over from *Beckett* and one or two other films that were very, very well done. We revised them and pulled them out of the scene docket at the studio and used them for both pictures. One other thing about *Masque*—I always considered it to be one of Poe's best stories and after *House of Usher* it was my original choice for the second film, rather than *The Pit and the Pendulum*. The reason I chose *The Pit and the Pendulum* over *Masque* is that the hooded figure of Death walking through a plague-stricken country is the essential feature of *The Masque of the Red Death* and also of Ingmar Bergman's picture *The Seventh Seal*, and I didn't want to be in a position of doing a picture based upon a nineteenth-century short story and possibly be accused of taking ideas from a film that was shot in the 1950s. As a matter of fact, I think it's highly probable that when Bergman did *The Seventh Seal* he was aware of *The Masque of the Red Death*.

I think Roger was getting better and better. And as the pictures became more and more popular, and his style and everything was accepted, they became sort of cult things—and people write about them now in great glowing terms. Their original reception was terrible, except for, strangely enough, House of Usher, *for which I was given the* Herald Tribune *award for the best performance of the year.*

—VINCENT PRICE, actor

In *Tales of Terror* (1962) we decided to do three fragments, just to do three separate stories. One of them, to be played for humor, was "The Black Cat." This was my first working association with Peter Lorre. Peter was a very funny man, and he played the husband of Joyce Jamieson. Vincent Price played a famous wine taster, a very cultivated man. Peter was just a drunk—a total drunken bum—who at the beginning of the picture was thrown out of the house by Joyce Jamieson and went stumbling down the street. (Incidentally, I built that street on a medium-sized sound stage. It was an example of how to construct a street that's maybe only fifty or sixty feet long. We shot from various angles and hung different street signs to create the impression that Lorre was walking a great distance. I'd like to see the movie again to see whether it still does look as though he's walking a longer distance.) Walking down the street, Peter saw a sign for a wine taster's convention. He went in and there was Vincent, the famous wine taster,

Boris Karloff in *The Terror*, 1962

saying that anyone who wanted to compete in the tasting could come forward. Peter, still half drunk, stumbled up and said that he'd compete. Vincent, ever the gentleman, said, "Give him a seat," and took out some of his materials. Vincent had a little silver cup with a chain hung around his neck, and when they gave him the wine, rather than putting it in a glass, he poured the wine into the silver cup, held the cup over its candle, and sniffed the aroma of the heated wine. He then took a little bit of the wine into his mouth and swished it around in his mouth for a moment before drinking it—it was a super-elegant, meticulous routine. Then he would announce what the wine was, and he was always right. Everybody would applaud. Then it was Peter's turn. He was slouched down in the chair, and when they gave him a bottle and all of the material, he just took the bottle of wine, held it up in the air over his head, and poured it all over himself. Some of it ran into his mouth; the rest of it poured all over his body and on the table and floor and everything. The people were ready to throw him out, thinking this was the worst guy they had ever seen. But he roused himself up and called the name of the wine instantly. At that point Vincent realized Peter was a great wine taster, and the two began their competition. Neither ever missed. Vincent got progressively drunker, but always remained elegant. Peter just got so smashed that he didn't know what was happening. The routine ended with Peter lying on his back on the floor, pouring wine all over everything and still calling the names of the wines correctly. Finally the competition was over. The two of them, now great buddies, went stumbling, totally drunk, out into the street and back to Peter's house—where we got into the story of "The Black Cat," in which Vincent stole Peter's wife.

A professional wine taster showed us the whole thing about testing the wine and breathing it in and doing all that stuff—then Peter and I just went a little further. I was trying to do it in an exaggerated fashion, which made it so funny. To this day, people still talk about that scene. I was doing it the way wine testers do it, and Peter was doing it the way they didn't do it. But here was an example again where I think Roger was so bright—he had two actors who were very inventive, who had this opportunity to see how it was actually done, and we were allowed to "comedy" it up.

—VINCENT PRICE, actor

We also played *The Raven* (1962) for humor, and had a really good cast: Vincent Price, Peter Lorre, and Boris Karloff. They were just wonderful to work with, and each a little bit different in the way in which he worked. Boris Karloff was a very

Basil Rathbone, Vincent Price and Peter Lorre in *Tales of Terror*, 1961

meticulous actor who would learn his lines to the letter; he would come in prepared to do them just so. Peter Lorre would more or less know his lines but was very creative and would improvise on the set and come up with wonderful stuff, which I would try to integrate into the script as much as I could. Vincent was more or less in between. He would come in as well prepared as Boris, but he would be prepared to improvise and play around a little bit with Peter. They all got along very well, but it did drive Boris a little crazy, because he would have done all this preparation and they would be changing scenes at the last minute. For instance, the coffin was always buried in the crypt beneath the house—nobody ever buried anybody in a graveyard, always in a crypt beneath the house. When Vincent said to Peter, "My wife's body is buried in a crypt beneath the house," and Peter said, "Where else?" we knew we were taking off. When they came down the stairs for the take we had the crypt really decorated. There were cobwebs and dust and rats running around, and it was just the dirtiest place ever. Peter came down the stairs, looked around, and said "Hard place to keep clean, eh?"

But I liked the picture, knowing we went for comedy for a variety of reasons. We never had very much money in these things. We would save the units of the sets, so each film would get a little bit bigger—we'd bring them back, repaint them, and make bigger castles. *The Raven* had about the biggest look of any of the Poe films. At the end of the film there was a very nice duel between Vincent and Boris—they were musicians and they were hurling thunderbolts at each other. You have to know that this is within the confines of a fifteen-day picture with a budget of three hundred thousand to four hundred thousand dollars. Within those limitations, the climactic duel between Vincent and Boris came off well.

The Tomb of Ligeia *was vaguely based on an idea that Roger and I had once. I had said I had always wanted to do a picture in a ruin, but actually using the ruin as an actual place, with real furniture in it and the ruin around it, which I thought would be very effective. Well, this is sort of what he adapted to* The Tomb of Ligeia, *which I think was the best one we ever did.*

—VINCENT PRICE, actor

The Tomb of Ligeia was the last Poe picture—I just didn't want to do any more. In order to make it somewhat interesting for me, I broke almost all of my rules. For instance, I had never wanted to shoot in real situations. I felt we were dealing with the world beyond the conscious, a closed, somewhat artificial world, so I tried to shoot everything in

Vincent Price in *The Raven*, 1962

studios. Everything was constructed, and maybe built a little off scale. When necessary, I would have to occasionally photograph the real world. In *House of Usher* Mark Damon, playing the young man coming into the house, had to ride across a landscape. There had been a fire in the Hollywood Hills, and I went up there and shot out of sequence to have him ride through this burned-out wooded area, which gave it a very eerie and very nice feeling. So I tried not to show reality. But with *The Tomb of Ligeia* I said, "Okay, I'm gonna show reality." We went into the English countryside and photographed a fox hunt, a wedding at a very pretty English church, a sixteenth-century monastery in ruins, to be used as the exterior of the house. It was very, very interesting. As a result, *Ligeia* had a very different look from the other Poe films, because it was the first and only time the sun ever shone in one of them—I did it just to see what would happen when I broke the rules. In retrospect, it gave the picture a good look, but I think the original theory was right: it was better to keep it a closed, dark world.

It was the second screenplay by Bob Towne, who wrote it as a love story. We picked it for that reason —just so I wouldn't be continually reworking the same ground. Although every one of the Poe pictures was commercially successful and, so far as I know, got very good reviews, I just stopped, because I just didn't want to do any more. AIP suspended the series for a year and then asked me to do one more. I said no. I think they did two or three more Poe films in England.

Tomb of Ligeia, 1964

Ray Milland in *The Man with the X-Ray Eyes*, 1963

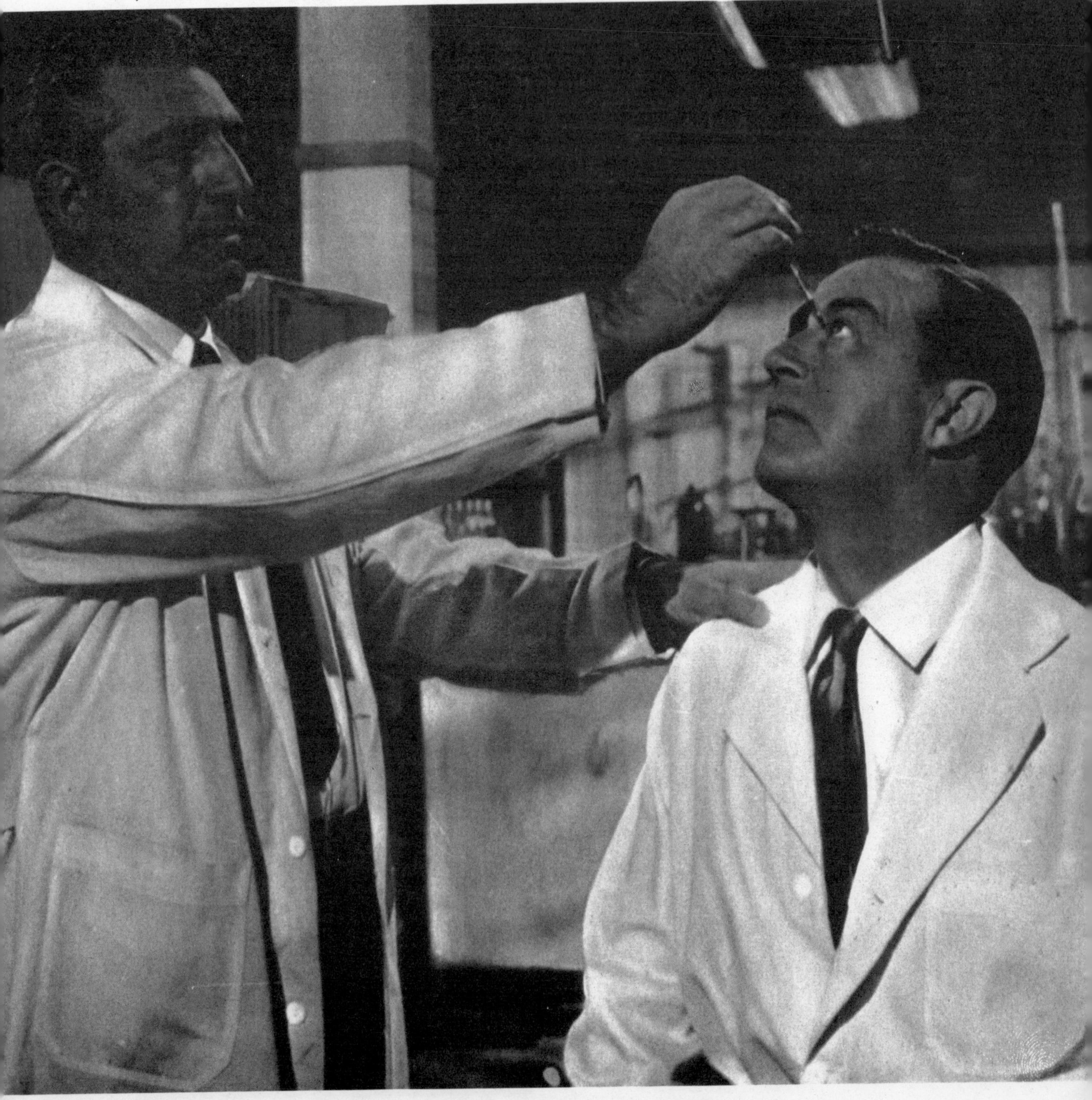

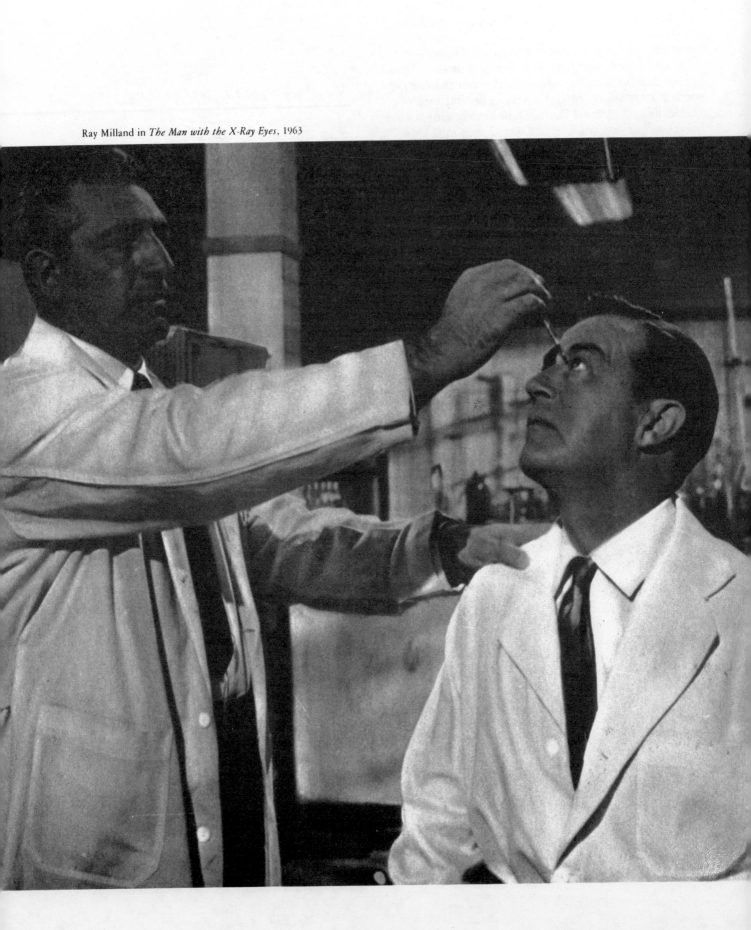

CHAPTER FOUR

WILL SUCCESS SPOIL ROGER CORMAN?

He was a normal kid.
—*MRS. ANN CORMAN, Roger's mother*

The Man with the X-Ray Eyes (1963) did reasonably well. In my opinion, it was a good idea that never developed as well into the final picture. But I won a couple of film-festival prizes with it and got just wonderful reviews, and it's been mentioned often in anthologies. Ray Milland played a doctor who experimented on himself and developed progressive X-ray vision. At first he could see through paper and wood, then metal, and finally through to the center of the universe. It had a religious-mystical theme throughout, and I think the critics were picking up on that. It was rather nicely done from that standpoint. But it didn't turn out as well as I'd hoped because, after developing the script, I told AIP that on a fifteen-day schedule, with a budget of three hundred thousand dollars, I thought the special effects were too big; they should abandon the project, and I wouldn't charge them for the work I had put in. Whenever I had tried to do big special effects on low budget, the cheapness always showed through, and I just didn't want to do it again. However, AIP was very pleased with the script and really felt we could pull it off. They said to go ahead and try it. Finally I said yes and I did it. When the doctor was supposed to see through the exterior of a building to its framework, I photographed a building under construction and we just saw the framework of the building. The effects were like that. It never really did come together because of all the special-effects compromises.

What I learned from Roger, although I tend to forget it now and then, but I think is a good rule to go back to, is that it is good to be real clear with yourself about what you're trying to do. The audience really appreciates that. Even in the more artistic films, it's important to set up what it is your time will accomplish, what you are going to express, what you're going for, things you will go and try to do. That's something I learned from Roger. Also that moviemaking is a practical business, like building a building. You have wonderful forms and drawings and build a building of the future, but you have to build it out of materials and cement and resources—and that's something that Roger fundamentally taught me.
—*FRANCIS FORD COPPOLA, director, writer, producer*

The Young Racers was something else. I was going to do another picture for AIP, which was still fairly small, although they were doing well. I had blocked out a certain amount of time in the summer, and shortly before we were ready to go they told me they were short of money and couldn't

The Man with the X-Ray Eyes, 1963

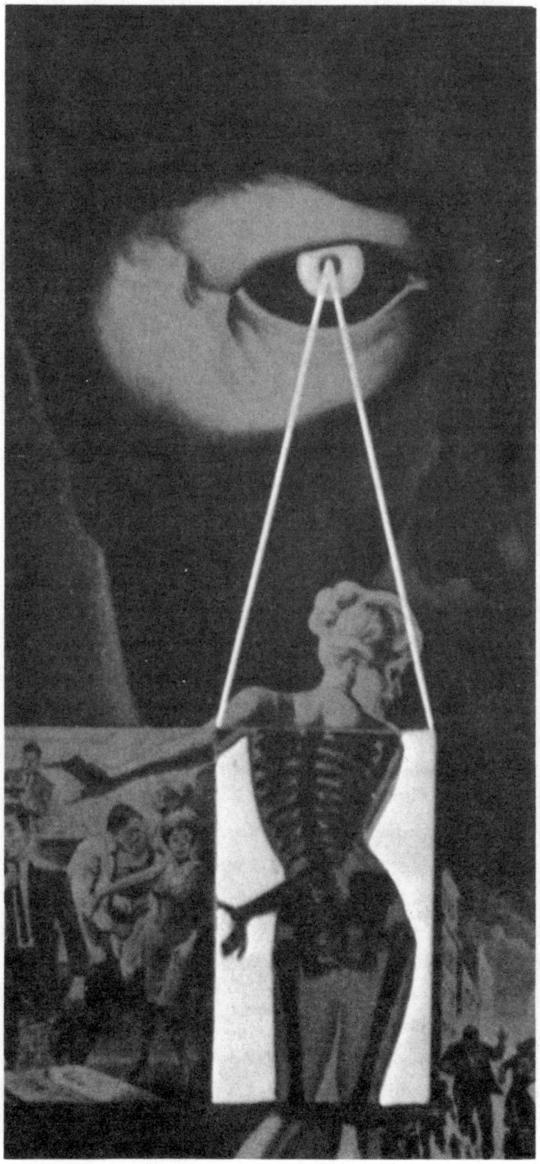

make a film that summer. I said, "How much do you have?" and they told me, "About a hundred and fifty to a hundred and eighty thousand dollars," and I said, "Maybe I'll come up with an idea for that amount of money," and they said, "Fine." I'd always been interested in Grand Prix racing, and I thought it would be nice to go to Europe for the summer and follow the Grand Prix circuit. Bob Campbell, who was another young writer, had a script about bullfighting that I thought was pretty good, which he had never been able to sell to anybody. I said, "Do you feel there is some similarity between bullfighting and motor racing?" Frankly, you're playing with death in both areas, despite what else he said about motor racing. I said, "Could you rewrite this script very quickly in a couple of weeks and make it a racing picture?" He said yes, and I told AIP I would do *The Young Racers*.

I made a deal with a lot of friends of mine to go to Europe; there wasn't that much money, but essentially it would be partly work and partly vacation. "We'll be all over Europe at the tracks watching the races and you'll have time off between the races, so it'll be vacation time in between." I got almost everybody working for me to come along, including Francis Ford Coppola, fresh out of UCLA, as a soundman. He also helped Chuck Hanawalt, my key grip, rebuild my Volkswagen into one of the first cinemobile-type vehicles.

I then flew to Munich and bought an Arriflex camera and had it shipped to Monte Carlo, where we opened the picture with the Monte Carlo Grand Prix. I made a deal with Sunbeam to use a Sunbeam Alpine sports car, which we would introduce as part of the picture in the Monte Carlo Grand Prix. Then we all drove up to Paris for some scenes there, and on to the Belgium Grand Prix afterward. Chuck Griffith, who was working as a writer and also an assistant director, totaled the car in Provence the first day out. Poor Bill Campbell, who played the lead, never had a chance to drive the Sunbeam—he ended up walking into the scene. These are the problems of low-budget films. There isn't much you can do about them.

With Roger I learned a practical approach to making a film: you give your best shot, find what it is you're trying to pull off, and go for that. It's very hard to consider Roger as a director, because Roger never gave himself half a chance to be a director. Roger basically went into directing because with the director he'd hired he figured, "Hey, I can do it as well as he." And he would save the director's salary. So Roger went into the movie business to make money and to succeed.

—FRANCIS FORD COPPOLA, director, writer, producer

Mark Damon in *The Young Racers*, 1962

The Intruder (1961) is the most acclaimed film I had made up to that time, and maybe ever. It got magnificent reviews and won several film festival awards. It was also the first film I had ever made that lost money. It had to do with the integration of the schools in the South. I was very much concerned with the subject and believed heavily in this picture. Up until that time I never developed a screenplay that hadn't been financed; normally my record was so good that I would just tell people the idea and immediately get financing. On this one I bought a novel and developed the screenplay and nobody would back me. They were probably right—it was very much a socially concerned picture without heavy commercial overtones. So I finally put up some of my own money and some money from Pathé American, a new distribution company at the time, and I had only a three-week schedule. I hoped to have more than the ninety thousand dollars I was prepared to invest. The locale was the South; the cast was headed by William Shatner, with the rest of the cast played by townspeople. As a result, the film has a very gritty, honest look, primarily because I wanted it that way, and secondarily because there was no other way to do it. There was no money to build sets. I think the fact that some of the townspeople were not brilliant actors was made up for by the fact that their faces were right, they looked good, and their accents were really right. We recruited a bunch of guys sitting around the central square of the town to be kind of the cohorts of the segregationists. They loved everything Shatner said and cheered and applauded when he gave his speeches. They had never read the script, and were really upset at the end of the picture to find out that he was the villain. It really broke them up. They thought everything he said—"Don't let these niggers get into the school"—was right on, and they would applaud and cheer every time he said it. Finding out he was the bad guy was a blow to them.

I have a high regard for the man. But the thing that struck me so much about him was that here, relatively early in his career, he put what was for him a lot of money into The Intruder, *a picture that was clearly a gamble, a picture that had to do with intolerance, that had to do with racial bigotry, that involved lynching, and didn't come up with any easy happy ending. And it was a film that he believed in. I'm not saying it was a great movie—it wasn't. Certainly it was not badly made—on the technical level it seemed more than passingly competent. But I think at that time it was a daring movie. I don't think the ending was fully resolved, but there were very intriguing things in it. I'm sure that if that picture had been more understandingly accepted, Roger would have stuck with making a*

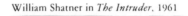

William Shatner in *The Intruder*, 1961

lot more like that. I think what he does do, exploitation films that he has made and exploitation films that he has produced, are generally more than competent on their level.

—ARTHUR KNIGHT, film critic

We had some difficulty on the final sequence of *The Intruder*—it's something of a mess. It was supposed to take place outside a certain school, and I was to shoot the sequence in two days. At the end of the first day of shooting they threw us out of town. I was really in some trouble, because I only had half the ending of the picture and had used all the money there was. So I scouted around that night and found a playground with swings in another town—swings were a key part of it. But the problem was the swings were a different height. Also, it was in a park instead of in front of a school, so I couldn't show any backgrounds. The police of that town evidently had heard from the other town that we were bad people and shouldn't be allowed to make this film. I directed as fast as I could to get these shots while my brother, Gene, a co-producer, talked to the police at the edge of the park. I could hear them from time to time, and he was doing better than I was; he was saying, "Well now, we understand that you don't want us here just now. What are the reasons? What is the legal situation? We of course want to cooperate in every possible way. Can we discuss this? Would you gentlemen like some coffee? Why don't we come over here, we have a little wagon with coffee, would you like some doughnuts, let's sit down, have a chair, let's discuss it. We certainly don't want to stay." He talked for three hours, stalling these guys, discussing aspects of the film, saying we certainly would leave. I got all my key dialogue during that three-hour period. I needed only a few more shots, and I knew my brother couldn't keep it up forever. We were about to break for lunch anyway. I gave my brother the signal, and he said, "All right, all right, there's nothing else to do. We certainly wanna cooperate. We'll leave." So we broke for lunch—but my brother stayed with the police—and I told the production manager to get everything packed up so after lunch we could get out of there. Meanwhile, I would find an out-of-the-way country school somewhere.

There was a girl there from the town who was working with us. She went with us in the car to scout the area. We drove all over the place, and I finally found one place that was really no match whatsoever, but we had no choice. I came back at the end of the lunch break and said, "Okay, here's where we go." We had no permit, but we figured we could set up and shoot and be out of there before anybody found out. So the climax of that

The Intruder, 1961

picture was shot in three different areas.
We shot a Ku Klux Klan raid by some motels in the black section of town on the final night—we figured we already had death threats, we certainly want to hold this for the last shot in the picture. Finally we drove all the way up to St. Louis in the middle of the night and arrived in the morning, grabbed a few hours' sleep, and took a plane back to Los Angeles.
The reviews were magnificent—one that I still remember said this motion picture was a major credit to the entire American film industry—but the film was a financial failure. Despite all these problems, I believe it was and it is still a good film. I think the honesty and the intent really showed through. I reassessed certain aspects of my filmmaking, and probably the thoughts I came out with have influenced most if not all of the other films I've made; as a result, the thought processes after *The Intruder* were probably more important than the picture itself, at least to me. I decided that never again would I make what was overtly a "statement" film, a "theme" film, or what is called a "personal statement" film. And I would not attack an audience directly. From then on I would make entertainment films that would have my personal statement underneath as a subtext, so that the audience could buy it on its entertainment level first and then take the textual level secondarily. I followed that concept through most of my filmmaking.

The key point or film for Roger was The Intruder. *This film changed the course of the Motion Picture Code. Before that, the word "nigger" had* never *been used in a film—you couldn't have gotten the seal of approval—but in our film the word was acceptable in the context of reality. At first we didn't get the seal, then we did, and it was a major breakthrough for the code. Charles Barnes, the star of* The Intruder, *was a young black teenager, an athlete, in the local high school in the South, an area called "the Badlands." While we were filming, everyone thought we were "commie nigger-lovers."*
We had put in our own money, and we got caught in a terrible trap when the film was released. Some distributors said, "We don't have this racial problem, so we won't show it," and some said "We do *have this racial problem, so we won't show it." We were invited to the Cannes Film Festival; then we were told we couldn't show* The Intruder. *The reactionary element was concerned, "in the best interest of Hollywood and all concerned, that this film not be invited as representative of the current motion picture scene." The film was ahead of its time, it was far out in front, but no major distributor would touch it—it got no distribution. The*

Roger Corman directing *The Intruder*, 1961

following year One Potato, Two Potato *came out, which was not as visceral as ours.*

—*GENE CORMAN, producer, Roger's brother*

I'd been making some pictures in Europe and Columbia had asked me to come to them; they would give me the opportunity to do major films. They said the usual things: "Okay, you've had success with low-budget films, we'll give you the chance to make big pictures if you'll sign a contract." I'd never been under contract with a studio before. So I signed a contract, and the first thing they did was offer me a low-budget film. I said, "This is really terrible. I was making more money as an independent—I took a cut in salary to come here for the chance to make big films." And they said, "Well, make one low-budget film and then you'll make a big one." I said, "No. I absolutely will not make a low-budget film. Why should I make a low-budget film for short money for you when I can go back to AIP and get more money for making a low-budget film, plus a piece of the profits?" I fought with Columbia for about a year and ended up breaking the contract and walking away.
At any rate, in the midst of it, AIP's Jim Nicholson called me, and I said, "Sure, I'd be delighted to come back and do a film if you can get me out of my contract with Columbia." Luckily, Jim was a friend of Mike Frankovich, who was the head of the studio, and he arranged with him to give me a leave of absence, which really suited Columbia, because they were paying me every week and I was just sitting there doing nothing. It is really difficult to get a picture through the bureaucracy of the majors. Intelligent people run the majors, very intelligent people, but the heaviness of the studio bureaucracy slows everything down. It takes them years to develop a script. I know people who spend two or three years developing a picture and the picture's canceled before it's ever made.

I've always said that you could throw Roger up in the air and he would land on his feet. He's rarely rattled. He has an easygoing manner, and in those days particularly he was a very hard worker. Once he was on a picture, he had to be his own producer. He didn't have much money, so he almost had *to direct to be able to get on the screen in the short period of time with the amount of money available. He had to produce and direct.*

—*SAM ARKOFF, president and co-founder, American International Pictures*

AIP wanted a contemporary film. I had seen a picture in *Time* magazine of a funeral of a member of the Hell's Angels and been really struck by the graphics of it. The Hell's Angels were in the news media all the time then. So I said I wanted to do a

The Wild Angels, 1966

picture about the Hell's Angels. They said fine. It was really that fast. I mean, it took something like ten seconds to decide on the film to be called *The Wild Angels* (1966). It was the story of the townspeople and what happened to them when the Hell's Angels came into town.

I got a little money to finance a Hell's Angels party and it was really wild. We went through a whole series of Hell's Angels parties. The story could go on forever. We would buy them marijuana and beer—their essentials. They didn't take any drugs other than marijuana then, and they didn't seem to drink whiskey. Beer and marijuana was their trip. And they would tell us these stories of sexual action, fights, raids with other gangs—one time they stole a member of their gang out of a hospital in Tijuana because he'd been arrested and they knew that as soon as he came out of the hospital he was going to be thrown into a Mexican jail. We used that as a sample fight. Peter Fonda with Nancy Sinatra and group broke Bruce Dern out of the hospital for the same reason. The entire story line of the Hell's Angels or of *The Wild Angels,* which I shot under the title of *All the Fallen Angels,* is based upon a story the Hell's Angels told us. As a result, it is not much of a plot picture—it's more of a picturesque story of a way of life.

On a Friday Roger called and said he was starting to shoot a picture that was titled All the Fallen Angels, *and he asked me if I would like to work on the picture. I said, "I'm working on this other script for you." "Put that aside," he said. "Would you like to work on this picture?" I said, "What would I do?" He said, "Well, just . . . I don't know. Just hang around and help me. Be my assistant. There's no script yet. Chuck Griffith is writing the script, but it's not in yet. We'll have it in a week or so, but I want you to look at some locations." I said, "Well, what the hell do I look for?" He said, "Why don't you take your wife and I'll give you some expense money." Roger never said, "Did you look for locations before?" He just said, "Go look for locations." Well, to make a long story short, this job, which had started as a six-week job, stretched out to twenty-two weeks. And I swear to God, it was the greatest lesson learning about movies right on the spot.*

—PETER BOGDANOVICH, *director*

I liked *The Wild Angels.* It had certain limitations—a fifteen-day schedule and not too much money. It had some good actors, and we used the Hell's Angels themselves to play the members of the gang, a development of what I'd done on *The Intruder* a few years earlier. I used the local townspeople. I used professional actors only for the leads. One thing I insisted upon—all of the profes-

The Wild Angels, 1966

sional actors had to ride the bikes themselves. I wanted to be as authentic as possible. I did not want to do what they did sometimes in the westerns, where the leading man jumps on the horse in the close shot, you cut to the long shot, and the stunt man rides the horse out. As a matter of fact, originally Peter Fonda was not going to be the lead. Peter was going to be the second lead and Bruce Dern was going to be the third lead. We had George Chakiris for the lead. AIP had some theory—which was probably correct—that since he'd been the lead in *West Side Story* as the leader of a Puerto Rican gang, he would be a natural here. I said to him, "Okay, George, you've got to learn to ride the bike with the Hell's Angels." They put him on a bike and gave him one lesson and he came in at the end of the lesson and said, "I'm not going to ride the bike. I'll be happy to play the picture, but you're going to have to get a double." I said, "George, it can't be that way," and I told Jim Nicholson we could not use him. Nicholson said okay. This happened just before shooting. I immediately moved Peter Fonda up from the second lead to the first lead, and moved Bruce Dern from the third lead to the second lead; everybody else moved up one.

The state police were tracking us. We were shooting on location, and they were with us every day. They had warrants out for the arrest of every single one of the Angels; they all had records a mile long. Jack Boyer, just as my brother had done on *The Intruder,* was talking to the state police and the local county sheriff's people. The Hell's Angels were really feared at that time. Jack said to them, "Look, these guys are working legitimately, we're paying them a salary, probably the only honest work they may ever do in their lives, why arrest them now? Let them work and earn their money. If they break the law, that's one thing." And we told the Angels, "Look, these guys are looking for you. We advise you to get out when we finish shooting on the last day, get out of here. Don't even come back. Just spread. Meanwhile they're not going to hassle you during the shooting, providing you're straight." And they were.

We were shooting in Mecca, which is a town near the Salt 'n' Sea, and I was setting up a long shot of the Hell's Angels coming into town down this dusty street. At the same time, my brother was doing a war picture called *Tobruk* in the desert outside of Mecca. He was shooting some close-ups one day and as a gag sent a group of Nazi half-tracks to raid my set. We were photographing the Hell's Angels coming down the street and suddenly from the other end of the street in came these Nazi half-tracks firing machine guns at the Hell's Angels. The Hell's Angels' motorcycles and the Nazi half-

The Wild Angels, 1966

tracks were sweeping together in the middle of the street, and I said to the cameraman, "Cut!" but my assistant director, Paul Rapp, said, "Don't cut. This is great footage!" It was really insane.

Roger is the last adventurer in movies, because he's still making pictures the way they did in 1914 or 1910. He's still getting a bunch of people, talented or not, and saying, "Here's some film and a camera, go out and shoot something. You don't know about the 180-degree line? Well, I'll show you." And "Just go out and shoot it. You can do it. Hurry up! What are you waiting for?" That spirit of adventure is what the movies were born in and what they have lost to a great degree, and starting that way with Roger made me feel that that was the way it always was.

—PETER BOGDANOVICH, director

When *The Wild Angels* was completed, and it turned out to be rather successful, the Hell's Angels sued me for defamation of character. I had a contract with them and they'd been fully paid, but they were looking for a way to pick up a few bucks. Once a Hell's Angel, always a Hell's Angel, only now they were trying to do it a little legitimately, which was at least a step up. They got a lawyer. A television news broadcaster laughingly reported that the Venice and San Bernardino chapters of the Hell's Angels sued Roger Corman and New World Pictures for defamation of character because they were portrayed in the picture as an outlaw and motorcycle gang whereas in reality they were a social organization dedicated to spreading technical information about the motorcycles. The suit dragged on—they were asking for two million dollars—and then the word got out that they were going to kill me. Big Otto Friedly, the head of the Hell's Angels, called me up one day to tell me, "We're gonna snuff you out." I said, "Otto, this doesn't make any sense whatsoever. You are suing me for two million dollars, and you also stated to everybody you're gonna snuff me out. Now in the first place, if you do snuff me out, since you've announced it in public, the police are going to be all over you immediately. You should really be protecting me and saving my life so that the police don't come after you. They are going to you first if I die. So you should really protect me, plus let me give you one bit of advice. Your two goals are mutually contradictory. If indeed you snuff me out, you cannot collect two million dollars from me. And since I'm covered by insurance anyway, my advice to you is to forget the momentary pleasure of snuffing me out and go for the two million." There was silence on the phone, and then Otto said, "Yes, that makes sense. I will do that, we'll do that, we'll go for the two million."

The Wild Angels, 1966

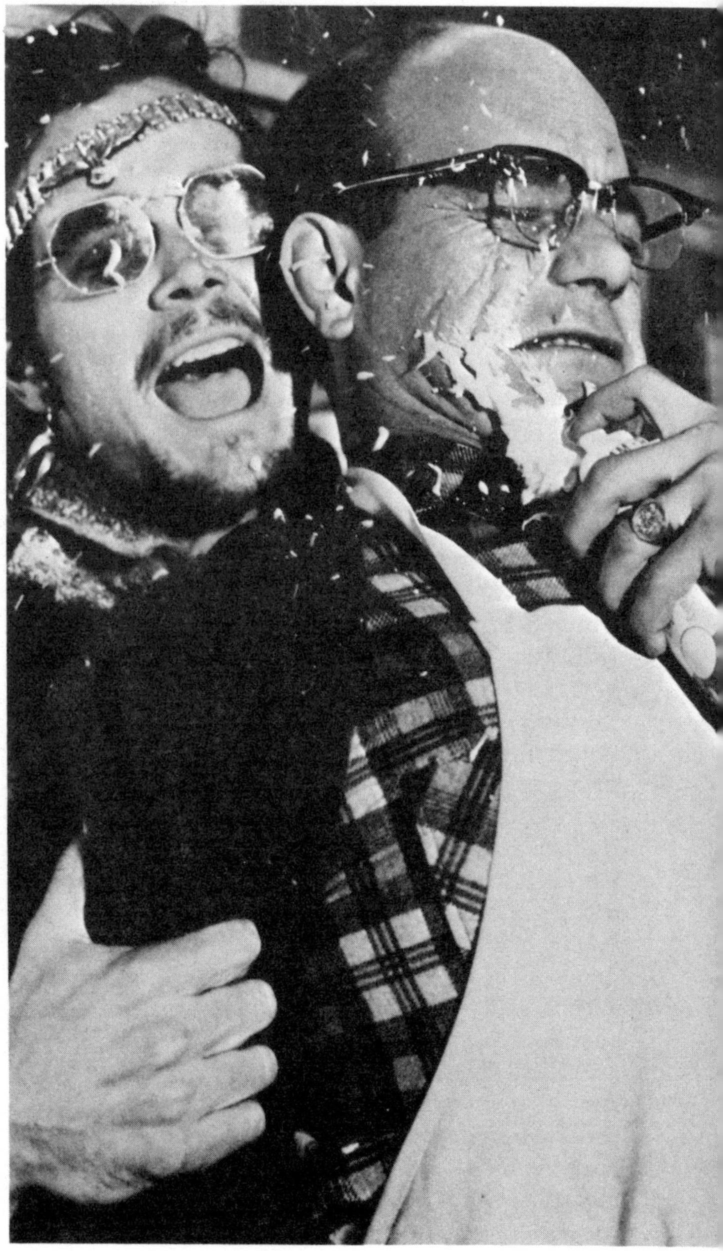

So—needless to say—they never snuffed me out. The lawyer for the insurance company was still talking to me about it two years later; the suit was still dragging on. I said, "Can't it be settled?" He said, "Look, we have a really dull law practice, we're insurance lawyers. There's not much interest. From time to time we call in a Hell's Angel and have him give us a deposition. We ask him what he's been doing. He tells us all these wild stories . . . just to pass the time." A year later it was still going on, and the Hell's Angels were willing to settle for ten thousand dollars. I said to the lawyer, "Look, you're a big insurance company, why not pay them the ten grand? It would cost you that much to go to court." He said, "Well, I'll get a few more stories and we finally will." I think they settled finally for two thousand dollars—just a nuisance kind of thing.

The Secret Invasion (1963) was my first film for United Artists. The story line was similar to that of *Five Guns West,* the first picture I had made. Somehow the idea of criminals involved in war has always appealed to me. Weirdly enough, there's another, more famous picture with the same idea, *The Dirty Dozen,* which followed *The Secret Invasion.* I don't think anybody stole anybody's ideas, but my picture was first, so I couldn't have stolen from them, and I don't think they stole from mine. I've been told that picture was held up—that they were getting ready to shoot when my picture came out and they suddenly realized they had a very similar story to mine and said, "Hey, let's postpone this picture a year, we can't come in right on its heels with this." *The Secret Invasion* was shot rather inexpensively, five hundred and ninety thousand dollars, in Yugoslavia with a group of stars who weren't that big at this time, in the mid-1960's: Stewart Granger, Raf Vallone, Mickey Rooney, Edd Byrnes, and Henry Silva. I enjoyed filming it because it was a bigger picture for me and an attempt to make a picture on a medium budget. Previously I'd had difficulty with films like *Atlas* and other epics on eighty thousand or ninety thousand dollars. Here I found that with at least five hundred thousand or six hundred thousand dollars I could come a little closer to achievement. But as a film it would really be remembered just as a straight medium-budget action picture with a little bit of thought about essentially bad men and a good cause.

I called Roger or he called me, I can't remember now, and he said, "I'd like you to write a script for me." I don't remember what the deal was—it was very low money, five hundred dollars or a thousand, not very much money. He said, "Now what I'm looking for is an adventure picture, kind of a combination of The Bridge on the River Kwai *and*

Edd Byrnes in *The Secret Invasion*, 1963

Lawrence of Arabia, *but cheap.*"
Then we found in a history book one sentence that gave us an idea for a picture set in Poland during World War II, during the Nazi occupation. It was something that really happened, which I won't go into in detail except that Roger liked it. It had to do with something that happened in the underground, the release of some criminals.
—*PETER BOGDANOVICH, director*

I Mobster (1958) was a script I had not developed. After *Machine Gun Kelly* I'd had some success, and Eddie Albertson brought me his script of *I Mobster* and asked me if I would do it for him. It was a straight gangster film. I don't remember a great deal about it other than a nice chase that I shot down at Terminal Island for the climax of the film.

The St. Valentine's Day Massacre (1966) was more important to me. I had finally broken my contract with Columbia, with some bad feelings on both sides that had to be negotiated by lawyers, and signed with Twentieth Century–Fox determined to make it all work this time. They liked the idea of doing a picture of the St. Valentine's Day Massacre, and other than the fact that they didn't go along with my original casting suggeston, everything turned out well. I'd wanted Orson Welles for the part of Al Capone and Jason Robards for Bugs Moran, and they said that Orson Welles was too tough to work with and anyway we couldn't get him, so I switched Jason to Al Capone and brought in Ralph Meeker as Bugs Moran, and it threw the casting off slightly. Other than that, essentially it was a good picture. (I later met Orson and he said he would have loved to play Capone. My idea was to have very distinguished actors playing these gangsters, and since Capone was a slightly overweight man, as is Orson, I felt it fit. And Jason being Irish and Moran being Irish, I felt it would have pulled the film together.)

Basically I liked *The St. Valentine's Day Massacre,* the only picture I ever shot in a major studio. As a result, it has a slightly bigger look. There is something you get from a major studio. I think you overpay in terms of overhead and costs; I could have made the picture for half the money. At the same time, I think it was good to work on a major lot and get that slightly glossier appearance.

We had some good supporting actors in the film—George Segal, Bruce Dern, Jack Nicholson in a bit part. I had offered Jack a bigger role, but he really needed some money at the time, and he said, "Hey, do you have anything that works a little longer?" Sometimes an actor gets a role that plays one week and then doesn't work for a couple of weeks because there's a break in the schedule, but he gets paid for the whole time. I showed him the

Jason Robards in *The St. Valentine's Day Massacre*, 1966

board, and he said, "Let me play this one." So he played a driver in a getaway car, getting more money for the smaller role because he worked longer.

Everything Roger did, every choice Roger made, was his. He is exactly what he wanted to be. He is the most honest movie executive I've met to date. In all the seven years I worked for him, I don't believe I ever had a contract. He never reneged on anything he ever said to me.

—*JACK NICHOLSON, actor*

The Trip. 1967

After the success of *The Wild Angels* AIP asked me to do another contemporary film. This was still the mid-1960s, and the hippie scene, the anti-establishment drug-oriented society, was building, particularly on the West Coast in Haight Ashbury and on Sunset Strip and in Venice, L.A. I determined to make an honest film about the drug scene and specifically LSD, which had really incredible powers attributed to it. I called Peter Fonda again and got a cast that was connected with this movement: Peter Fonda, Dennis Hopper, Jack Nicholson, who also wrote the script, Bruce Dern, who was the only principal not really into experimenting with LSD. I was not particularly into LSD, but I was interested in it, and it may have been this interest that led me to make a film about it—that often happens.

I decided to take LSD before making the picture and read Timothy Leary's book on the subject. He talked about "set and setting," which should be a beautiful place, and being with friends so you go into the trip with a good experience. I decided to go to Big Sur, which to me is one of the most beautiful places in the world, and told a few friends to meet me there. Suddenly the whole thing mushroomed into a caravan of cars going up to Big Sur, and so many people were up there that we had to work out a schedule, just like a motion picture schedule: so many will take a trip at this time and their guides will be so and so and the next trip will be these persons.

Mine was just a wonderful experience—it was just spectacular. It was so good that as I was coming down the thought occurred to me that there was no particular reason to go back to Hollywood, no particular reason to exist in the "real world" at all. I would simply rest a little bit and go right back up. I remember feeling that making a motion picture really was not the way to create art or to transmit art. I was lying on the ground and a girl who was my guide said, "We came all the way up to Big Sur so you'd be in a beautiful place and here you spend eight hours lying face down on the ground, staring at the dirt." While I was lying on the ground it occurred to me that the way to create was to spread yourself out against the ground so as much of your body touched it as possible. Then you could create the piece of art in your mind, and anybody who wanted to partake of that art could lie against the earth anyplace else and the image would form in their mind; this would be a pure art form, simply from the mind of the creator to the mind of the spectator-participant, and there could be one or one hundred million spectator-participants who took part in the creation and the experience of the art. I felt it was a pretty good idea. I didn't know exactly how to do it.

The Trip (1967) won a major award at the Italian National Film Festival, and I flew there from Rome with a psychiatrist who was going to be on the jury. He had had some experience with LSD. I told him about this one great image I had had of floating through space in kind of a golden outer space. It was very beautiful, and I saw a ship coming to me—an old clipper ship, very beautiful—and as I swam, as it were, through space to this ship, the ship approached me and I knew I loved the ship and the ship loved me and it was a wonderful experience. As the ship came closer I realized that the sails, which were moving slowly, under "galactic wind," were actually a woman's body and the body was moving in space, and as it came closer still I realized that the ship was also jeweled. So this jeweled, undulating woman's body in the form of a clipper ship was sailing toward me with great love.

We were always experimenting. I think the first hand-held camera sequences were done in The Trip, *in the riot in the church at the end. And Roger—somehow or other, with a kind of rigid personality, he is really not able to let go—he let me direct these kinds of things. We developed a system in which we would hold the cameraman with the Arriflex camera and I would steer him through and talk to him about what to shoot. I would break hundreds of amyl nitrates all over the set and get everybody just freaked. I did all this stuff in the freak-out scene, and Sam Arkoff came walking through the set while I was popping these amyl nitrates all over the place. Of course, Roger would giggle his ass off—he thought it was funny! And like he used to say to me, "Paul, you get all the* girls *and I do all the* work." *I'd say, "Yeah, Roger, but you get all the* money!"

—*PAUL RAPP, production manager*

Making the film was a lot of fun because we improvised a little bit, working with a basically good script by Jack Nicholson. But Jack had written some portions which were just too extensive—I think it was the first script he had ever written, and on a

The Trip, 1967

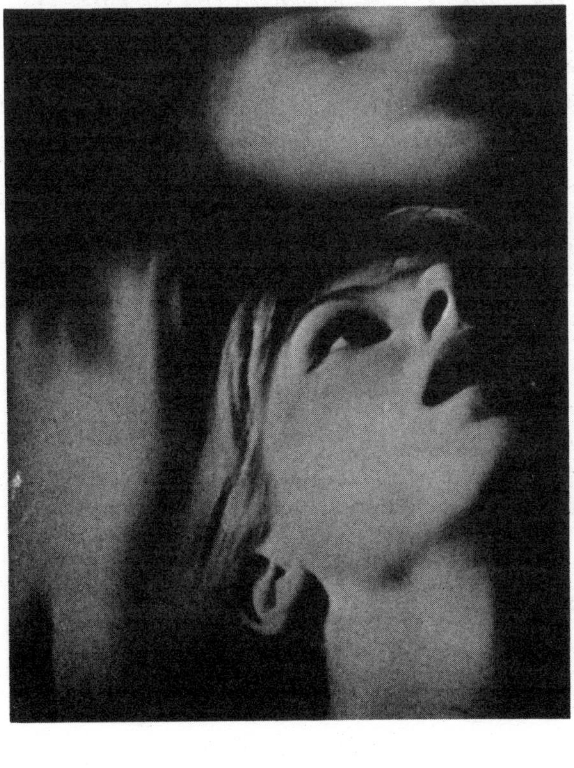

fifteen-day schedule and a hundred-thousand-dollar budget we had to find alternatives for some of the scenes which were just too big. I think in general we succeeded, at least reasonably well. As I say, the film won awards and made quite a bit of money. The thing that I regret about the film was the fact that AIP put in a disclaimer at the beginning of the picture saying that LSD was not good and that the makers of this film wanted everybody to know that it was not a good thing. They even changed the ending of the picture. We had made it an open ending: the morning after the trip, Peter Fonda walked onto the deck of a beach house and just looked at the rising sun, and it was left ambiguous as to what results of the trip were going to be, although there were certain hints within the picture. AIP cut the shot in half and put a big sheet of shattered glass over it to imply that his life was ruined because he had taken a trip, which of course totally distorted the meaning of the picture. The only solace I can find in the whole thing is the fact that I don't think anybody understood what the shattered image was supposed to mean. All it did was mess up the end of the picture. I think they cut one or two things out of the picture, too. It was that plus some cutting on some later films that really led to New World Pictures, which I started so I could have some control.

Roger really understands the numbers when it comes to filmmaking—the costs, the profits, etc. He understands what goes into making a film; he has a great understanding of how to structure a story. Someone must understand the money—he does. Also, the strength of an executive is in choosing the right people—Roger has this strength. He always understood the contemporary scene and he always strove for originality.

—GENE CORMAN, producer, Roger's brother

Bloody Mama (1969) was an interesting picture. It was written by Bob Towne and on the surface was simply the story of the Ma Barker Gang in the 1930s. Beneath the surface it was a look at blood relations and family ties. Contrasting the primitive and blood is very important in this. *Bloody Mama* was the title and more than that, kind of a theme. We got into incest at one time. But we were really very strong on blood relations in the family and the primitive powerful relationships within the family unit, as contrasted to the breaking up of the family unit and society. That was a very strong subjective part of the picture.

AIP wanted me to shoot it on the back lot at Warner Brothers and they had a very good deal, but I was determined to shoot this on location, and I feel the locations added a great deal to it. We shot in the Ozarks and then down in southern Ar-

Shelley Winters in *Bloody Mama*, 1969

kansas. We had a four-week schedule on this one, so we were slightly in the big time here, and we had a very good cast. It was the first film that cinematographer John Alonzo did, and he won an Academy Award for his photography.

Bloody Mama *was my first feature film as a director of photography. I had been a photographer for documentary films, and Roger gave me that first real break we all wait for to make the jump to features. I still do not know what gave him the idea or inspiration to use me. Roger is an excellent director and producer or putter-together of films, and he combines the perfect balance of commercial qualities with aesthetic qualities. If he only directed, we would lose our number one champion of hiring new talent. On the set, I found him to be shy in relation to the shooting of the sex scenes, whereas I expected him to be above it all. He is the best kind of filmmaker in the truest sense of the word.*

—JOHN ALONZO, director of photography

It had one of the best casts I ever worked with. Shelley Winters was Ma Barker. Her four sons were Robert De Niro, Robert Walden, Don Stroud, and Clint Kimbrough. Every one of them is an outstanding young actor. De Niro, of course, has gone on to big things, and I think the rest of them will also. The young man who came into the gang as a stranger was Bruce Dern, and the other supporting actor, a man named "Kidnap," was Pat Hingle. Just working with so many good actors added a great deal to the film.

If I had anything to say against the film, it would be about the cuts AIP made in the finished print. This was strange—in my early days with AIP they left my films alone. As my pictures made more and more money, they started to make little cuts. You know, not heavy. I'd make a ninety-minute film and they'd cut it down to eighty seven, weirdly and abruptly, without even fixing the sound track, which could have been done for a thousand dollars. Perhaps they felt that I was saying things a little bit too strongly. *Bloody Mama* was considered a violent picture at the time, but today it would probably be considered a mild picture.

Boxcar Bertha, *the sequel to* Bloody Mama, *was supposed to be a New World picture, but it was switched over to AIP for some weird reason. I'm still not quite sure why. I was given freedom within the limitations of the genre and the shooting schedule. Without having made that film, I couldn't have made* Mean Streets, *because I used all the same people basically, especially Paul Rapp, who had helped me through* Boxcar Bertha.

David Carridine and Barbara Hershey in *Boxcar Bertha*, 1972

It was his idea to shoot most of Mean Streets *in LA. The budget was much lower than that of* Boxcar, *but it was the only way it could be done—a hundred and fifty thousand dollars cash and a hundred and fifty thousand deferred. Roger suggested that* Mean Streets *be made about blacks instead of Italians because his brother had just made* Cool Breeze. *Roger said to me, "I'll give you a hundred thousand dollars—you go to New York and shoot it nonunion. The only thing is, are you willing to sway a little and make it black?" I wanted to make the picture so bad that I said, "Let me think about it." But then I decided I'd better stay straight with the Italians—I just couldn't see the blacks saying all those Hail Marys in the* festa di San Genaro. *Wouldn't work at all!*

—MARTIN SCORSESE, director

Gas-s-s-s (1969) was the last picture I did for AIP—they did some heavy cuts at the end, and I ended the association. *Gas-s-s-s* was an interesting idea that frankly failed. I felt that I didn't really do my best work and the script wasn't quite right. And I had to shoot in the fall, because I had another commitment to do a picture in Ireland. It was a somewhat topical picture, about the death of everyone over the age of twenty-five and what happened to the young people when they took over the world. I started out doing a satirical comedy with a comment behind it, but the script wasn't quite right so I went to the location with the writer, who was also one of the actors, feeling we could rewrite as we went. It didn't quite come off. It's got some interesting visual effects, and I think there are some interesting ideas in it. Some scenes I love, but overall I did not pull the picture together, and AIP cut very heavily. For instance, they cut the character of God right out of the picture, and God was one of the funniest characters.

A number of young actors in the film have gone on to big things: Talia Shire, Ben Vereen, Cindy Williams, and Bud Cort. By the end of the 1960s I was able to pay a little bit over scale, and therefore to star more talented young people.

Part of my job on The Terror *(1962) was to get the props. I was the wake-up-call person—I did it all. I also had to dress the set for* Dementia 13, *for an underwater sequence we were going to do in a lake but ended up doing in somebody's swimming pool. In one month with Roger I learned much more than in a drama-school situation. It was a real place to learn. He was getting something too—he got all of your energy, your innocence, your youth, and he got you for pennies—but he gave you something back.*

I was rotten in Gas-s-s-s, *really rotten. It was the beginning of stage fright for me, a classic case. I*

Gas-s-s-s, 1969

guess it was because I was working for the man himself. I had known him for so long and I felt like he was a relative. I felt that he was very protective of me and I had disappointed him. He had launched my brother (Francis Ford Coppola), who had since become famous, so I felt trapped by many elements—my brother, myself—and I didn't want to displease him. He's a wonderful director.

TALIA SHIRE, actress

Von Richthofen and Brown (1970) was the last film I directed. The experience of these last films really led to the start of my own production and distribution company, New World Pictures. I didn't get exactly the cast I wanted and relations with United Artists really hampered the film.
The picture was shot inexpensively, for nine hundred thousand dollars, but the flying sequences took three weeks. Probably the most enjoyable part of the picture was the pure flying. It was very nice. When we finally got to do the ground sequences it seemed as if the picture was over.

Economy of gesture, and the economy of getting on with it, of being prepared—I realized with Roger that time is money, that indecision and lack of preparation cost money, lose you time, and end up costing everybody money and enthusiasm. As a result, I've always tried to be as prepared as possible when I step onto the set. I learned about the practical aspects and the technical and physical aspects of making movies by actually doing it for Roger and watching him work. Mainly Roger had tremendous expertise in terms of where to place the camera, knowing how much footage he needed and how much he would need to make something cut and not cut, and so on.

—PETER BOGDANOVICH, director

Von Richthofen and Brown, 1970

Big Doll House, 1971

CHAPTER FIVE

A NEW WORLD FOR ROGER CORMAN

There is a clear and surface reason I haven't directed since *Von Richthofen and Brown.* I expected New World Pictures would be built over a period of time. It took off on its first picture at the end of the first year, which I hadn't planned on at all. Suddenly I found myself working six or seven days a week running a production and distribution company, with no time to do anything else. It just took all of my time away from directing. At the same time I may have made too many films too fast. I think probably I've made more films in a short period of time than anybody else, and I was just tired.

It was clearly more fun when I was an independent producer-director—I think I led a more interesting life. I was always all over the world. I spent about half of my time in Europe and in the Near East, shooting in Turkey, Yugoslavia, Greece, England, France, Italy, and Spain. It was a more international life. It was more stimulating. This is a grind, to a certain extent. I'd never been in a position of coming to the office every morning, and I simply do not like it. My wife commented one time that I refer to New World Pictures as "they"—the company is almost the enemy. We have our own building; we have a big staff. And I think somehow they're all working against me. I wasn't cut out to come and do this. So the thought occurs to me to cut out for a while and maybe do one picture. And I may do it if it ever gets to the point where it isn't a one-man operation. It's necessary. And I think we are getting that way.

Angels Die Hard (1970), our first film, was a surprising winner, and the first film we produced ourselves, *Student Nurses* (1970), was a big winner. Everybody was jumping up and down and saying we were making money hand over fist. Our theater owners made commitments with us on what we were going to do, and I got into a whole lot of preproduction planning and took off immediately. I went to the Philippines to set up the preproduction for *Big Doll House* (1971), which Jack Hill made. This film became a bigger winner than the previous two. Suddenly we couldn't do anything wrong.

There was a male sexual fantasy to be exploited, comedic subplot, action/violence, and a slightly-to-the-left-of-center social subplot. Those were the four elements that were required in the nurses' pictures. And then frontal nudity from the waist up and total nudity from behind and no pubic hair and get the title of the picture somewhere into the film and go to work. So that was essentially it.

—*JONATHAN KAPLAN, director*

The whole thing was very exhilarating for a while. I thought it held various connotations. I was turned down by the corporations commissioner on my first

Big Doll House, 1971

choice of a name for my company because a public broadcasting company in San Francisco, a foundation called Pacifica, had first claim on the title. I came up with New World Films after reading a book written by an advertising executive who said that the two most important words in advertising are "new" and "improved." You look on boxes and "new improved" is there all the time, it's all over everything. So I came up with New World Films. It seemed to be right. "New World" meant the United States, and at the same time "World" meant the whole world. I wanted to have a company that would be worldwide in scope, with headquarters in the United States, and I felt the word "New" was important—my company would always be new. Then I dropped the word "Films" at the last minute, and decided on New World Pictures.

We made Big Doll House, *one of our very first pictures, for a hundred and twenty-five thousand dollars, and it did one and a half million. But it didn't go to television, it didn't go to foreign. We had made a foreign deal with MGM; we licensed it against an enormous guarantee, and the guarantee was reduced to nothing because it was censored in so many places.*
We took Cries And Whispers *for no reason whatsoever, except to avoid an AIP image, and Corman figured out that between the advance, the New York opening, and the prints, it would be a complete and utter loss. But what it would do for New World publicity-wise was worth it, because we would never be caught in the niche of* Summer School Teachers *(1975) and* Big Doll House, *extremely successful films financially, but hardly reputation-building.*

—BARBARA BOYLE, vice-president, New World Pictures

In 1973 I acquired Ingmar Bergman's *Cries and Whispers* (released in 1976), which was our first art-house release, and it was nominated for a number of Academy Awards, won one Academy Award, and was the highest-grossing Ingmar Bergman picture ever in the United States. Surprisingly, the picture had been turned down by all of the major studios; I acquired it simply because I wanted to distribute that particular film, and beyond that, I wanted to distribute art films in general. I felt it would be good for the company to have an almost schizophrenic image, in that we would deal with definitely commercial pictures and with art films. The type of film we would stay away from would be the middle-of-the-road average normal film, and we've continued that pattern. We've gone from Bergman's *Cries and Whispers* to *Amarcord* (1974). We have two films by Francois Truffaut, *The Story of Adele H.* (1975) and *Small Change* (1977); we have *The Romantic Englishwoman*

Cries and Whispers, 1976

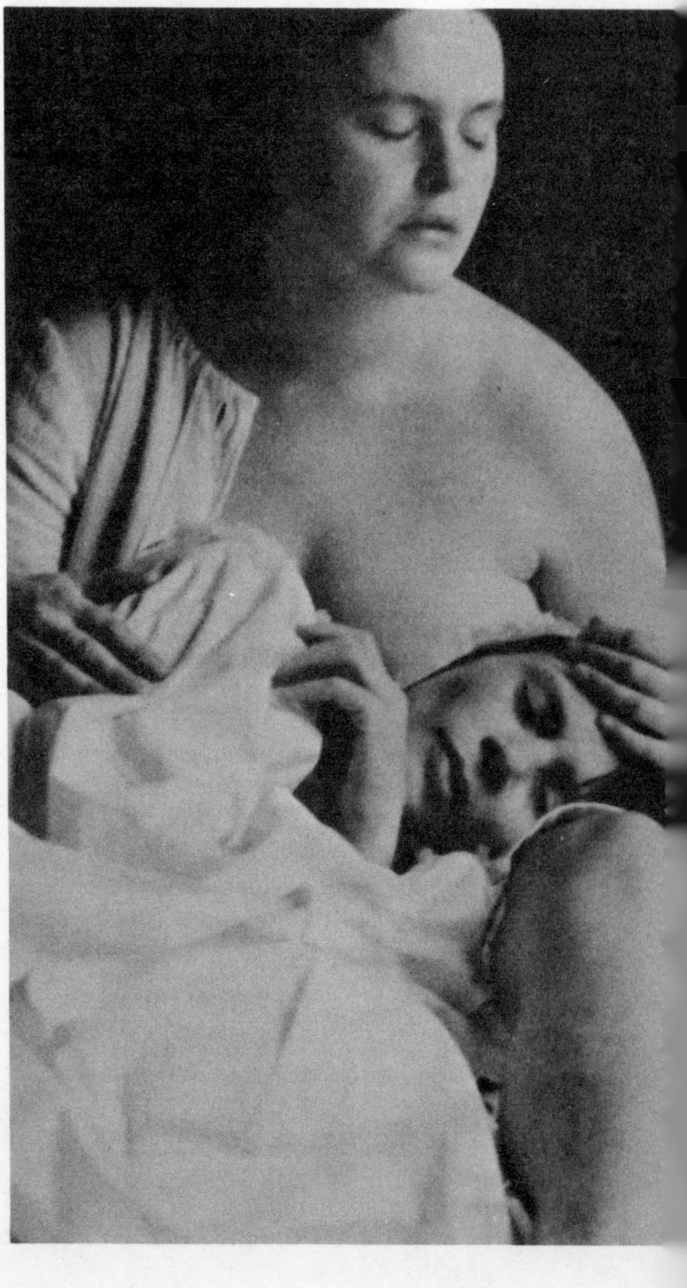

(1975) from Joseph Losey. These foreign films have won four Academy Awards and ten or twelve Academy nominations, and every single one of them has been profitable for us. It's been a very good experience. I like the idea of handling what are essentially some of the finest films in the world. Beyond making a certain amount of money, they are good for our company, in that my staff is very young, very much committed to films—and I think that's one of the reasons we've been able to do a better, profitable job.

I don't think there is anything to suggest flights of imagination or creative insight on the level of a Bergman or a Truffaut. On the other hand, it is marvelous that there is a man in Roger's position who can appreciate the work of Fellini, Bergman, or Truffaut and who helps get their films to a wide audience.

—ARTHUR KNIGHT, *film critic*

At the same time, with films we've made ourselves, we have gradually upped the budget and, I believe, upped the quality. Our first films were made for about a hundred to a hundred and fifty thousand dollars; we gradually moved it up to two hundred thousand dollars. In 1974 we made a picture with Angie Dickinson called *Big Bad Mama,* which cost us four hundred thousand dollars on a four-week shooting schedule, and that was a major step up for us. It was more than double the budget of anything we had done before. *Cries and Whispers* was a significant film because it began our involvement in the art market; *Big Bad Mama* began our involvement with slightly bigger films. The film did very well. It made quite a bit of money. It got very good reviews. It was well received in Europe, and it established us on a different level, and even though four hundred thousand dollars may still seem very cheap, it looked as though a major studio had made it for a million dollars.

The head of our company is a filmmaker. So the first thing that happens, be it a production or an acquisition, is Roger will say, "I want this picture." The next thing he will say is "Does the deal work?" I may look at a picture and say I really like the film, or I may read a script and say, "Gee, this seems good to me." But by and large the film idea starts with Corman or someone in his department. Then he'll come to me and say, "Do the terms work?" I will talk to our general sales manager, our advertising department, etc., and if the deal doesn't work we'll have to pass. If we really like the film and the deal works, then I will go and try to effectuate what he wants. For example, in New York I saw The Story of Adele H. *I just*

The Story of Adele H., 1975

happened to see it. I called Roger up, and he said, "Yes, I've heard great things about it. Acquire the film if the deal makes sense."

—*BARBARA BOYLE, vice president, New World Pictures*

The next step up was a science-fiction picture we did with David Carradine, called *Death Race 2000* (1975), which was the highest-grossing film we had up through 1975. Again, it went to a number of festivals and got some nice reviews. We followed that in 1976 with a car-chase picture with Ron Howard called *Eat My Dust,* which was the first film we made that earned over five million dollars in film rental. We came back in 1977 with *Grand Theft Auto,* which is now our highest-grossing film, also with Ron Howard. Our first budgeted million-dollar film, also in 1977, was *I Never Promised You a Rose Garden,* which received really extraordinary reviews in major newspapers. *I Never Promised You a Rose Garden, Cries and Whispers,* and *Big Bad Mama* were probably the three most significant films we've been involved in, because each put us into a different area.

Roger is an enigma, a very contradictory kind of person. He is extremely hip and at the same time very square. He is a person who has vast understanding of the social inequities of the world, and yet he lives in a closed, rich community. Roger seems to be able to find a space of his own, however—right in between everyone else's space. Or perhaps it includes everyone else's—I can't explain it. It's difficult. But, y' know, Roger is a genius. There's no doubt about it. Roger's genius expresses itself in the way he makes a picture. He will foster the creation of the script. He won't write it, but he will definitely foster it.

—*DAVID CARRADINE, actor*

We shoot almost everything on natural locations. Our films have the look of reality plus a somewhat liberal-to-radical political viewpoint. We don't take the time for wonderful lighting—our cameraman doesn't have the time—so the look is a somewhat rough version of reality, although we've been getting a little bit smoother. It's a rough version of reality with a somewhat rebellious viewpoint. We cannot spend as much money as Columbia spends. And I think we're a slightly more socially conscious company than Columbia was. The comparison is not bad at all. And, moving into art films, we are specifically concerned with certain levels that Columbia is not.

With Roger there's an expediency in shooting, first getting yourself what you need, then allowing youself a few frills. It's not just getting what you want in a utilitarian fashion, it's getting it artistically too. If you want a moving camera, you can

Kathleen Quinlan in
I Never Promised You a Rose Garden, 1977

get it in such a way that you don't waste a whole afternoon setting it up. This is something you begin to forget, especially after doing a film like New York, New York, *and hopefully I'll begin to remember. I'll never do a picture like that again. I mean, you can shoot a picture for nine million dollars and still make every shot count, but very often you have weaknesses in the script, and for every two days of shooting, you lose three. Working in a big studio, there's this attitude of how things are done here, and you do it.* New York, New York *was the first film I ever had a dressing room on. Before that, I stayed in the streets of New York City while Bobby De Niro changed in a Winnebago. Here, we were in the studio all the time—no locations. I had this cubicle on the set, and I would stay in there while the set with nine hundred extras was being lit. There are these long waiting periods for lighting, and you lose your enthusiasm. It takes you twenty minutes to get back up in energy—you even begin to resent getting up to take the shot—but you get up, you get going. But it costs a lot.*

—MARTIN SCORSESE, director

Here's the way a normal picture is done in the real world. I will decide on an idea. I'll decide on what I want to make. I will then bring in a writer (sometimes a writer-director), generally one I've worked with before, sometimes a new writer. I work with the writer and with my story editor, Frances Kimbrough, in a joint effort to create first an understanding. We do not put anything on paper in the beginning. We get to the point where all three of us understand what the picture is about and the line it will take. Only at that time, when we have really made most of the decisions, is the writer sent home to do a treatment. The story line is generally pretty fully worked before anything is put on paper. The writer then does the treatment. He brings in the treatment, and we have another series of discussions. Then the writer goes for his first draft.

Our normal policy is a first-draft script, a second-draft script, and dialogue from the second draft. I will very often hold the dialogue polish until I've selected a director. Then I bring the director into the consultations. The director knows that this is the basic story. He's not here to make any drastic changes. But I welcome his ideas, because he'll be the man with the actors and camera, and we will generally work together with the writer, making minor refinements and dialogue polish so that the director's viewpoints start to come in. Then I work very closely with the director in preproduction so that we're agreed as to who the actors will be, what camera style he will be working with, what locations he'll be shooting, the schedule, how much of

Grand Theft Auto, 1977

a second unit (if there is a second unit) and the basic themes of the film. When that's done, the director has been thoroughly briefed on what we're doing and he and I are in essentially full agreement.

I give the director a great deal of freedom on the set. I'm generally on the set the first few days of shooting; after that I don't even go back. I look at the rushes. I talk to the director on the phone. The director is given so much freedom because I wouldn't have hired him if I didn't have faith in him, and by the time shooting begins his thoughts and mine are the same. That doesn't mean I dictated all the thoughts. Probably the majority come from me, but he has thoughts and it is a give-and-take process so that there is a synthesis of our ideas. As I say, if it's going well I don't go to the set after the first couple of days. Then I give the director the first complete cut of the film. I don't even go into the cutting room. I have him sit with the editor and cut the film the way he thinks it should be cut. At that point I have a screening, and we jointly go over several cuts and fine polishing and bringing it down.

Roger called me in New York and asked me if I'd direct Deathrace 2000, *which I did. I also worked on the script. It was rather chaotic working for Roger then. There were times when Roger preferred not to communicate with me directly on this film. It was canceled several times—there was somewhat of a disagreement on the comedy-violence mixture. I wanted more comedy and less gore. He wanted more gore and less comedy. However, in the compromise the film was successful. The MPAA made us take out some of the gore, and Roger compromised and left in some of the gags.*

Roger is a very clever man. At the same time that he exploits people—and he does exploit people—he is also giving them a chance to make their first film, and sometimes their second film when their first film hasn't worked out. He has a keen ability to recognize talent, and that plus his ability to know the market is a beautiful formula for success.

—PAUL BARTEL, director

I think our films were geared very much to the domestic market—we made the right film at the right time. Every film was made right, because we had really studied what we wanted to make. We did not have the same foreign success, however. It's only been within the last couple of years that our foreign department has become strong, and it is still not as strong as our domestic department. That's one area we're working on.

We will probably go into higher-budget films. We are the biggest independent in the United States, if you consider AIP to be a major. If not, we're the second biggest and closing the gap on AIP.

Death Race 2000, 1975

I don't want New World to distribute thirty pictures a year. Now, maybe it's just the nature of free enterprise that you have to grow that way. I hope not. Maybe as you open your own exchanges, as your overhead increases, you need more garbage to feed the garbage disposal. I don't buy that philosophy, and neither does Roger. I wouldn't be here if he and I had different philosophies about the company. He would like to also limit our distribution to somewhere between twelve and eighteen pictures a year, which leaves us at fifteen, with that great wonderful mixture of a Grand Theft Auto *or whatever its new equivalent will be, with a* Rose Garden *or the art pictures, so that it would cover a spectrum of films. I mean, Roger is our company; the man does move to his own beat. We all tease Roger about how he's a terrible manager. All we have to do at staff meetings is talk about "management" and he just shrivels up and hates all those words. You send him a memo and he says, "Why have you sent me this?" We have constant arguments on why are we spending time writing memos with all these people getting copies. The whole idea of organization really goes against his grain.*

—BARBARA BOYLE, vice-president, New World Pictures

I don't think New World Pictures will ever be a major in the sense that we will have a hundred million dollars to play with in the foreseeable future. But now that we've more or less established ourselves in the million-dollar bracket, I think we can make and distribute just about any kind of film we want, barring the super-expensive film—the film with ten million dollars in special effects, or five giant stars lumped together. I'm not particularly interested in either of those types of films, however, so, within reason, I now think that there are no practical limits as to what we can do.
I may direct again. I may not. It's one of those things. There's a lot of time; I'll be making films for a long time. At the moment I'm interested in producing and distributing and spending a little more time with my family.

Now with New World there is far more flexibility in the type of deal that we will strike if we like a picture. That's the first part. Also, producers are now coming to us (and directors and creative people) because, even when they've had a winner at the studio, they haven't realized any income, because of the nature of the deal. When I'm talking about revenue, I'm talking about pictures that cost a million to a million and a half, that had film rental of five to seven million dollars. Under a major you are barely breaking even under a traditional studio formula. For us, at seven million dollars a lot would be returned to the producer. Okay,

Ron Howard in *Eat My Dust!*, 1977

that's the first reason. The second reason is that our own reputation is catching up with us. People are now saying, "We want New World to distribute the picture." So we are not ending up in last place, certainly not in the art market—because we returned more to Mr. Fellini in actual film rental on Amarcord *than he ever saw from* Casanova *at Universal, except for whatever they paid him in front. I don't want to equate the two pictures, because even if you say* Casanova*'s not near the picture* Amarcord *is, New World does not have the power of Universal to get the play dates, the theaters, the terms—but we shared the film rental. So now people are coming to us and saying, "We want New World to distribute because of the unique way you handle pictures."*

—BARBARA BOYLE, vice-president, New World Pictures

I am interested more and more in films that reflect the world around us. I've done horror films, I've done science-fiction films, I've done just about every genre it's possible to do, with the exception of porno films. If I directed again, it would be something dealing either directly or indirectly with the world around us.

I would hope that at some point Roger would try again to make a film that is as felt a statement as The Intruder. *I would think that now, with the passing of the years, he may well have acquired the skills to do better than he did in 1962. I would also like to see him try again a film that deals with something* he really feels strongly about *rather than a film that he thinks is going to make him a couple hundred thousand dollars more this time out. I think he's got the ability to do it. I think all it needs is a certain amount of disengagement from what has become the routine of New World, and the determination to strike out one more time. I think it's going to have to come from within.*

—ARTHUR KNIGHT, film critic

I was born in Detroit but I moved to California as a boy and graduated from Beverly Hills High School, then went to Stanford University. I began graduate work at England's Oxford University. My background is primarily middle class or upper-middle class. I was never the richest kid in Beverly Hills. I was a guy in Beverly Hills. I've never known poverty and I've never known great wealth. I think my background makes me somewhat representative of the mainstream of America—Beverly Hills is not exactly the mainstream, but Detroit sure is representative of a mainstream American city. And my father was an engineer and as such middle class. I wasn't poor, I wasn't rich, and that probably formed me to a certain extent. Politically, I'm very much to the left. I'm

Amarcord, 1974

somewhere between liberal and radical, depending on how I wake up that particular morning, and I think that permeates my work. Also, I think I am very much of an individual, which may be one of the reasons I am an independent director-producer rather than a studio type. Recently, as a matter of fact, I was offered a position as president of a major studio.

I once schlepped over to Europe on the cheapest charter I could find—twenty-eight hours in the air. I flew to Ireland and spent four weeks in Europe. I spent my last dime and got back on the plane, this dinky plane with one engine, and they're crowding millions of people in like sardines—it was insane and horrible—and I sit down next to a man who is fast asleep. I nudge my boyfriend, who was with me, and I say, "God, I think it's Roger Corman sitting next to me, on this shitty plane!" He was a really well-known guy at this time, and he hears his name, looks up and says, "Lynn!" I say, "Roger, why aren't you flying a huge DC-10 or 747? Why are you flying on this piece of shit?" He says, "Trying to save a dime!"

—*LYNN BERNAY, actress in many Corman films*

As to who am I and where do I want to go—do I want to stay as president of New World Pictures, or become president of a major studio?—very likely I will stay as president of my own small company. I am not a team player, the corporate organization man, which you must be to head a major studio. I function best as an individual. I'm not so much a loner as an individual. I work as an individual, and my beliefs are somewhat to the left of a certain collectivist thinking—it does set up a certain dichotomy in what I'm doing, and I think a lot of things are worked out in my films. But in most of them you have to dig for my beliefs because of *The Intruder* and other things. They're not that easy to find; however, they are there if a person wants to look at the films.

I think that he has an intuitive sense of what people want to see, which is the requirement for somebody who's in the distribution of motion pictures. And I think he's got a tremendous visual sense—a very good intuition for talent. He's able to perceive by sitting and talking to somebody whether he'll be able to handle the job that Roger's giving him. I think that his overall asset as someone to work with is his confidence, his strength. He certainly has that.

—*JONATHAN KAPLAN, director*

Amarcord, 1974

Roger Corman, age 7

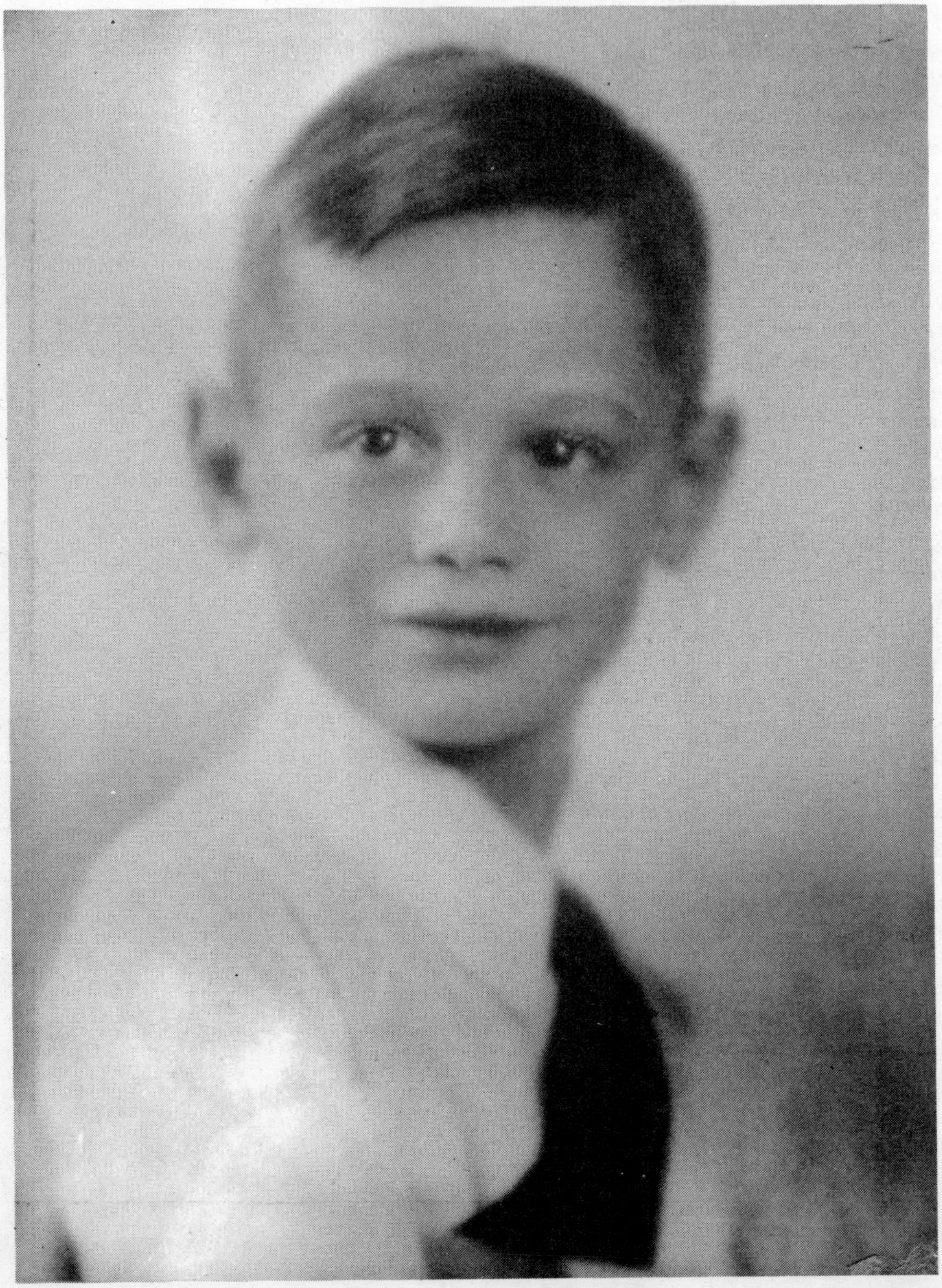

CHAPTER SIX

THE CORMAN PHILOSOPHY

Roger Corman, 1977

I think you have to be intelligent, dedicated, and willing to work very, very hard. Creativity, talent—these are intangibles. But I believe an intelligent and hardworking man or woman who has learned the craft can make good pictures, and if he has certain other attributes, he might make brilliant films. I do think making films is one way that has enabled me to function. Motion pictures are *the* art form of the twentieth century, and one of the reasons they are *the* art form of the twentieth century is the fact that films are a slightly corrupted art form. They fit this century—they combine art and business. And, with the possible exception of one or two great creators, I think everybody who is doing good work must to a greater or lesser extent combine both ends, but probably the great creators have to combine a little bit too.

From a commercial standpoint, obviously producing is running the show. But from the artistic standpoint it depends upon any given picture. Sometimes it's the director; sometimes it's the writer; sometimes it can be an actor; and sometimes it's the producer. Under most circumstances, it's likely to be either the director or the producer, but almost as many times the director is the key artistic man. One of the reasons it's very often the producer is because he makes the most important decisions regarding a film—what film he's going to make and how he's going to make it. Everything stems from that. His original creative vision is what starts everything. That one bit of creativity is the cornerstone of the entire edifice.

In Europe a director is very often a director-producer; the producer is the financier. I think the European critics got a little bit confused. In Europe a director will very often have the original idea and will pull the elements together; in America, the producer has the original idea. Very seldom does he draft the story; he'll go to a writer first. Generally, the project is created and implemented in the minds of the producer and the writer. Gore Vidal overstated it one time when he was a contract writer at Metro in his youth; he said at that time it was clear that the producers and the writers created the film and the directors were the brothers-in-law. That's an overstatement. I don't subscribe to that. Having worked as a writer and as a director and as a producer, I know I don't want to knock any of the three areas. All I'm saying is that, depending upon the picture and the personalities, the writer, the director, or the producer may emerge as the key artistic contributor.

One of the reasons a producer's job seems so intangible and so multifaceted is that it's hard to pin it down. People don't know what he does because he does almost everything. You can envision a writer sitting at a typewriter, and you can see the director standing behind the camera, and you can see the cameraman's work, and you can see the editor's work—everybody is doing something specific. But the producer can be lying on the beach, working in his mind. You can't really photograph a mind. The true filmmaker would be a producer-director. He would be a writer-producer-director, as a matter of fact, if one man can do that. Only a few people in the world can do it. I think probably the greatest films are made by people who are writer-producer-directors. I think of Bergman as a writer-producer-director; I think of Truffaut as one; I think of Fellini as one. Even though they may not take all those jobs, they usually encompass all of those jobs.

I think anybody who's working in a creative area is working partly out of his unconscious and partly out of his conscious mind. I think all decisions are a combination of both, with almost everybody able to state their conscious reasons, which may only be a part of the reason or may not be the reason at all.

If there are any heroes today, they are heroes who stand against certain aspects of the times. What they stand for varies from time to time, but for a long, long time, not just at the moment and not just in the 1960s, there's been a feeling that something is wrong with this system. But there hasn't always been a coherent theory as to what should replace it.

In *The Wild Angels* the hero, played by Peter Fonda, was against the system but had no coherent view of his own. All he knew was "This is wrong." And he had a vague idea that he wanted to be free, but he was not an intellectual man and could not express any more than that—a desire to lead a free life against the strictures of society. Peter Fonda in *The Trip* was the equivalent man but more highly educated, more intelligent, and more articulate, and through LSD was attempting to find answers. I was thinking very much in terms of post-industrial society when I made *The Trip*, and about how very possibly in the future work will not be necessary. What is man to do with his time? LSD and various aspects of that culture, I thought, would be the beginning of experiments to find alternate ways to live.

I had action in both *The Wild Angels* and *The Trip*—excitement, sex, visual images, plot, and story line. But these other elements carry the viewer on the surface, and beneath the surface I have these ideas, so that those people who want to find them can do so. The viewer who is not interested in them may be only vaguely aware that they are there, or not aware at all.

I believe that unless a writer, director, producer, actor—whatever—has some idea other than just to tell an action story, he's going to be working on a

Peter Fonda in *The Trip*, 1967

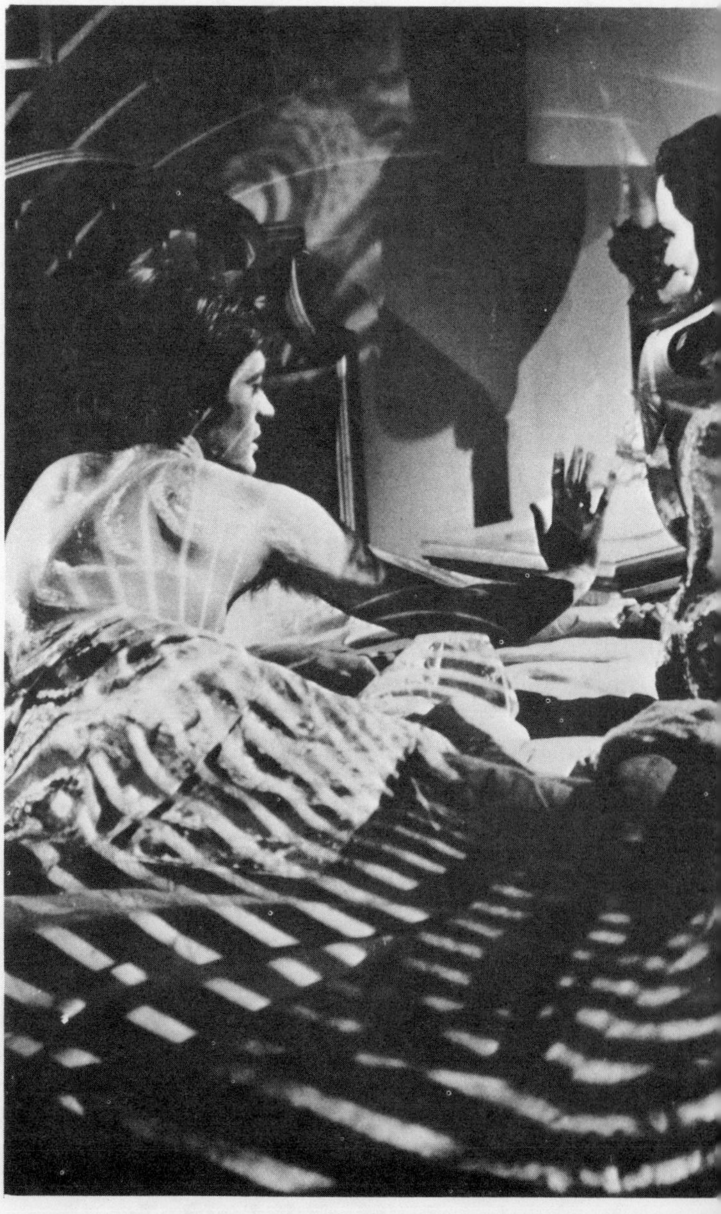

very limited basis and making a very elementary type of film. His ideas can be wrong. I think it's good if his ideas are right. But it's better for his ideas to be wrong than for him not to have any ideas—at least it brings a coherence in shape and meaning to the film. Without it there are just images on film. Even if the unifying factor is wrong, it's better than not having a unifying factor. Of course, it's better to have it right if you can.

We live in a compromised society, and I would think of myself as something of a compromised artist. I think one of the great things about motion pictures is that it is a compromised art form. So, much as I work on the basis of what I want to put into a film and the reaction I want from the audience, at the same time I want my films to make money. I think almost everybody rides the path of looking for commercial success while doing good work. Some people will say they're not looking for commercial success, they only want to do good work, and they are generally not telling the truth. There are other people who say they are looking only for commercial success and they don't care about the quality of the films, and I don't think they are telling the truth either. I think they do care but they just don't want to say it.

I have more fun with the ideas and the concepts. That may be one of the reasons I haven't directed recently, because the actual process of directing is somewhat mechanical. You're simply putting on film what you thought of before. I get more fun out of thinking up and the putting together the idea of what the film should be about.

Sometimes I wake up in the middle of the night and work. I work at the beach—anyplace where I can relax (although sometimes fresh ideas come to me in traffic). The problem, of course, is that the film on film is never as good as the film I have in my mind. It's part of the compromise. It's part of the mechanics, obviously—you can see things more in your mind than by the camera. In my mind the visions are always beautiful—the actors are always magnificent, down to bit actors; the sets are as great as they can be, and the music is the best.

I was starting to do bigger films when I stopped directing. I had done *The St. Valentine's Day Massacre*, which cost a million dollars or a little more. By Hollywood standards this was not expensive. As a matter of fact, I think *Sight and Sound* magazine said that money and Corman go together. After doing all those little films, my strong point was really doing big films. I handled the sets, the crowds, and all of that well.

Forming my own distribution company forced me back to low budget. In other words, I had worked up from low budget to high budget and then formed my own company, which meant I had to

George Segal in *The St. Valentine's Day Massacre*, 1966

finance my films myself or get some people to help me with the financing, which forced me back ten years in budgets. New World Pictures is now in our ninth year and just beginning to climb up with slightly higher budgets. This company will become more established.

I would like to remain diversified. Primarily on behalf of my children, I would like to have investments in other fields, but I have no intention of ever leaving motion pictures. This is my primary activity. The others really are side investments, although I bought a vineyard recently, which I have taken some interest in as a hobby. We try to raise grapes and market some good wine. I enjoy making films most of all. I have a feeling, however, that I've made too many films, and I want to ease back.

Jason Robards in *The St. Valentine's Day Massacre*, 1966

FILMS DIRECTED BY ROGER CORMAN

DIRECTED

THE OKLAHOMA WOMAN

During my first years as a director, budget limitations imposed a six- to ten- day schedule on everything I made. Of the four westerns I made for American International Pictures, two were AIP's ideas and two were mine—the titles reflect the difference between our conceptions of a western. AIP's titles were Apache Woman and Oklahoma Woman. Five Guns West and Gunslinger were mine. I always helped to develop the scripts, because I realized very early on that the script is the key to a coherent film. In Apache Woman I made a first attempt at dealing with racial prejudice as a thematic element within the framework of a commercial picture.—CORMAN

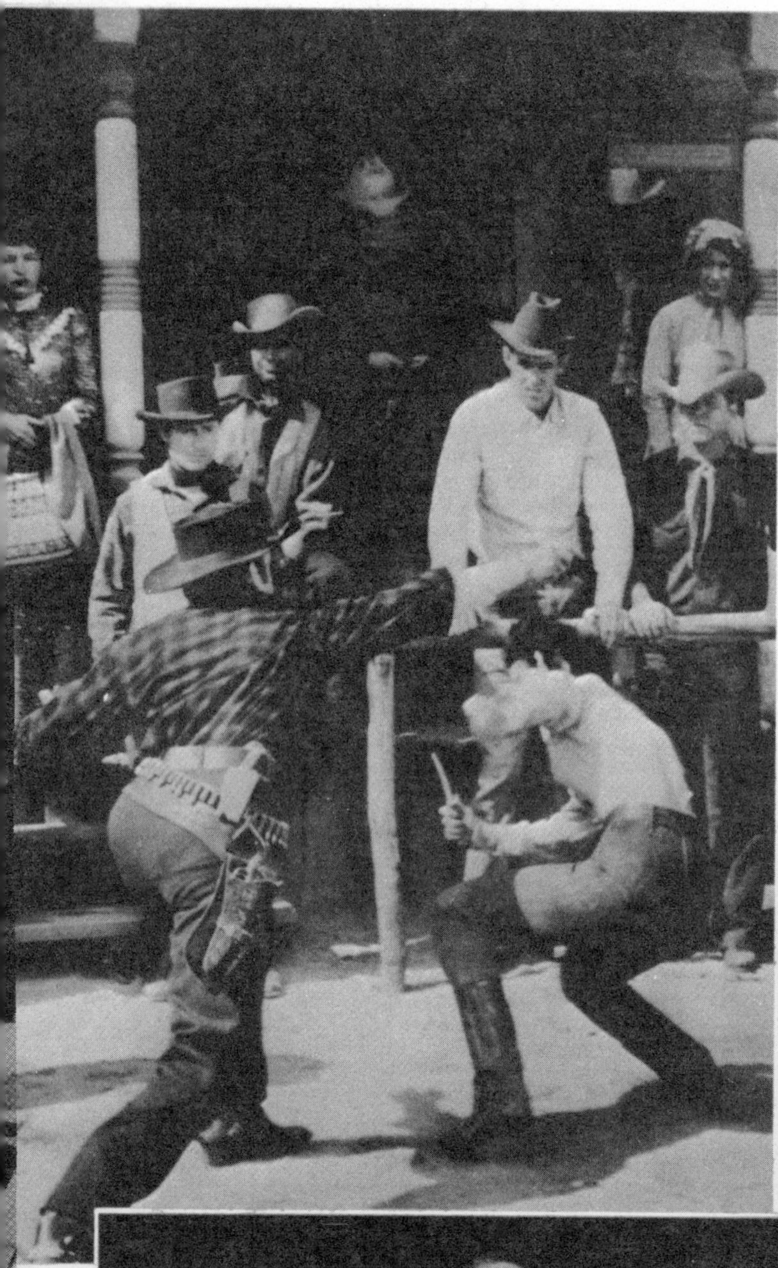

APACHE WOMAN
LLOYD BRIDGES
JOAN TAYLOR
LANCE FULLER
with MORGAN JONES • PAUL BIRCH
LOU PLACE • PAUL DUBOV

Five Guns West

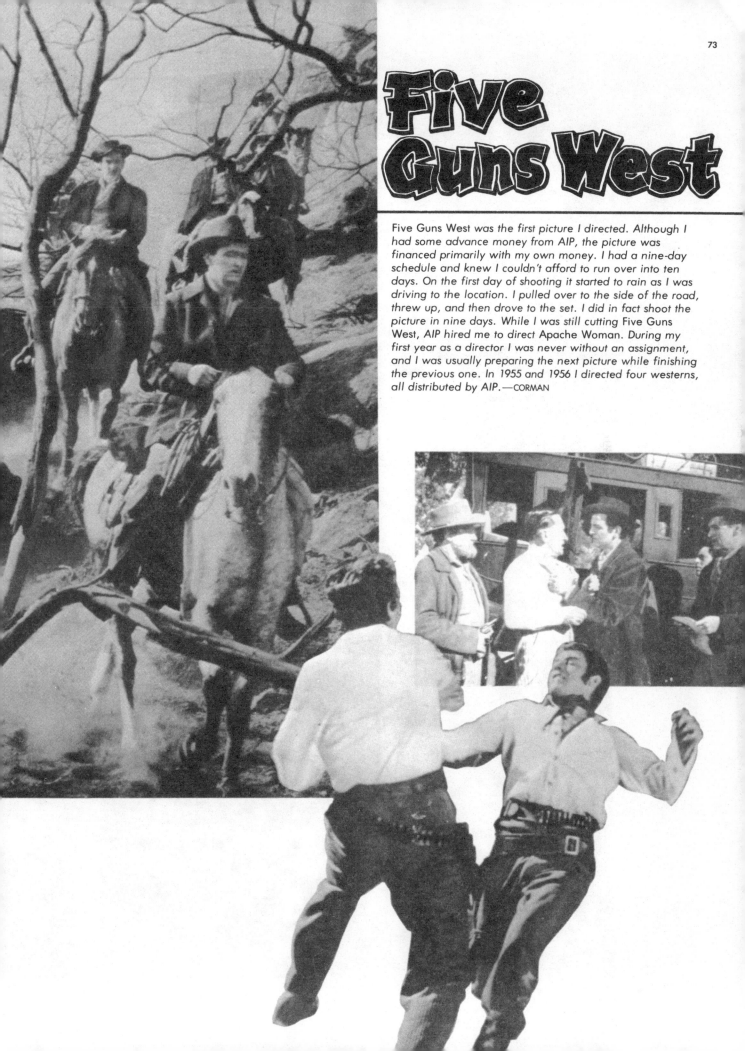

Five Guns West was the first picture I directed. Although I had some advance money from AIP, the picture was financed primarily with my own money. I had a nine-day schedule and knew I couldn't afford to run over into ten days. On the first day of shooting it started to rain as I was driving to the location. I pulled over to the side of the road, threw up, and then drove to the set. I did in fact shoot the picture in nine days. While I was still cutting Five Guns West, *AIP hired me to direct* Apache Woman. *During my first year as a director I was never without an assignment, and I was usually preparing the next picture while finishing the previous one. In 1955 and 1956 I directed four westerns, all distributed by AIP.*—CORMAN

SUPERSCOPE
Starring RICHARD DENNING
LORI NELSON
ADÈLE JERGENS
with TOUCH CONNORS
PAUL BIRCH
ATTACKED... by a creature from hell!
RAYMOND HATTON • PAUL DUBOV
JONATHAN HAZE • PAUL BLAISEDELL
Produced and Directed by ROGER CORMAN
Story and Screenplay by LOU RUSOFF
A Golden State Production
Presented by JAMES H. NICHOLSON
and SAMUEL Z. ARKOFF
Executive Producer ALEX GORDON

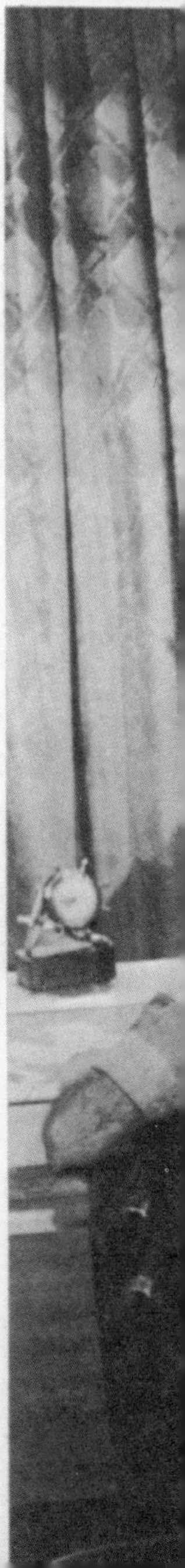

DAY THE WORLD ENDED

This was my first science-fiction film, and it became AIP's first really large success. The story dealt with the after-effects of atomic war and the concept of starting life anew—whether man can shape his destiny or is driven by irrational forces within. I have always believed it is essential to find a unifying idea or theme to work with; otherwise, a picture lacks meaningful impact, no matter how much action and special effects there may be on the screen.—CORMAN

GUNSLINGER
Hired to kill
the woman
he loved!
STARRING
JOHN IRELAND
BEVERLY GARLAND
ALLISON HAYES
A ROGER CORMAN PRODUCTION
Distributed by AMERICAN RELEASING CORP.

THE GUNSLINGER

I shot this picture in six days. It stands out in my memory as the first time I failed to finish on schedule. The picture had been budgeted for only five days, and it rained heavily fo. the five consecutive days of shooting. As a result of shooting continually in pouring rain, the picture has a misty, somewhat beautiful quality.—CORMAN

IT CONQUERED THE WORLD

The basic idea for this was the invasion of earth by an alien force. The creature came from a planet much larger than earth. Since I had majored in engineering, with a minor in physics, I set about designing the creature according to scientific principles. To function on a planet with heavy gravity, life forms would have to be very massive and low to the ground; the creature was designed to match these specifications. When the creature was brought onto the set, Beverly Garland, the leading lady (who excelled in spirited-female-protagonist roles), walked over to it, looked down at it, said, "So you've come to conquer the world? Take that!" and kicked it. I immediately subordinated scientific theory to dramatic logic, and reworked the schedule to allow for a drastic revamping of the design. What was formerly the creature became the new creature's head, and a new framework was erected beneath that, so that the creature finally towered over the human cast.—CORMAN

ATTACK OF THE CRAB MONSTER

A science-fiction idea of mutation was the starting point for this story: the threat of individual minds being absorbed into one giant mind. This premise provided strong suspense, since each time the predatory mind took a victim it acquired his knowledge and thus became harder to defeat. One of the dramatic problems was the amount of exposition required to carry the plot. To counteract this, Chuck Griffith, the writer, and I worked on the principle that in every scene there must be horror or suspense, so that there would never be a straight expository scene. Also, this was the first time I used market research to come up with a title. The picture was very successful: it was made for about seventy thousand dollars and grossed over a million dollars. I believe its success was due to the combination of all these elements: the title, a strong story idea, the structuring of every scene for horror and suspense, and editing for rapid pace.—CORMAN

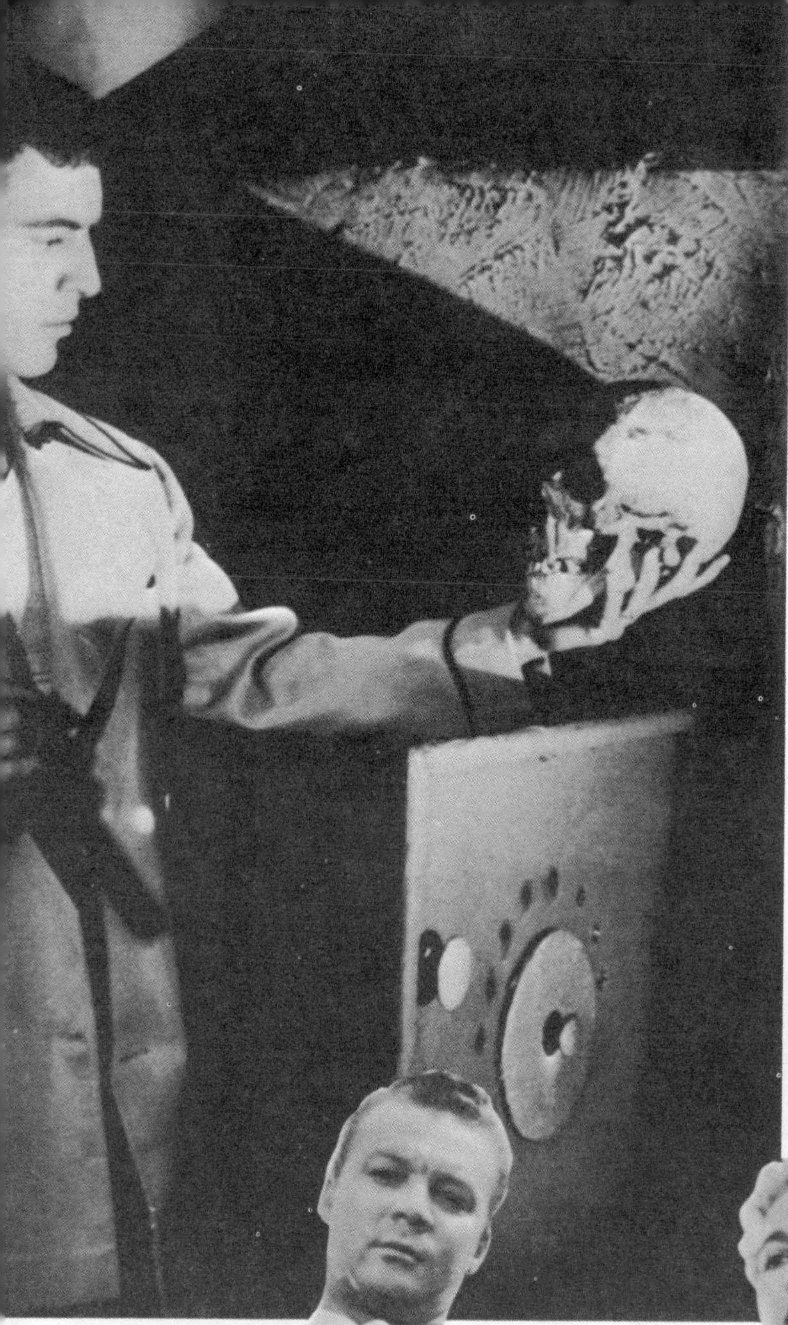

NOT OF THIS EARTH

The premise of this film was that a being from another planet comes to earth in order to experiment on the people of this planet. I have always liked the plot, because it combines humor with science fiction. Dick Miller plays a Fuller Brush salesman who comes to the house of the being from another planet, determined to get in to sell his brushes. The alien being, played by Paul Birch, wants to get him into the house for his own purposes. This became a very funny scene, and the humor of cross-purposes beneath apparently mutual aims is of course a classic comedy device. Audiences responded so enthusiastically to this combination of suspense and comedy that I continued to experiment with it, particularly in horror films.—CORMAN

THE UNDEAD

This is a story of reincarnation, and the first time I developed a story moving back and forth in time. It told the story of a girl in the present day with a parallel history of her life in medieval times. I tried to deal with a logical and philosophical problem that I still consider a real flaw in time-travel stories, namely that if you go back in time you alter history, and therefore the present time would be different.—CORMAN

ROCK ALL NIGHT

This was shot on one of my lowest budgets, in five days. Despite the budget limitations, I have always liked the picture. It was one of the first films to deal with rock 'n' roll; the hero was a little guy who was pushed around in the rock 'n' roll bar life while trying to win the pretty girl. The aim was to deal on multiple levels within the simple framework, to show the rock 'n' roll milieu, the explosion of something new in the culture, and at the same time people struggling toward something they want.—CORMAN

See and Hear
THE PLATTERS
and THE BLOCKBUSTERS
Some have to dance... Some have to kill!
ROCK ALL NIGHT
starring
DICK MILLER · RUSSELL JOHNSON · ABBY DALTON
A Sunset Production • An American-International Picture

SHE GODS OF SHARK REEF

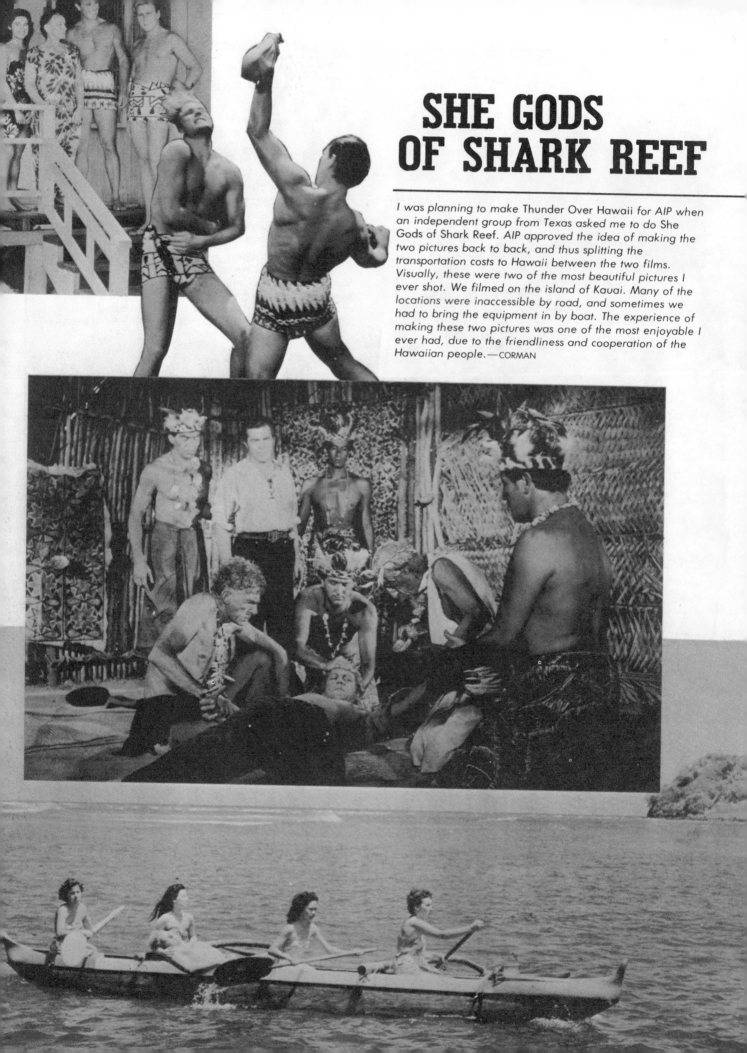

I was planning to make Thunder Over Hawaii for AIP when an independent group from Texas asked me to do She Gods of Shark Reef. AIP approved the idea of making the two pictures back to back, and thus splitting the transportation costs to Hawaii between the two films. Visually, these were two of the most beautiful pictures I ever shot. We filmed on the island of Kauai. Many of the locations were inaccessible by road, and sometimes we had to bring the equipment in by boat. The experience of making these two pictures was one of the most enjoyable I ever had, due to the friendliness and cooperation of the Hawaiian people.—CORMAN

THUNDER OVER HAWAII

(FORMERLY...NAKED PARADISE)

TEENAGE DOLL

This was one of a group of pictures I made for syndicates of theater owners. The general pattern was that they would provide the title and subject of the film and leave me free to develop whatever aspects and themes I wanted within the framework of the genre. In this picture I dealt with class/cultural conflict in a high school. The leading lady played a middle-class girl, and her story dramatized the clash between middle-class and working-class values.—CORMAN

CARNIVAL ROCK

This was another picture financed by theater owners. I remember it primarily for its extremely good rock music. The theater owners were from the South, and they sent me several young rock performers who were not stars, such as Bob Luman (left), but contributed a lot of infectious energy and enthusiasm to the picture.—CORMAN

Sorority Girl

I was a fraternity member in college, and my observation of the fraternity and sorority system left me somewhat ambivalent about many of its aspects. I tried to explore some of these aspects in the film. It was shot on the USC campus, and members of a sorority were used in supporting roles and as extras. Through a number of films I developed the technique of shooting on natural locations whenever possible, and using local talent to further augment the authenticity of the background.—CORMAN

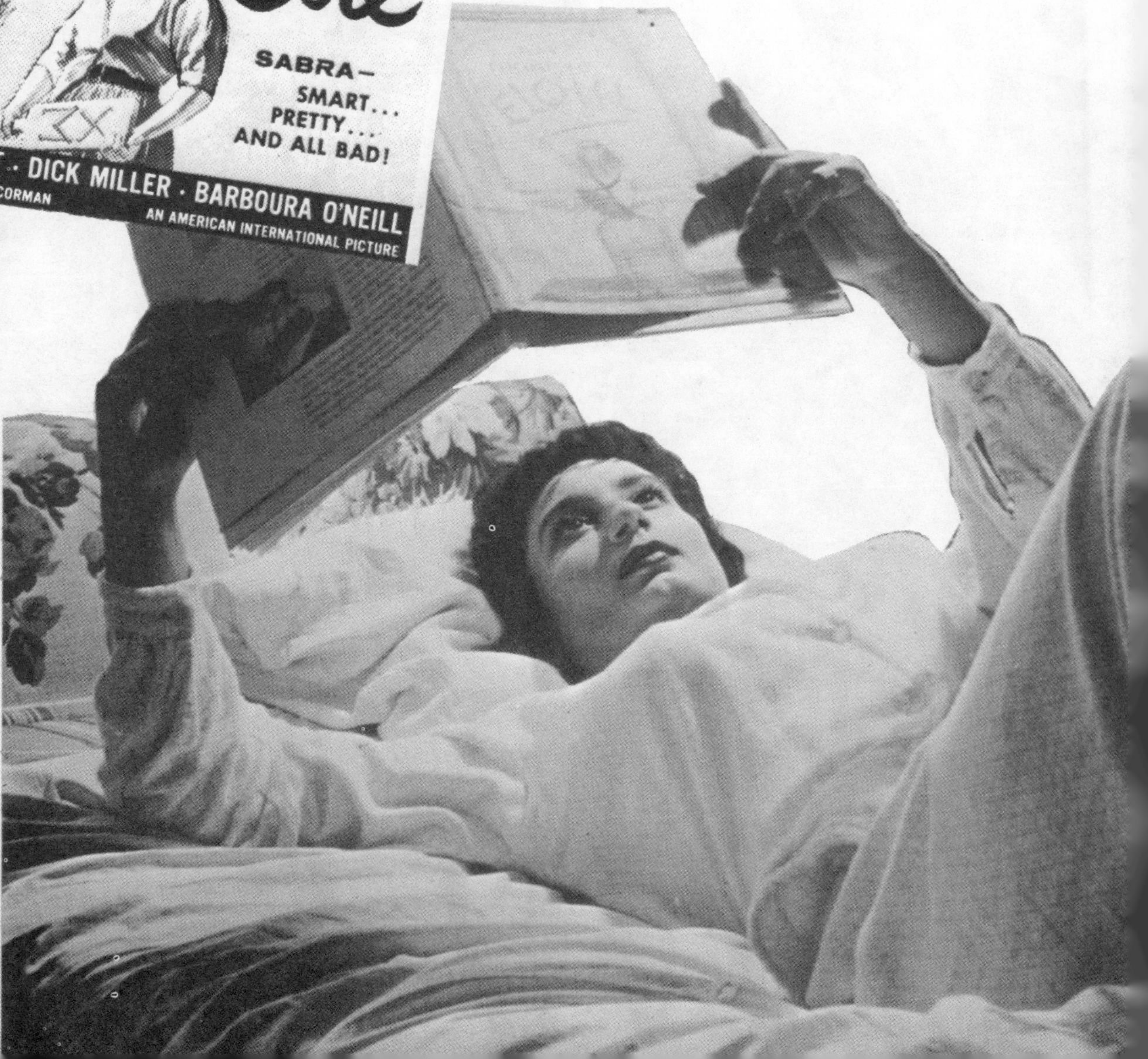

Viking Women and the SEA SERPENT

The full title of this film was The Voyage of the Viking Women to the Waters of the Great Sea Serpent. *AIP believed in short titles to express the essence of a movie, but this time I decided we couldn't capture what the movie promised in a short title, so we'd try the other route and go for the longest title ever. It was made for about a hundred thousand dollars on a ten-day schedule, but the scope of the picture really demanded a bigger budget. In general, when working on a low budget you are better off with material that does not depend primarily on spectacular special effects.*—CORMAN

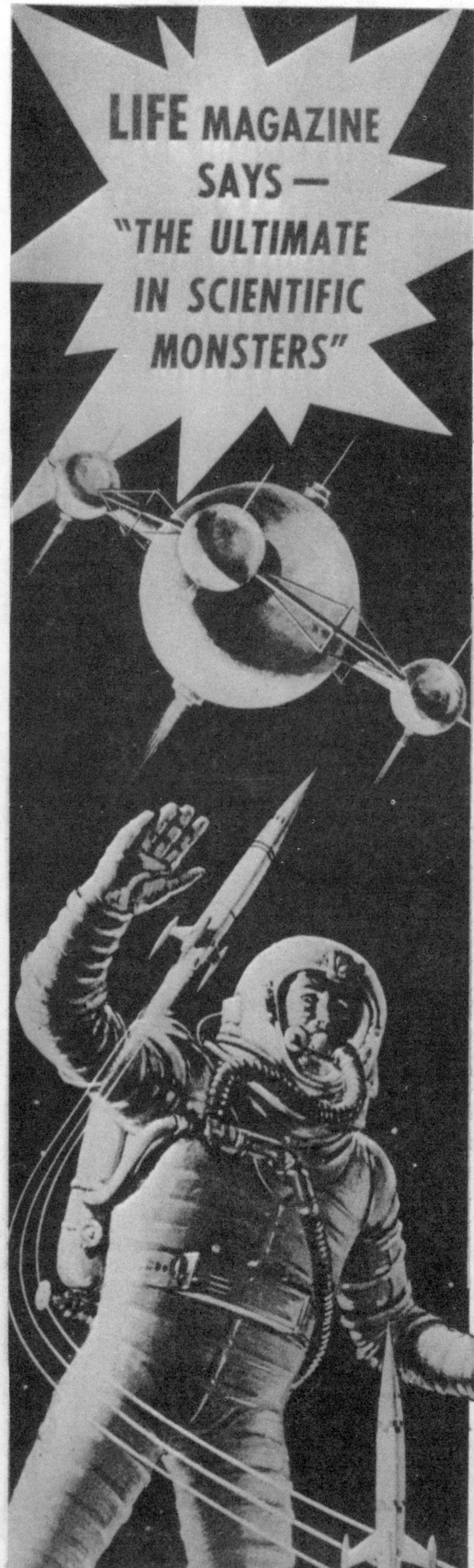
LIFE MAGAZINE
SAYS —
"THE ULTIMATE
IN SCIENTIFIC
MONSTERS"

WAR of the SATELLITES

This was a quintessential example of shooting from the headlines. The first Russian Sputnik had just been launched when a friend called me with a story idea about satellites. I called Allied Artists and said I would have a script in two weeks and the film could be shot in ten days and cut in three weeks. The film was actually shot in eight days, and within two months of the headline event we had the first movie about the new space age.—CORMAN

I MOBSTER

I Mobster was made for Alperson, a prominent independent producer. After seeing Machine Gun Kelley, he called me and asked me to do this picture. It was made on my customary low budget. Although it turned out well, I prefer Machine Gun Kelly, partly perhaps because I developed the script myself, but also because I believe Kelly had more of the true appeal and flavor of the period.—CORMAN

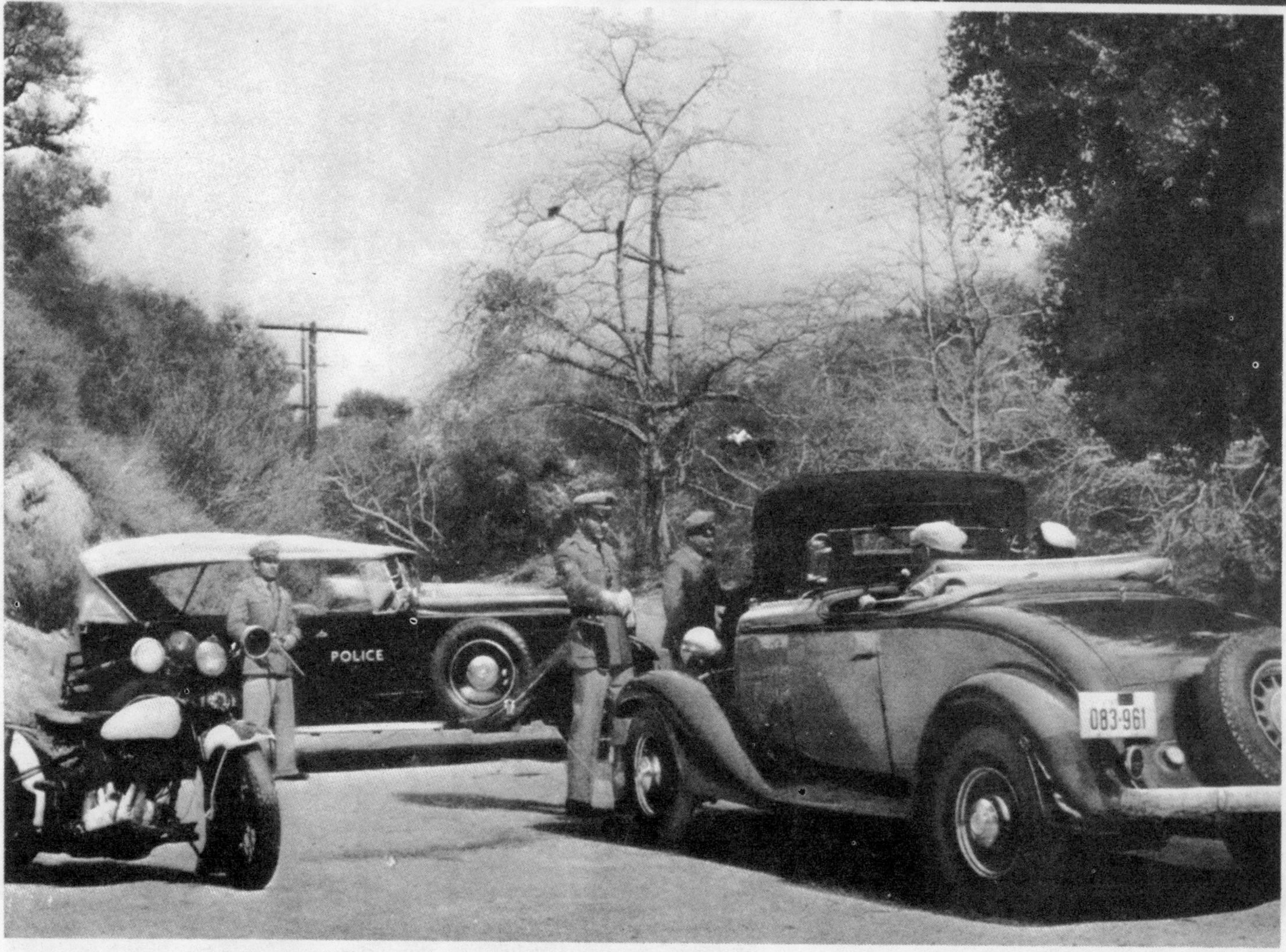
POLICE
083-961

MACHINE GUN KELLY

WITHOUT
HIS GUN
HE
WAS
NAKED
YELLOW!

AIP wanted a gangster picture, so I researched various possibilities and settled on Machine Gun Kelly because of an interesting angle. Research indicated that although he was Number One on the FBI's Most Wanted list, he was actually a coward. The picture was designed to lead up to its last line, which was taken from the testimony about his capture. They had him surrounded in a hideout in the mountains, and called out to him to throw down his gun and surrender. Which he did. The FBI agent said to him, "You're supposed to be the toughest man in the country—why'd you surrender?" Machine Gun Kelly replied, "Because I knew you'd kill me." Machine Gun Kelly was Charles Bronson's first starring role, and he was excellent. It is a further testimony to his gifts as an actor when you remember that there was almost no rehearsal time, and we very seldom went beyond a second or third take—this had to be the rule on those limited shooting schedules.—CORMAN

TEENAGE CAVEMAN

This was an example of AIP's penchant for commercial titles, sometimes at the expense of the film. The original title was Prehistoric World. After its first opening, the Los Angeles Times review stated: "Despite its 10 cent title, Teenage Caveman is a surprisingly good picture." That helped change the title back to the original. The picture followed the progress of a young man in a prehistoric tribe, showing religious taboos and initiation rites. At the end of the picture, the forbidden area is discovered to be contaminated by radiation, and we realize that the story is in fact taking place in the future, after civilization has been wiped out, and religion and myth are developing along the same lines as before. An optimistic note is sounded at the very end as people discover the artifacts of the previous civilization, and the idea that they can perhaps learn from history is introduced. Robert Vaughan (below) starred in the picture, in one of his first roles.—CORMAN

The Wasp Woman

This was one of the first pictures I made for my own company, Filmgroup. Since I was now financing films from my own savings, I budgeted the pictures at twenty to fifty thousand dollars. This one was made for fifty thousand dollars, and has a good performance by the leading lady, Susan Cabot. She plays the head of a cosmetics firm who tries to increase business by incorporating a rejuvenation wasp jelly into her products. The idea occurred to me after reading a magazine article about the use of bee jelly or some such thing in women's cosmetics.—CORMAN

A BEAUTIFUL WOMAN BY DAY-

A LUSTING QUEEN WASP BY NIGHT.

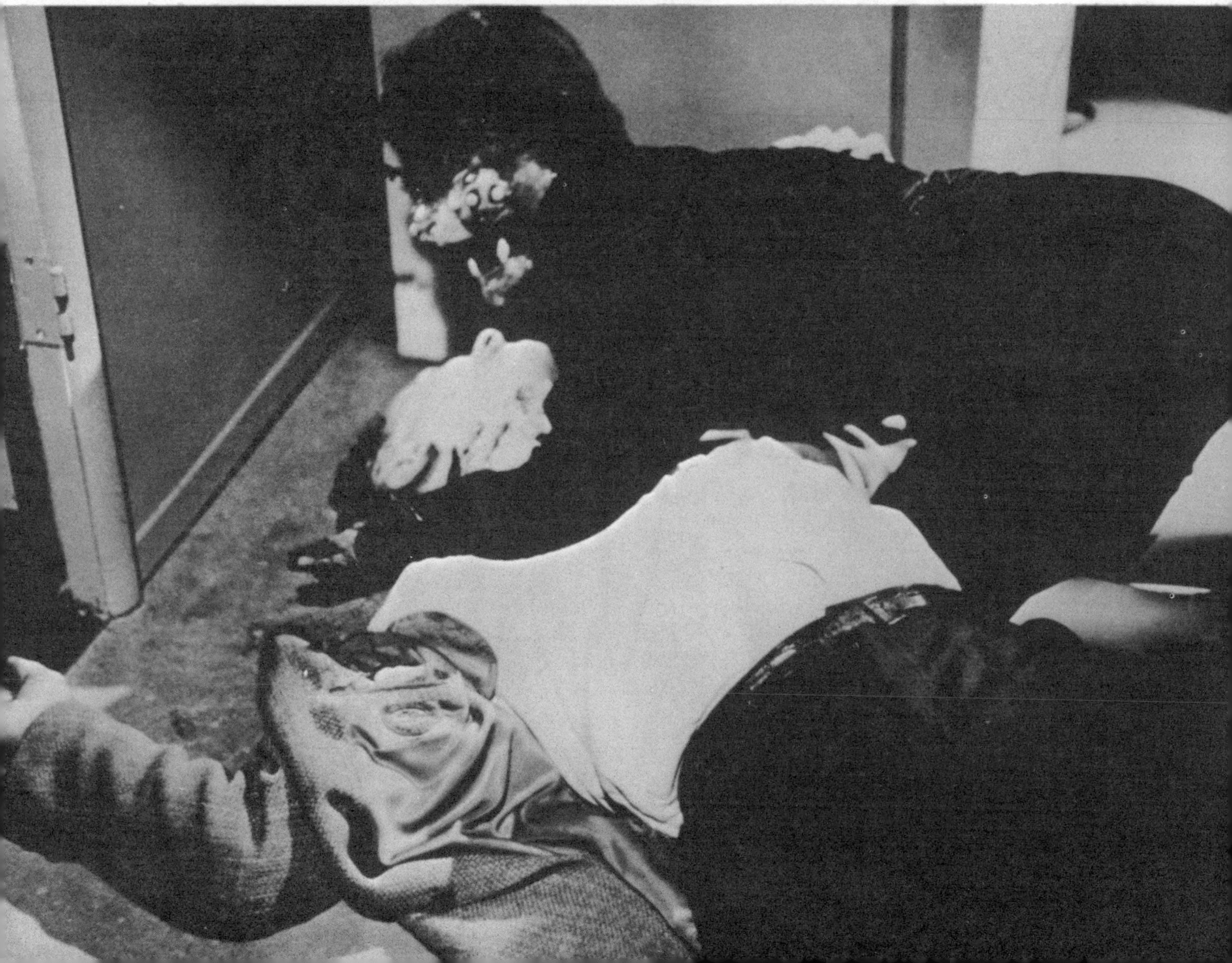

You'll be sick, sick, sick —from LAUGHING!

"Are you together?"

"All I said was, Bucket of Blood was coming on, lady. Please remove your hat."

"Okay, let's get a bite to eat...but nothing with tomato sauce."

"What a night! Fourteen people shrieked...nine people fainted and one of our ushers is missing!"

JAMES H. NICHOLSON and SAMUEL Z. ARKOFF present an AMERICAN-INTERNATIONAL picture

A BUCKET OF BLOOD

AIP asked me to make a horror film for fifty thousand dollars and I took it on as a challenge. My friend and scriptwriter, Chuck Griffith, worked out the story with me. We came up with a comic horror film which took place in a coffeehouse and centered around the beatnik movement. We had a five-day shooting schedule, and it was an enjoyable film to make because the spirit on the set was high. I was working with a group of actors who were mostly friends of mine, and they added improvised jokes and lines, taking off from the spirit of the script, as we went along.—CORMAN

SKI TROOP ATTACK

This was the only time I ever played a part amounting to more than a one- or two-line bit in any of my films. I had hired a former German skitrooper to play the leader of the German ski troop, but he broke his leg the day before we were to begin shooting. We were on location in Deadwood, South Dakota, with no time to replace him, so I had to play the role myself. The Deadwood High School ski team played the American skitroopers, and the Lead High School ski team played the German skitroopers. In some of the battles, of which I was unfortunately a part, the high-school rivalry made the fighting spirit only too authentic.
—CORMAN

IN CINEMASCOPE AND COLOR
starring
VINCENT PRICE
co-starring
MARK DAMON
MYRNA FAHEY
with HARRY ELLERBE
NOW SHOWING
in theatres and drive-ins
throughout Southern California

House of Usher

AIP had a practice of double-billing two black-and-white horror or science-fiction pictures. When they asked me to make two ten-day black-and-white horror films to play as a double feature, I convinced them instead to finance one horror film in color. I also picked the material—I had read this story of Poe's in high school, and had always liked it. This was the first picture for which I had more than a two-week schedule (I had fifteen days), and it was also, at two hundred thousand dollars, the biggest budget I'd ever had. It was exciting creatively to be working on something more substantial, combining all the elements to evoke a pervading sense of horror and mystery.—CORMAN

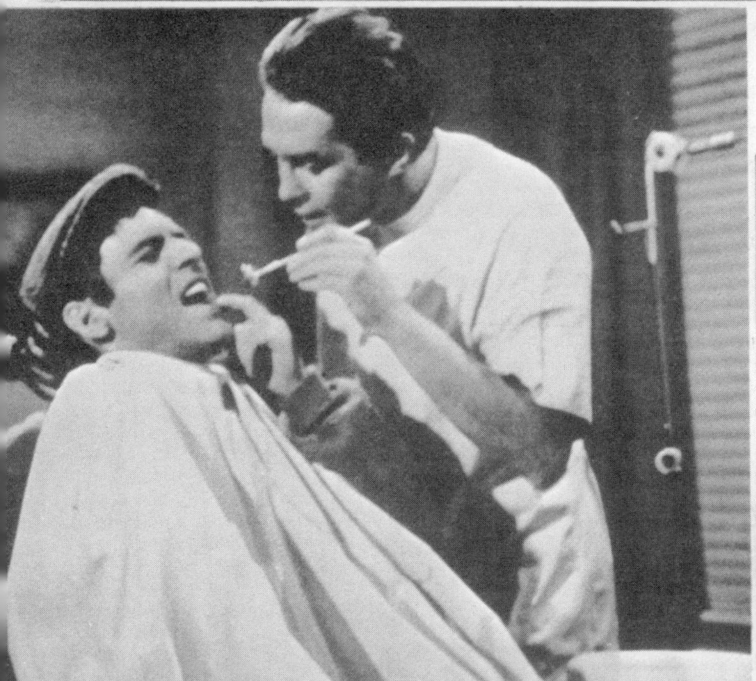

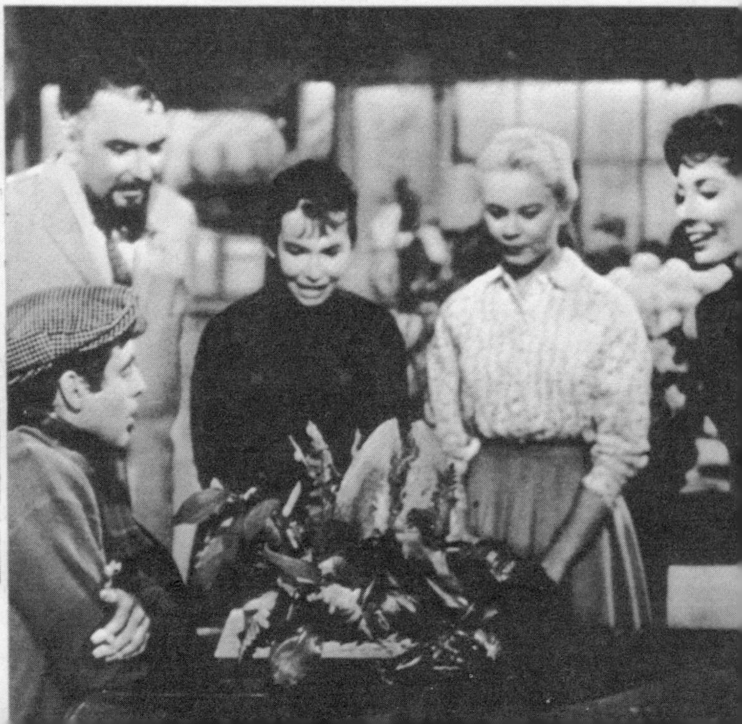

The Little Shop of Horrors

After the success of A Bucket of Blood, a comedy-horror picture shot on a five-day schedule, I determined to attempt a similar style of picture on a two-day schedule. Once again, since the cast and crew were mostly all friends, making this film was an enjoyable experience. At 9:00 a.m. on the first day of shooting the production manager informed us that we were already behind schedule and we'd have to pick up the pace. We did, and finished in two days. It still plays on college campuses and at midnight screenings, and has become something of a cult film.
—CORMAN

THE LAST WOMAN ON EARTH

This was a science-fiction idea, with a screenplay written by Robert Towne (later of Shampoo and Chinatown renown), a good friend of mine. Though talented, he was a somewhat slow writer, and hadn't finished the script by the time we were due to start shooting in Puerto Rico. Since I couldn't afford to bring him along just to finish the script, I had him play the second lead in the film, so he made his acting and writing debut at the same time (above, right).—CORMAN

I did Atlas for all the money I could scrape up, which was about seventy-five thousand dollars. This picture actually made a little money, but it was the same old story of inefficiently doing a giant film on a small budget. I played a small role, below, third from right.—CORMAN.

CREATURE FROM THE HAUNTED SEA

This was the third and last of the low-budget comedy-horror group of films (preceded by A Bucket of Blood and The Little Shop of Horrors). The film was shot in six days, and is notable for reversing the convention in which the monster was always defeated by the humans. In this picture the monster killed and ate all the actors; the last shot is of the monster sitting on the ocean floor amid a pile of bones, picking his teeth.—CORMAN

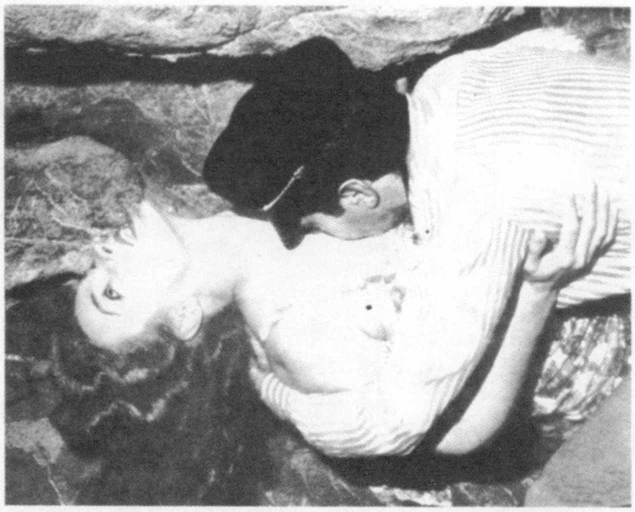

"WITHIN THE COFFIN I LIE... ALIVE!"

THE PREMATURE BURIAL

I had made several Poe pictures for AIP, and the customary disagreement between filmmaker and distributor had arisen over the division of profits. AIP's laboratory work was done by Pathé, which wanted to expand their distribution company. Pathé offered to back me on more attractive terms than AIP if I would make a feature for them. I started shooting Premature Burial for Pathé, and to my great surprise, on the second day of shooting, the heads of AIP, Sam Arkoff and Jim Nicholson, showed up on the set with big smiles and hearty handshakes, welcoming me back to AIP. They explained that Pathé had sold the picture to AIP after they had pointed out that AIP could well take all its lab work away from Pathé. I was happy enough, since AIP honored my deal with Pathé.—CORMAN

"Deep, deep, and forever, into some ordinary and nameless grave"... Poe

THE GREATEST TERROR TALE EVER TOLD!

Edgar Allan Poe's
THE PIT AND THE PENDULUM
"It was designed to cross the region of the heart... It would return again and again ...Down and still down it came!..."
–POE
FILMED IN PANAVISION AND COLOR
AN AMERICAN INTERNATIONAL PICTURE

STARRING VINCENT PRICE · JOHN KERR · BARBARA STEELE · LUANA ANDERS

SCREENPLAY BY RICHARD MATHESON · PRODUCED AND DIRECTED BY ROGER CORMAN MUSIC BY LES BAXTER

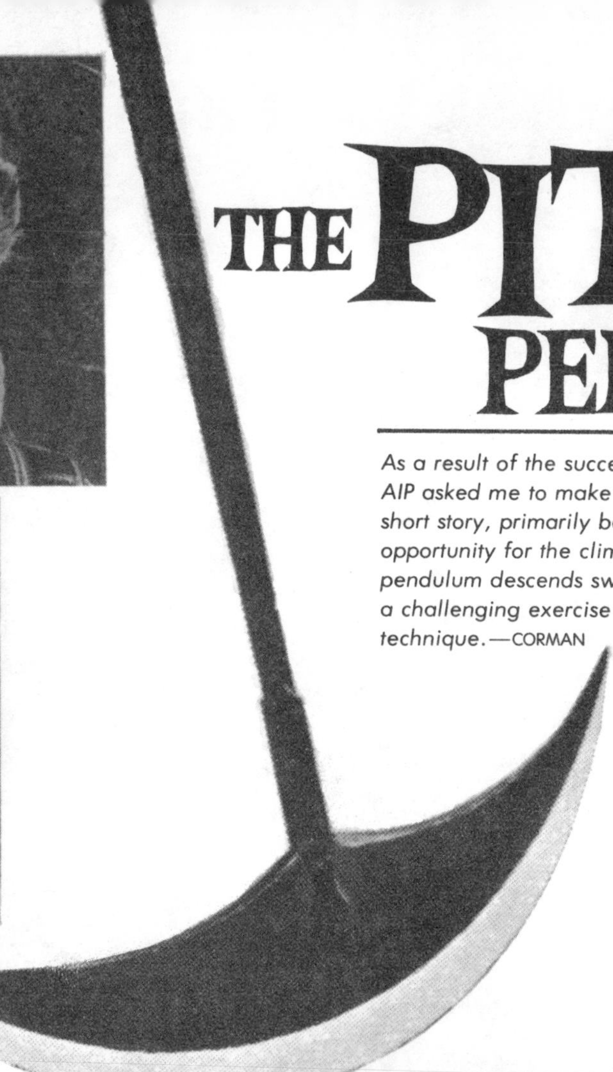

THE PIT AND THE PENDULUM

As a result of the success of The Fall of the House of Usher, AIP asked me to make another Poe picture, and I chose this short story, primarily because it provided a great visual opportunity for the climactic sequence, in which the pendulum descends swinging over its victim. This film was a challenging exercise in both shooting and editing technique. —CORMAN

MOMENT OF TERROR — Dreaded pendulum blade drops lower and lower on terrified John Kerr in dramatic highlight of American International's filmization of the Edgar Allan Poe terror classic, "The Pit and the Pendulum".

MARITAL DISHARMONY — Vincent Price, as the tormented Spanish nobleman in American International's filmization of the Edgar Allan Poe terror classic, "The Pit and the Pendulum", shows his displeasure with his wife, portrayed by Barbara Steele.

THE INTRUDER

The fate of this film was a paradox. It got magnificent reviews, won several film festivals, and was probably the most acclaimed film I had made at the time(1961) or since—yet it was also the first film I had ever made that lost money. It was concerned with the integration of schools in the South, and I believed strongly in the picture. I had never previously developed a screenplay speculatively—without backing; my record was so reliable that normally I could get financing for a screenplay and picture simply on the basis of an idea. On this project, I bought the novel rights and developed the screenplay only to find that nobody would back me. So I put up some of my own money and managed to raise some more from Pathé American, then a new distribution company. I'd hoped to have a decent budget and schedule, but I had only ninety thousand dollars and a three-week schedule. I shot on location in the South with a few professional actors, headed by Bill Shatner, and local people playing the rest of the roles. As a result, the film has a gritty, authentic look, which was in keeping with the kind of film I wanted to make—an honest look at a part of America at a critical time. The fact that some of the townspeople were not brilliant actors was compensated for by the fact that their faces were right, and of course their accents were absolutely authentic. I remember we recruited a group of guys sitting around the town square to be the cohorts of the segregationists. They loved everything Shatner said, cheered his speeches, and were really upset at the end of the picture to find out that he was the villain.—CORMAN

TALES OF TERROR

This was another in the series of Poe-based pictures. Most of the Poe short stories were no longer than two or three pages; they were essentially dramatic fragments . . . wonderful fragments. The method used in the first Poe pictures was to use the Poe story as the climax, and construct a line of development toward this climax which we tried to make faithful to Poe's quality of imagination. However, not all the short stories lent themselves to this method. So in this picture, I used three stories as the basis and, because I feared being repetitious, added some humor to one story, "The Black Cat."—CORMAN

TOWER OF LONDON

After the success of the Poe series, Eddie Small asked me to do a similar kind of film on a historical subject. This film was shot in black and white, and since I'd depended so heavily on color in the Poe films, it was an interesting challenge. —CORMAN.

DO YOU HAVE THE COURAGE TO SPEND 83 MINUTES IN
ADMIRAL PICTURES, INC. PRESENTS
VINCENT PRICE IN
TOWER OF LONDON
MICHAEL PATE · JOAN FREEMAN · ROBERT BROWN · SCREENPLAY BY LEO V. GORDON, AMOS POWELL AND JAMES B. GORDON
Story by Leo V. Gordon and Amos Powell · Music MICHAEL ANDERSEN · Directed by ROGER CORMAN · Produced by GENE CORMAN · Released thru UNITED ARTISTS

THE TERROR

This was the lowest-budgeted of the horror films I was making at that time. The picture ostensibly starred Boris Karloff, but since I could afford him for only two days, the real star of the film became Jack Nicholson, a good friend of mine. Several of my other horror films climaxed with fire. In this one, the house is destroyed by a flood at the end. In retrospect, I consider fire easier to work with, to control, than water, and more effective on the screen.—CORMAN

The Raven

The Raven was one of the last of the Poe series. As I felt the pictures were in danger of beginning to look and feel alike, I decided to play The Raven for humor. I had a really good cast: Vincent Price, Peter Lorre, and Boris Karloff, who were wonderful to work with. Boris was a meticulous actor who would learn his lines to the letter and come in prepared to deliver them just so. Peter would more or less know his lines but constantly improvised on the set. Vincent was somewhere in between—he was as well prepared as Boris but enjoyed improvising with Peter. The two of them drove Boris a little crazy. For example, a convention of the Poe pictures was that the coffin was always buried in a crypt beneath the house—no one was ever buried in a graveyard, always in a crypt beneath the house. So in this picture, when Vincent said to Peter, "My wife's body is buried in a crypt beneath the house," Peter replied, "Where else?" They continued down the stairs to the crypt, and there was the coffin covered with cobwebs, rats running around and dust all over the place. Peter looked around and said, "Hard place to keep clean, eh?"—CORMAN

THE YOUNG RACERS

I assembled a group of friends to go to Europe on a trip which would be part work, part vacation. We made a film which followed the Grand Prix racing circuit, incorporating the actual races into our story. A number of people who worked on this film as assistants have since gone on to acclaim on their own—including Francis Ford Coppola, Robert Towne, and Menachem Golan (the Israeli producer-director).—CORMAN

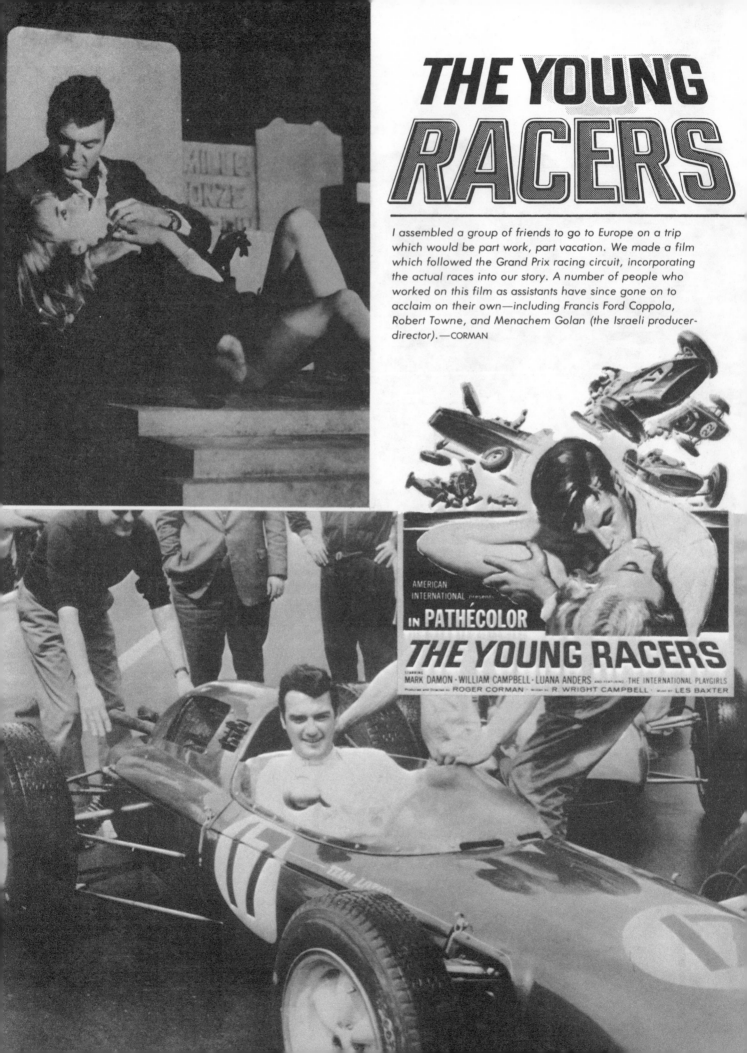

THE Haunted PALACE

Films in the Poe series were successful because they appealed on two levels: as horror films they drew the normal audience for that genre, but because they were based on the tales of Edgar Allan Poe and I tried to develop a cinematic style appropriate to the imaginative quality of Poe, the films received a certain amount of critical attention, sometimes played in art houses, and went beyond the normal horror market. I was particularly pleased by Penelope Houston's reference in her review of the Poe series in Sight and Sound to "Roger Corman's elegant arabesques of horror."—CORMAN

"X" THE MAN WITH THE X-RAY EYES

This was the story of a man experimenting with the nature of vision. First he developed x-ray vision in himself, and then he progressed until he was able to see deeper and deeper into the very core of the universe. Possibly because of the mystical implications of the theme, it got a great deal of critical attention.—CORMAN

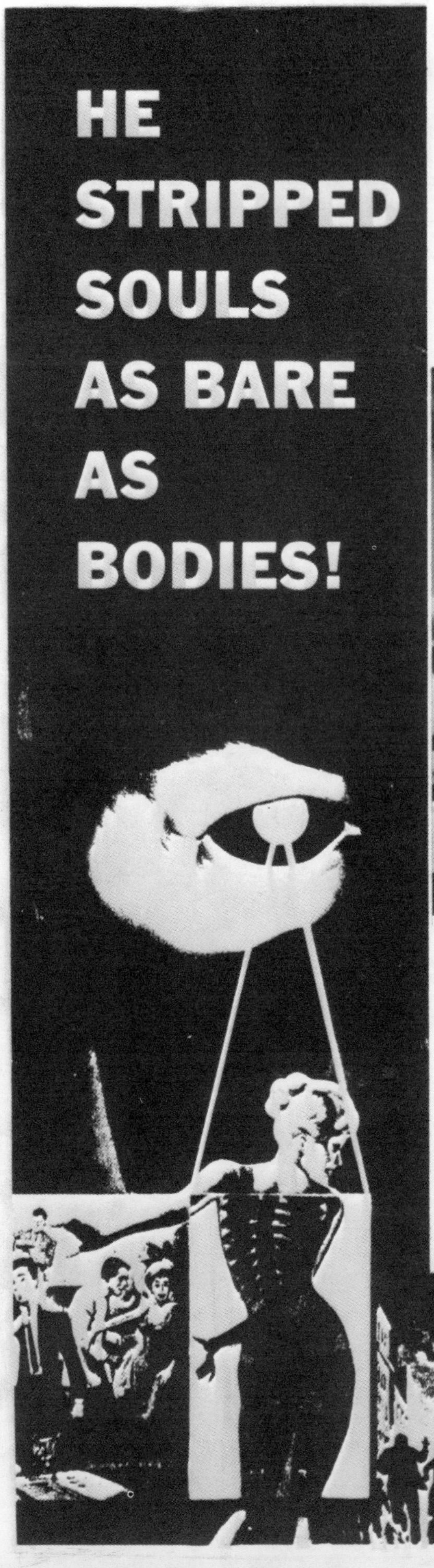
HE
STRIPPED
SOULS
AS BARE
AS
BODIES!

"THE SECRET INVASION"

This was my first film for a major company (United Artists), and at five hundred and ninety thousand dollars it was the biggest budget I'd ever had up to that time (1963). It was the story of a selected group of criminals used in war, based on the premise that war is itself a criminal activity and criminals are therefore potentially its most effective practitioners. It was simply a matter of fitting the outlaw, criminal mentality to the motivations of war. I had a very good cast: Stewart Granger, Edd Byrnes, Mickey Rooney, Raf Vallone, and Henry Silva.—CORMAN

THE DARING PLAN... THE STAGGERING ODDS... THESE ARE
THE INCREDIBLE 5 WHO LAUNCHED
THE CORMAN COMPANY presents
"THE SECRET INVASION"
Driven by the knowledge that history could not afford their failure.
The Mad Major
Destined against his will to be a hero. This genius outwitted all of Fortress Europe.
The Master Criminal
He could blow the crystal off a watch yet still keep it running!
The Demolition Demon
As good with a pen as he was with a gun!
The Forger
He didn't need a war to kill ...with him murder was an instinct!
The Assassin
STEWART GRANGER RAF VALLONE MICKEY ROONEY EDD BYRNES HENRY SILVA as Durrell
introducing MIA MASSINI
Written by R. WRIGHT CAMPBELL
Produced by GENE CORMAN
Directed by ROGER CORMAN
COLOR by DeLUXE
PANAVISION
Released thru UNITED ARTISTS

In The Tomb of Ligeia I departed from my usual practice in the Poe films by shooting a fair amount of the picture in the English countryside. I wanted to experiment on this picture, so I shot a great deal in natural sunlight. As a result, the picture has a bigger look, but I still think my original theory and practice were the most effective.—CORMAN

THE MASQUE OF THE RED DEATH

This was the first of the Poe pictures I shot entirely in England, which have a better look due to slightly larger budgets and longer shooting schedules (five weeks as opposed to three weeks). Visually these pictures represent my better work, as I could afford more elaborate sets, better costumes, and more time to work with the cameraman. On this picture the cinematographer was Nicholas Roeg, who has since become a director. I sometimes wonder about the number of people who started with me and later became directors—was it because they learned something working with me or because they thought if I could do it anybody could?—CORMAN

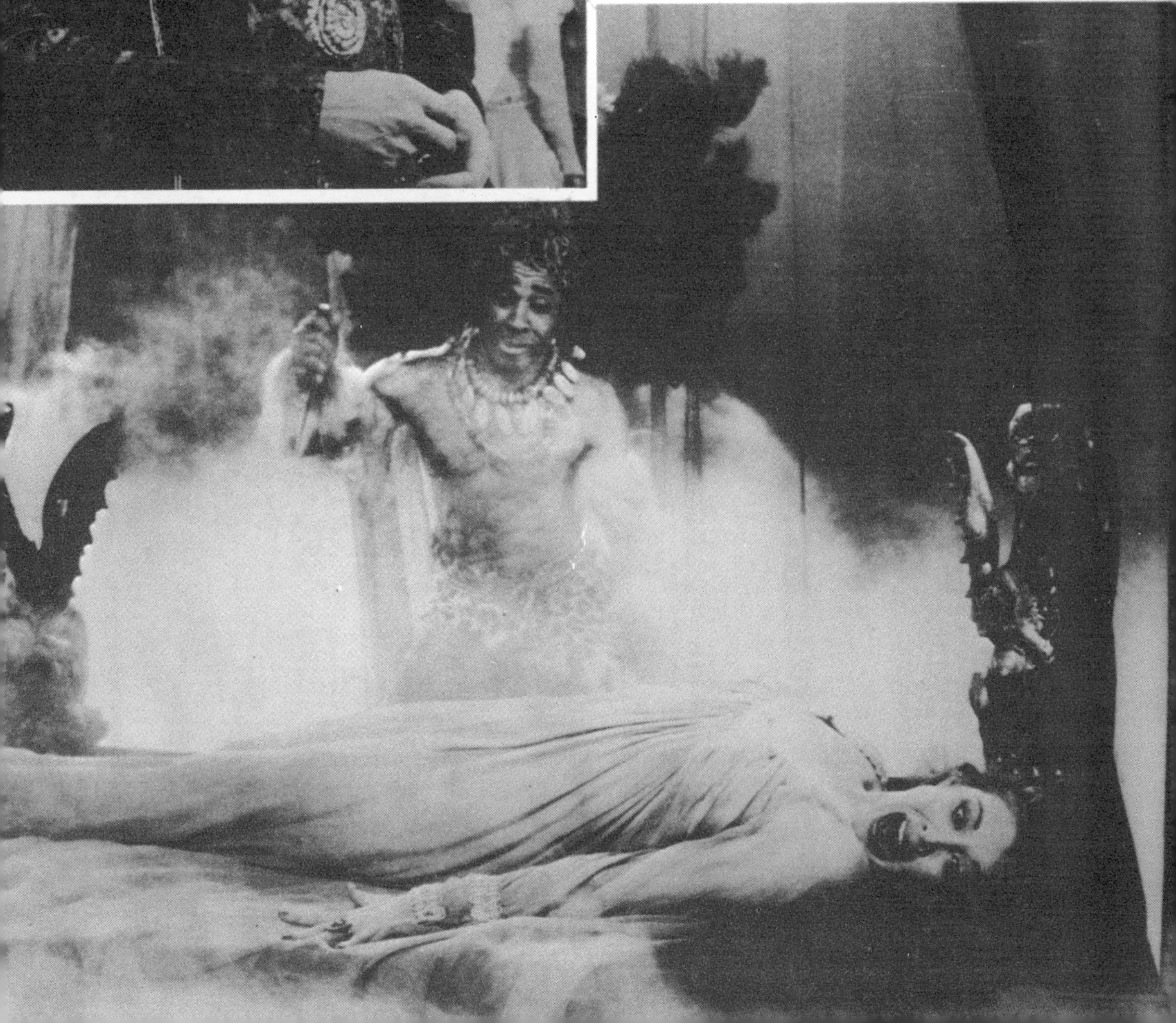

THE WILD ANGELS

Just as the Poe pictures gave rise to a series of similar horror films, The Wild Angels was the precursor of over fifty "biker films." It was the first film to deal with the notorious Hell's Angels motorcycle gang. In order to be as accurate as I could in depicting this phenomenon, I spent a fair amount of time hanging out with them, learning to ride a chopper, and financing some of their parties. The picture was shot on natural locations, and the Angels themselves were cast in it. The scenes were all based on stories they had told me. I felt the Angels were simply people who had no place in an increasingly technological, structured society, and so formed a rebellious counterculture—a few years before the concept of the countercultures of the late 1960s became fashionable. In terms of the story and the visual presentation I conceived them to be to a certain extent latter-day cowboys roaming free, on motorcycles rather than horses. A number of good actors, particularly Peter Fonda and Bruce Dern, benefited from a new momentum in their careers as a result of this film.—CORMAN

Against everything but each other–
these are today's real rebels, with a chip on their shoulder,
a monkey on their back and a hate for the world in their guts!

Their credo is violence... Their God is hate and they call themselves THE WILD ANGELS

AMERICAN INTERNATIONAL presents

PETER FONDA · NANCY SINATRA

CO-STARRING **BRUCE DERN and DIANE LADD**

WITH

MEMBERS OF HELL'S ANGELS OF VENICE, CALIFORNIA

This was the only picture I ever shot on a major-studio lot. The contrast with shooting independently on natural locations was considerable, and I found it hard to become reconciled to a certain amount of inefficiency and economic waste in production. There is, however, no question that a more polished, professional look is achieved under these conditions. The aim of this film was to provide an extremely accurate, semi-documentary account of the Chicago gang wars leading up to the St. Valentine's Day Massacre. Every aspect of the film was painstakingly researched, and, so far as I know, it is the most accurate feature made on the subject. Most gangster movies had been fictionalized and romanticized to such an extent that, as in westerns, the concept of historical reality had been lost. Almost every scene in the film can be corroborated by evidence that it really happened or could be deduced to have happened from available records.—CORMAN

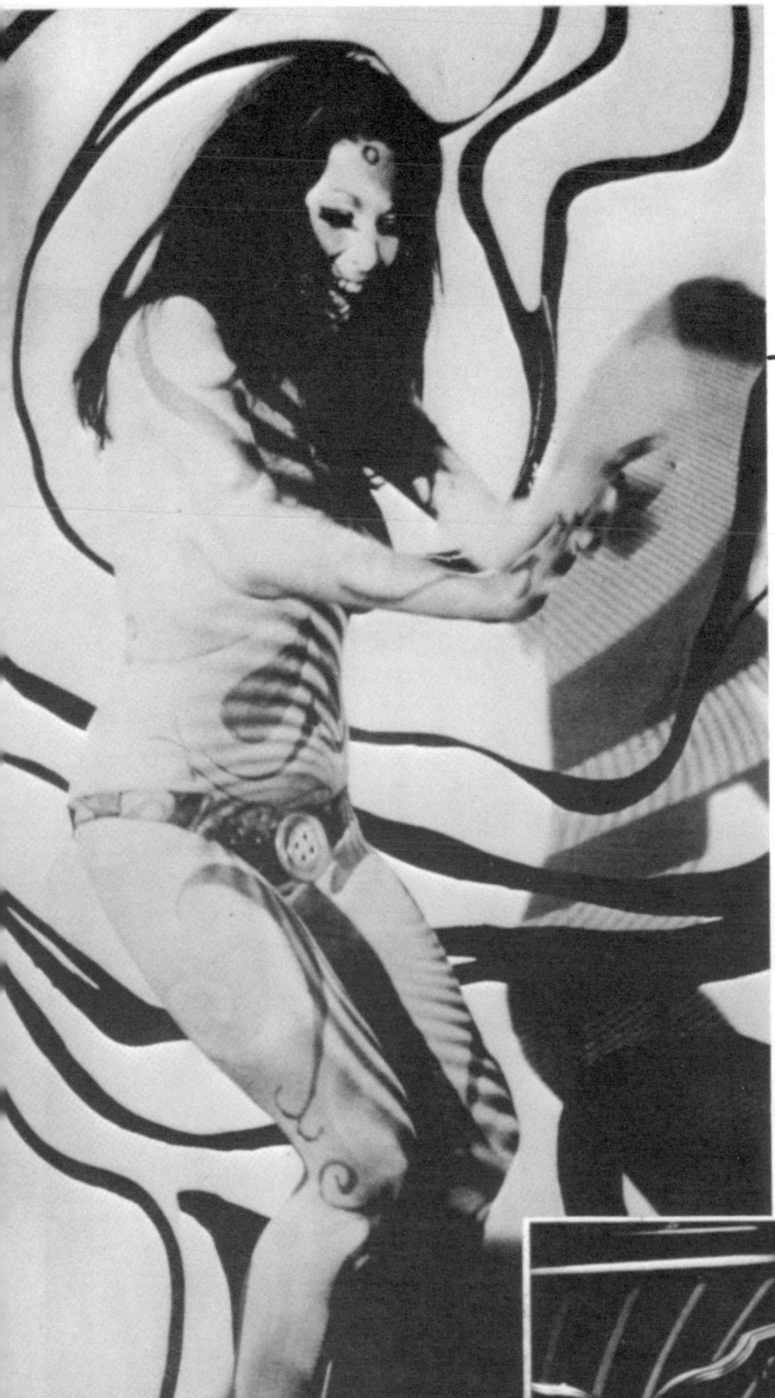

THE TRIP

Following the success of The Wild Angels, AIP asked for another film exploring the contemporary youth culture. Peter Fonda, who had become a star as the result of The Wild Angels, was again to play the lead. The drug scene, in particular the use of LSD, was burgeoning at the time. As in The Wild Angels, I again decided to dispense to a large extent with a conventional plot, and to build the picture around actual experiences. The screenplay was written by Jack Nicholson, who had worked with me as an actor on many films, and who brought a great deal of sympathy and insight to this project. The Trip told the story of one man on one particular LSD trip, his first, which lasted approximately twelve hours. Knowing it was impossible to reproduce on film the full effects of the drug experience, I tried to come as close as I could within the limitations of the medium and, as usual, the budget. I tried to present the hero's experience without moralizing, choosing an open-ended structure so that the audience could judge for itself whether the trip had been a good or a bad one.—CORMAN

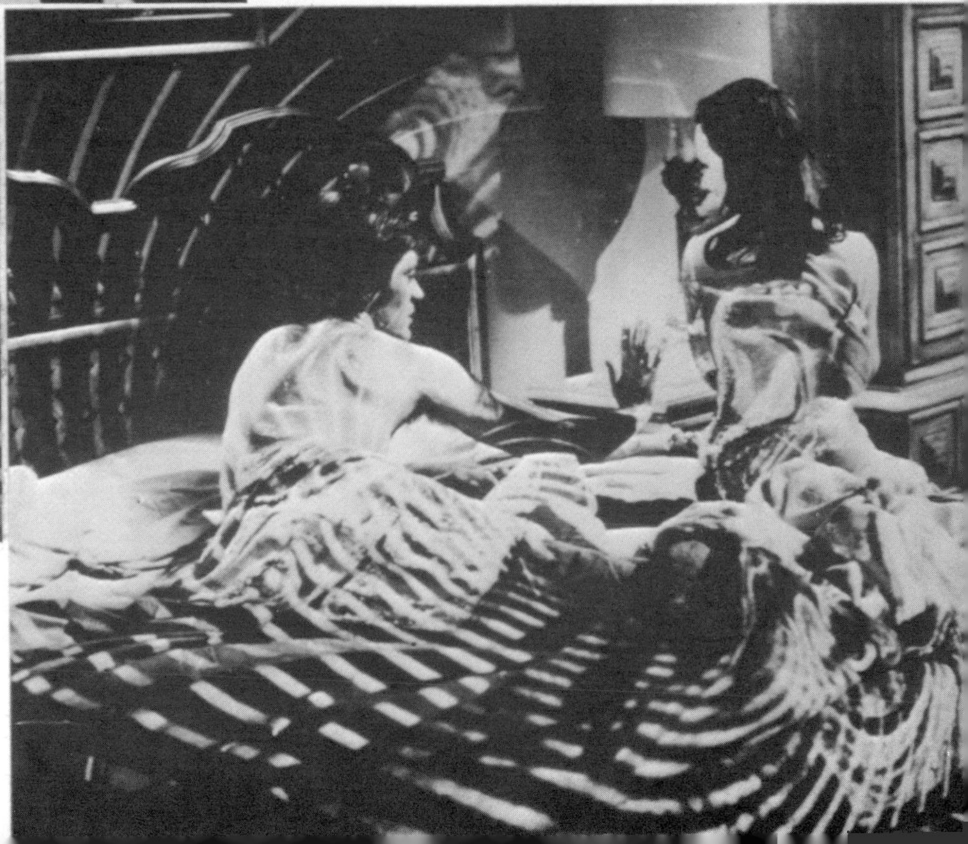

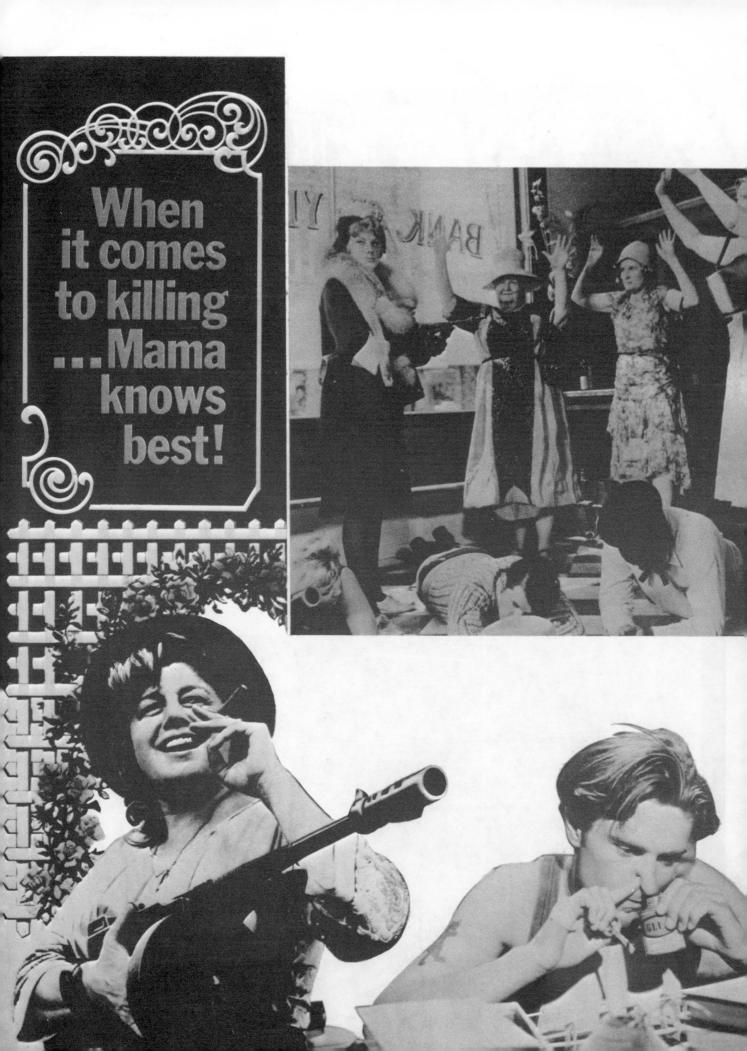

When it comes to killing ...Mama knows best!

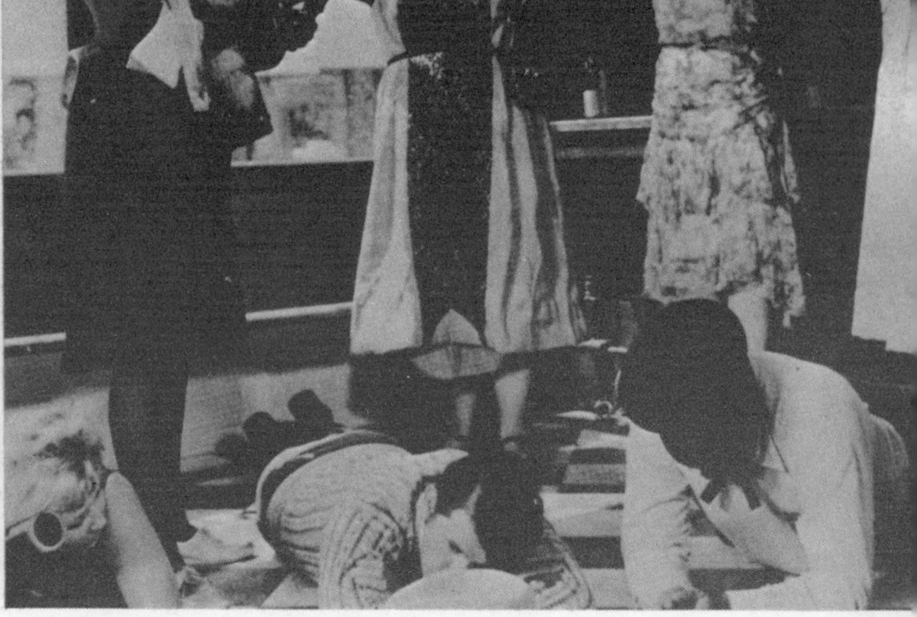

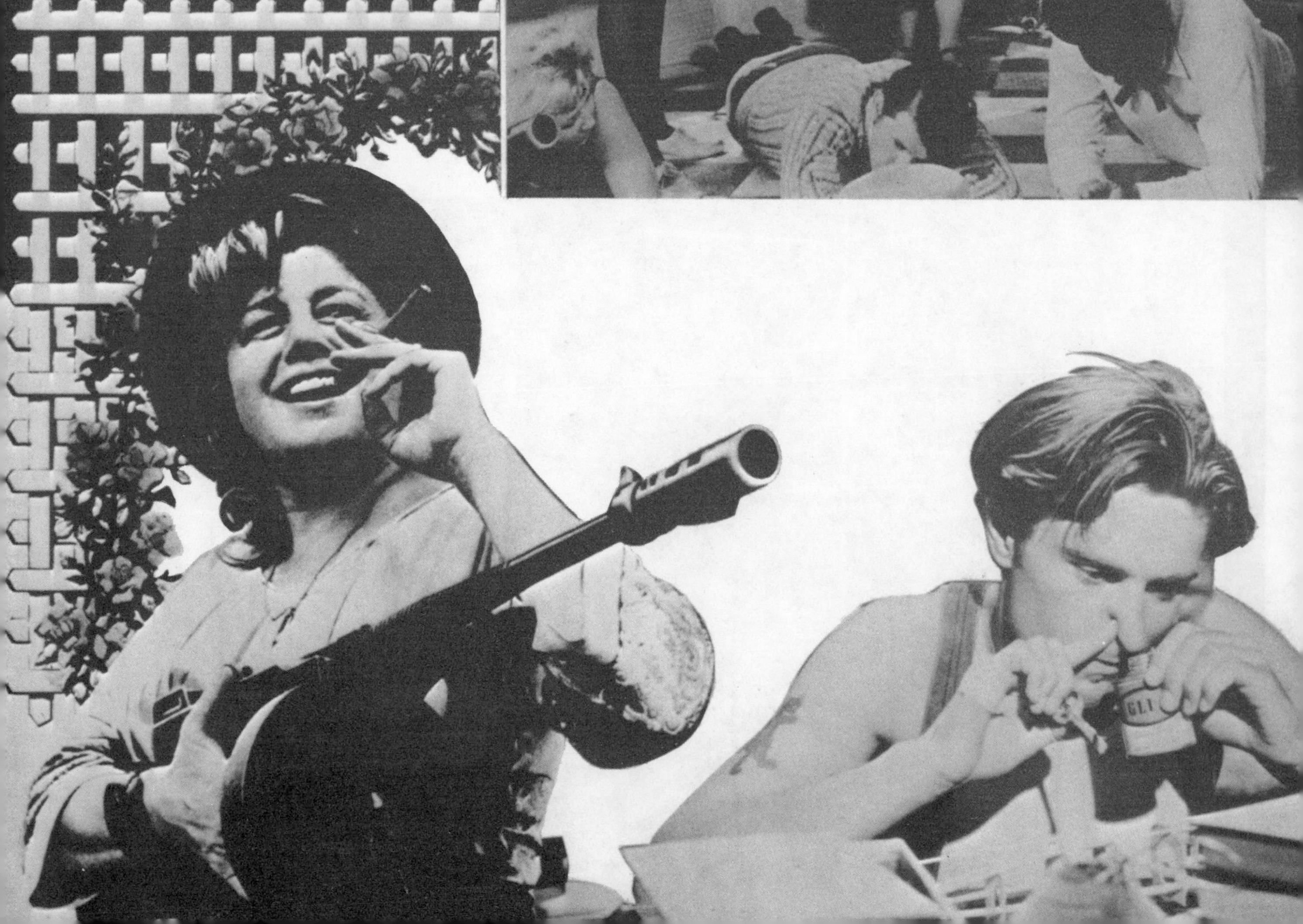

"BLOODY MAMA"

AIP had a deal with Warner Brothers at the time, and they wanted me to shoot the picture on the lot. I chose instead to shoot the picture on location in Arkansas, because I felt that while on the surface it was a period gangster picture, the story of the Barker gang in the 1930s, underneath it was really a psychodrama of pungently American family life, reflecting certain sociological influences best depicted through authentic surroundings. The drama of the story ultimately derived from the uprooting of a small agrarian family in which the father lacked the initiative to combat the encroachment of industrialization. Consequently, it was the mother, Ma Barker, powerfully played by Shelley Winters, who shaped the fate of the family. In many respects, it was a dark look at the matriarchal tradition in American family life, a kind of mythology of fatal blood ties and family relationships, in which the memory of the abandoned father plays havoc with the psychology of the gangster family. Bloody Mama had an excellent cast: Shelley Winters, Don Stroud, Robert Walden, Clint Kimbrough, Pat Hingle, and Robert De Niro (below) in one of his first roles.—CORMAN

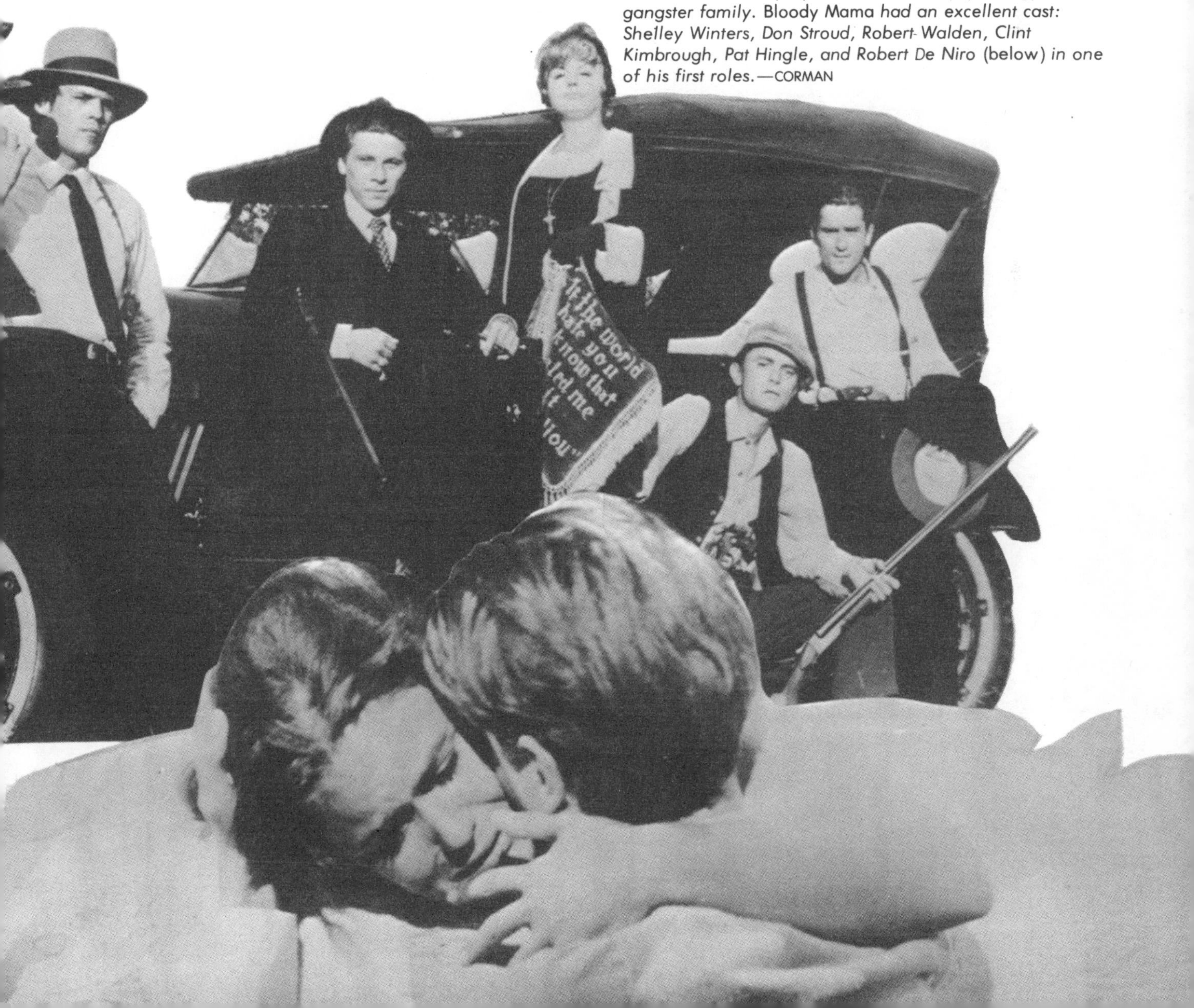

GAS-S-S-S

This was an almost surreal comedy. The premise was that as a result of the accidental leak of a nerve gas developed by the military-industrial complex, everyone in the world over the age of twenty-five died, leaving the young people free to take over. In the story, which was always comedically focused, various groups of young people attempted to cope with the conflicting beliefs and psychology they encountered in one another, on their way to a gathering place where they hoped to found a new utopia. Ultimately, the picture became a series of variations on the idea that those who fail to learn from history are destined to repeat it. There were a number of good actors in the film, then unknown, including Talia Shire (later in The Godfather and Rocky), Ben Vereen (Broadway and television star), Bud Cort (of Harold and Maude), and Cindy Williams (of ABC's Laverne and Shirley). The picture was the last I directed for AIP, and it was one of the experiences that prompted me to found my own production and distribution company, New World Pictures, since AIP found Gas-s-s-s overly controversial and made cuts in it which I believe damaged the picture. —CORMAN

"Von Richthofen and Brown"

This was the last picture I directed for United Artists, fulfilling a prior agreement, as I was then in the process of setting up my own company, New World Pictures. I had always considered that World War I ended the concept of chivalry, and that the pilots were the last of the knights. The script was developed with an excellent novelist and short-story writer, Bill Corrington, who dramatized and structured the story in accordance with this idea. Von Richthofen, who was an aristocrat, was defeated and killed by Brown, a Canadian garage mechanic, a climax which neatly symbolized the end of an era. This was a nine-hundred-thousand-dollar film, but the flying sequences were shot in three weeks.—CORMAN

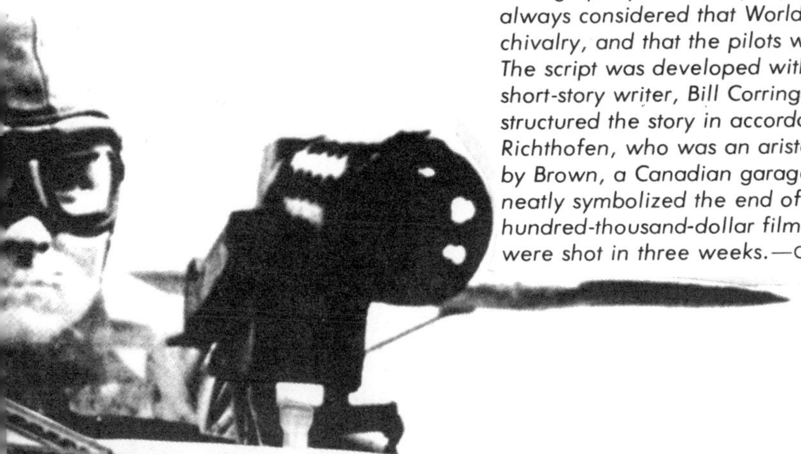

FILMS PRODUCED BY ROGER CORMAN

PRODUCED

HIGHWAY DRAGNET

My first significant job in films was as a writer. I called the script The House in the City, *but Allied Artists changed the title to* Highway Dragnet *because* Dragnet *was a popular TV series at the time. I took the money from that script, which was three thousand dollars, and put it together with a few thousand I had saved, borrowed a few thousand more, and made* It Stalked the Ocean Floor.—CORMAN

TERROR STRIKES
FROM BENEATH THE SEA!
SEE . . . MONSTER CREATURE OF THE ATOMIC AGE!
SEE . . . . . . ONE-MAN SUB IN UNDERWATER ACTION!
SEE . . . FIERCE BATTLE WITH MAN-EATING SHARKS
"MONSTER FROM THE OCEAN FLOOR"
"MONSTER FROM THE OCEAN FLOOR" with ANNE KIMBELL • STUART WADE • DICK PINNER
Produced by ROGER CORMAN • Directed by WYOTT ORDUNG • Screenplay by WILLIAM DANCH
A PALO ALTO PRODUCTION • A LIPPERT PICTURES PRESENTATION

THE FAST AND THE FURIOUS

WIDE SCREEN THRILLS!

The success of Highway Dragnet enabled me to set myself up as a producer—so I immediately sought to start other films to avoid the trap of waiting for a film to pay off before another could be started. Monster from the Ocean Floor was a science-fiction picture shot in six days for a budget of twelve thousand dollars, which was all the money I could raise. After this came The Fast and the Furious, which I made for AIP—although AIP was not a company then. Jim Nicholson approached me with the idea of starting his own company and wanted to use The Fast and the Furious as its first film. I agreed since Jim was a friend, but I wanted money in front so that I didn't have to wait for the picture to be released, and I wanted a commitment for financing two more films. Jim and his partner, Sam Arkoff, raised a small amount, something like a thousand dollars. Jim and I flew all around the country with the print of The Fast and the Furious, which we showed at key distribution centers. We wanted commitments and money for two more pictures, and we got it. That's how AIP started, and that's how I broke through.
—CORMAN

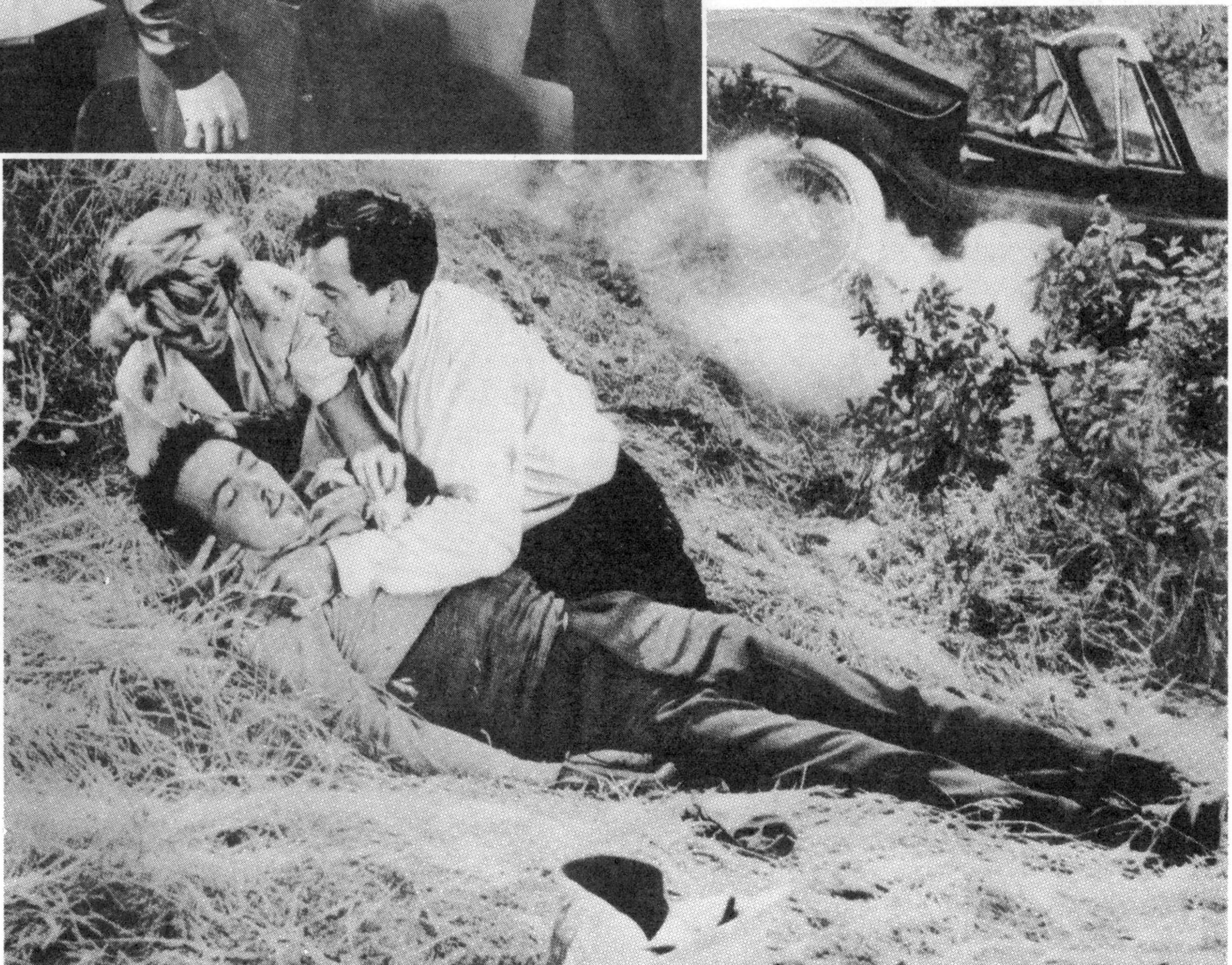

CRY BABY KILLER

Roger's a good friend. He saved all of our careers. He kept us working when no one else would hire us. For this, we are all eternally grateful. For the fact that he was able to underpay us, he is eternally grateful. —JACK NICHOLSON, actor

Crybaby Killer was the first picture I ever produced that did not make money, though it did get its money back off the television rights. The only good thing about the film was that Jack Nicholson made his debut in it. I remember one good line in the picture. Leo Gordon, who wrote it and played in it as an actor, said in the picture, "Teenagers—we never had 'em when I was a kid." I think it was true. The beauty of the line was the concept of the teenager.
—CORMAN

STAKEOUT ON DOPE STREET

Stakeout on Dope Street was one of the first pictures I financed but didn't directly produce myself. I functioned as executive producer. Stakeout on Dope Street was primarily an action picture and was made more than twenty years ago. Some teenagers inadvertently find a supply of dope that has been dropped by a group of mobsters. The gangsters and the police are both after the dope, and the teenagers become involved in the chase. The dope was simply a springboard, the valuable thing that set off the chase; it could have been diamonds or counterfeit money just as easily. There came a point of morals late in the picture when it was possible for the teenagers to make some money, and the question then became whether they wanted to profit from traffic in dope. At that time we said no.—CORMAN

HIGH SCHOOL BIG SHOT

High School Big Shot was a low-budget film that I financed and functioned as executiver producer on. It was written and directed by Joel Rapp and turned out rather well. It was the story of a rather quiet, shy, but intelligent boy in high school who becomes involved in a crime and really utilizes his intelligence to try to make some money very rapidly. It was a well-done picture, and there was a young actor who has since died—I think his name was Tom Pittman—who gave a very good performance in the lead role.—CORMAN

T-bird gang

T-Bird Gang was another picture I financed. High School Big Shot and T-Bird Gang went out as a double bill, and T-Bird Gang was the straight-out thriller with fast cars. The two pictures did well. I did not personally produce either of them. I was executive producer—CORMAN

WILD RIDE

On Wild Ride I was really executive producer. It was made by Harvey Berman, a high school drama teacher in northern California who had gone to the UCLA drama school with some friends of mine. He conceived the idea of making a picture during the summer using students from his high school drama class in the cast and crew and sending up a few professionals from Hollywood to work with them. It's notable in that the actor we sent up was Jack Nicholson (left), who plays the lead. This is one of the little pictures I remember with pleasure; it turned out very well.—CORMAN

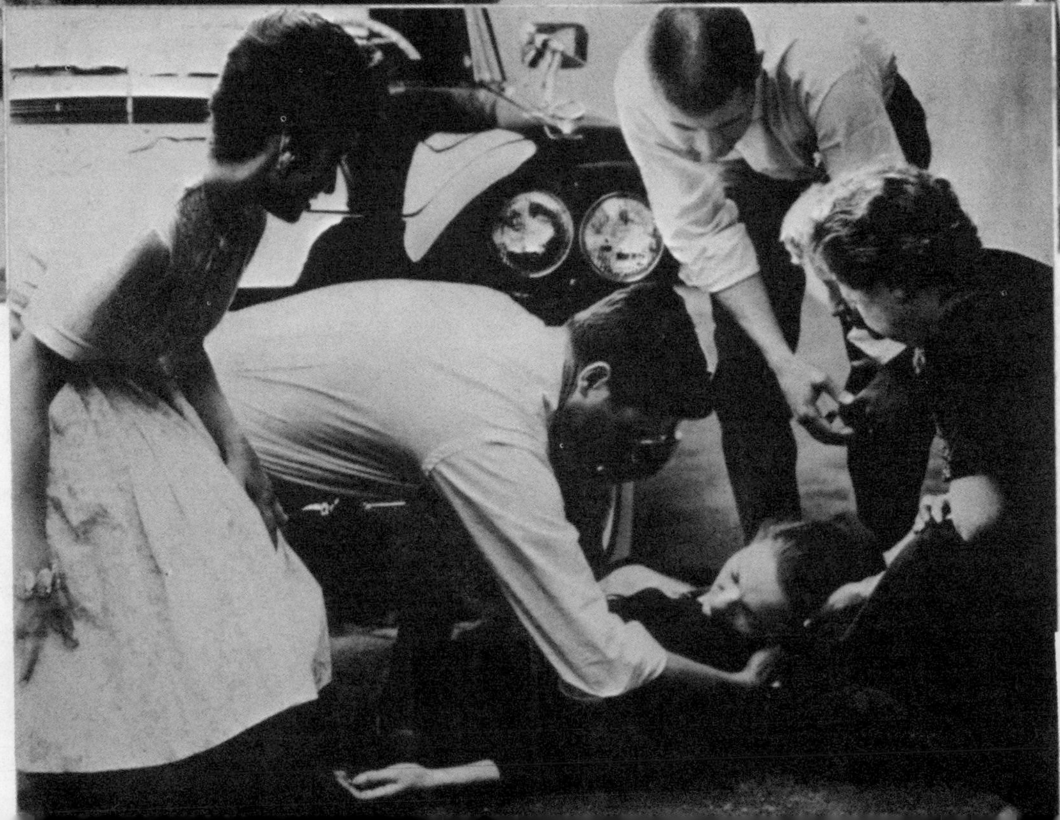

BATTLE OF BLOOD ISLAND

The Battle of Blood Island was written and directed by Joel Rapp and was one of three pictures we made in Puerto Rico. I produced and directed two of them and served as executive producer on this one. It was an action-adventure story set in World War II about a Japanese soldier and an American soldier who find themselves alone on a deserted island in the South Pacific. They start out at opposite ends, finally come together, and then the war that is raging around them engulfs the island. It turned out very nicely; it was a good little picture.—CORMAN

This was a picture with a cast of thousands—starring two actors. They all died in the attack; two survived. It was a war story about two men—and one of them was paralyzed and the other had to carry him around on his back. It was a gas. Then, the first day on the picture, the script girl quits. Roger gives me a fifteen-minute briefing course, puts the script in my hand, and says, "You're the script clerk."
—BEACH DICKERSON, actor

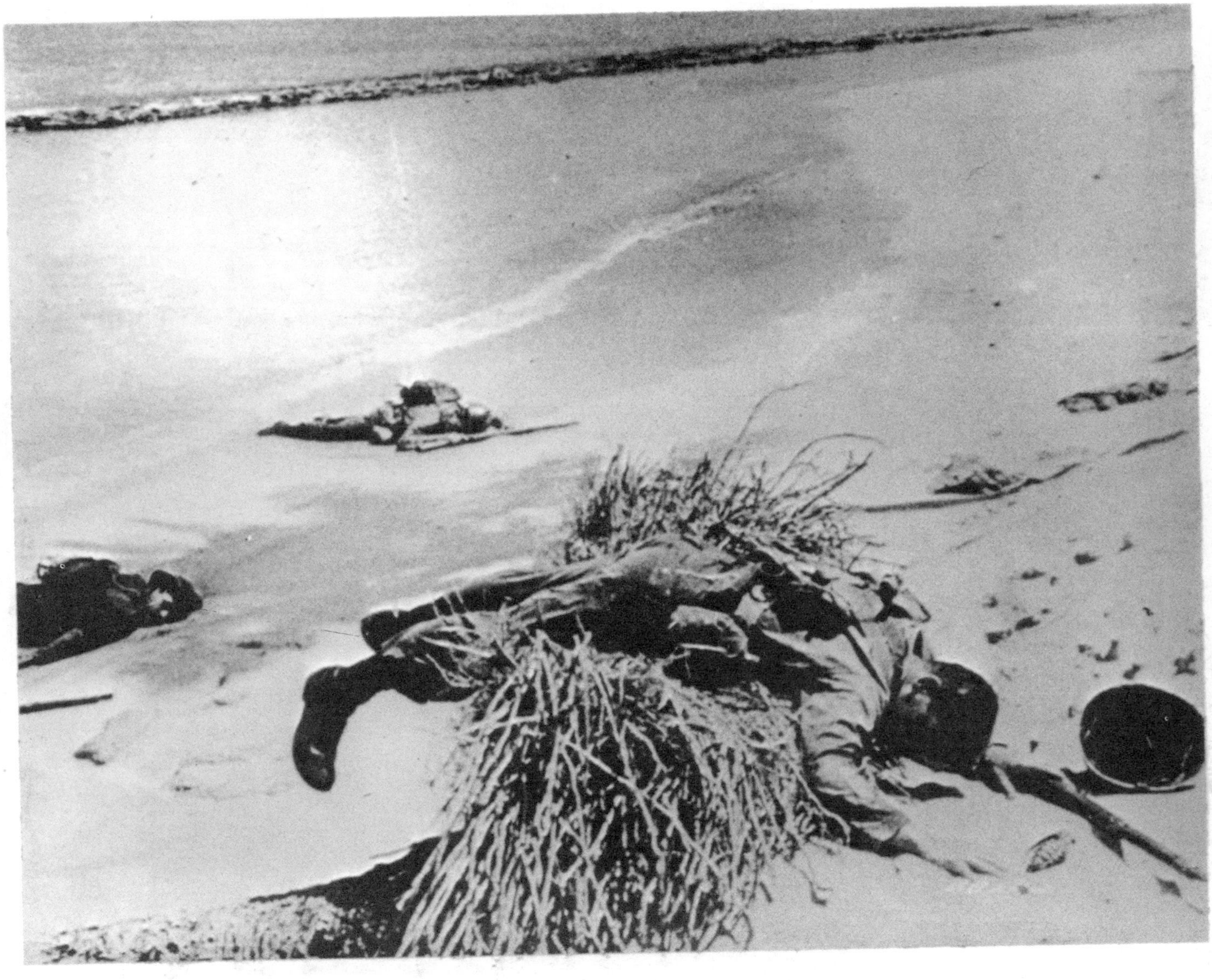

BATTLE BEYOND THE SUN
IN COLOR
SEE
The incredible meteorites from Mars!
The escape from the mysterious Sun!
The space station run amuk the Stars!
The rocket cruisers in the last war of the Worlds!
STARRING EDD PERRY · ARLA POWELL · A FILMGROUP Presentation · AN AMERICAN INTERNATIONA

The Magic Voyage Of Sinbad

Battle Beyond the Sun *and* The Magic Voyage of Sinbad *were both made by reworking some Russian science-fiction pictures. The footage was reedited and the pictures were dubbed into English.*—CORMAN

We wrote English dialogue that would more or less fit into the mouths of these characters. At one point in the original Russian version, one of the characters looks out and sees the astronauts holding the golden "torch of truth." Roger wanted to add some horrible battle scene with monsters fighting instead, so we ran around and shot some cockamamie monsters and put them in.—FRANCIS FORD COPPOLA, director

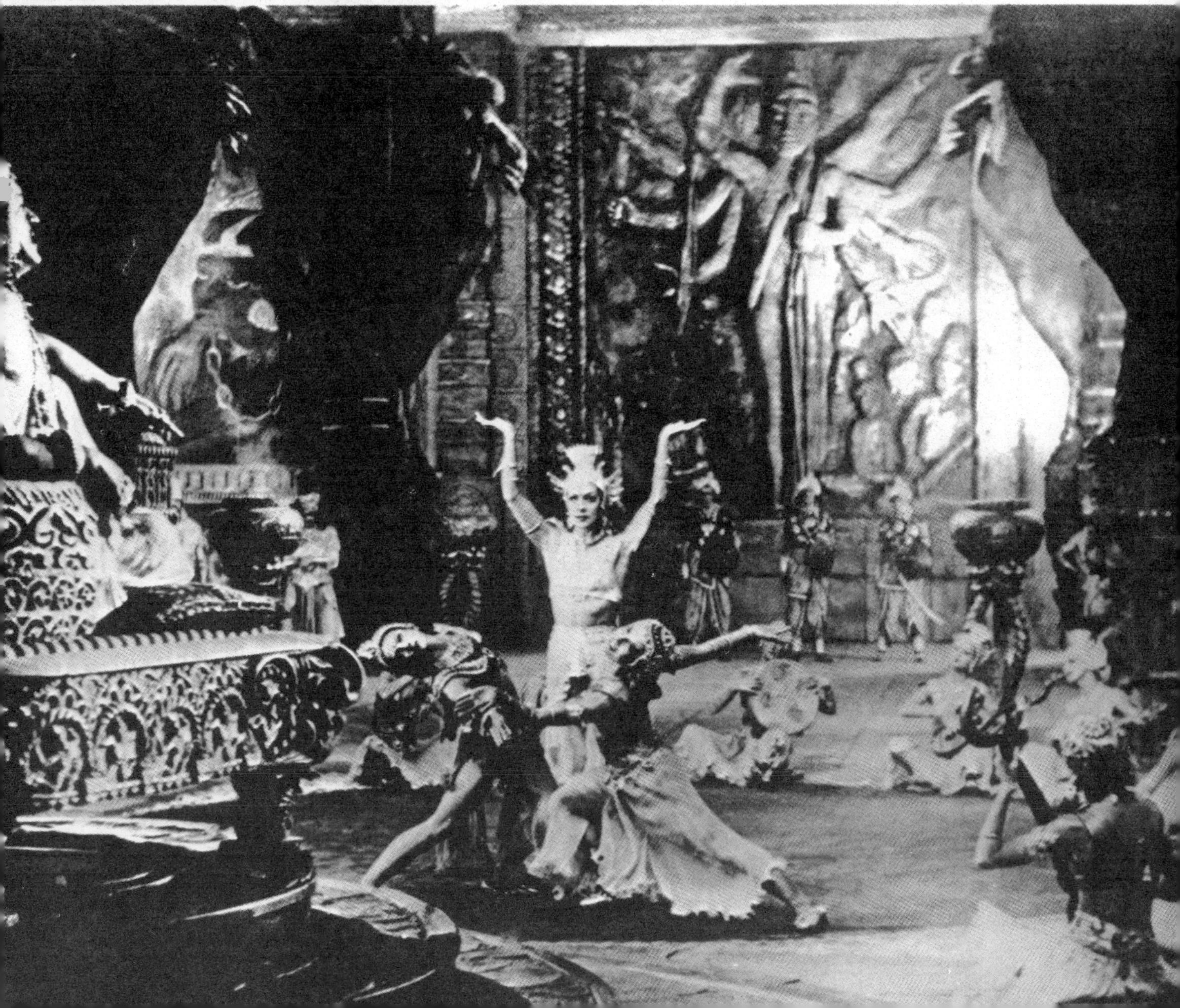

DEMENTIA 13

This was the first film directed by Francis Ford Coppola. Francis came up with the idea for Dementia 13 and wrote the script while moving between France and England—or rather, specifically while on the move between the various Grand Prix races we were filming for The Young Racers.
—CORMAN

Roger wanted to make Dementia 13 cheaply. He wanted it to be homicidal, sort of a copy of Psycho. You know, Gothic and psychological, with some kind of terrible knife killing scene thrown in. So I wrote the script to order.
—FRANCIS FORD COPPOLA, director

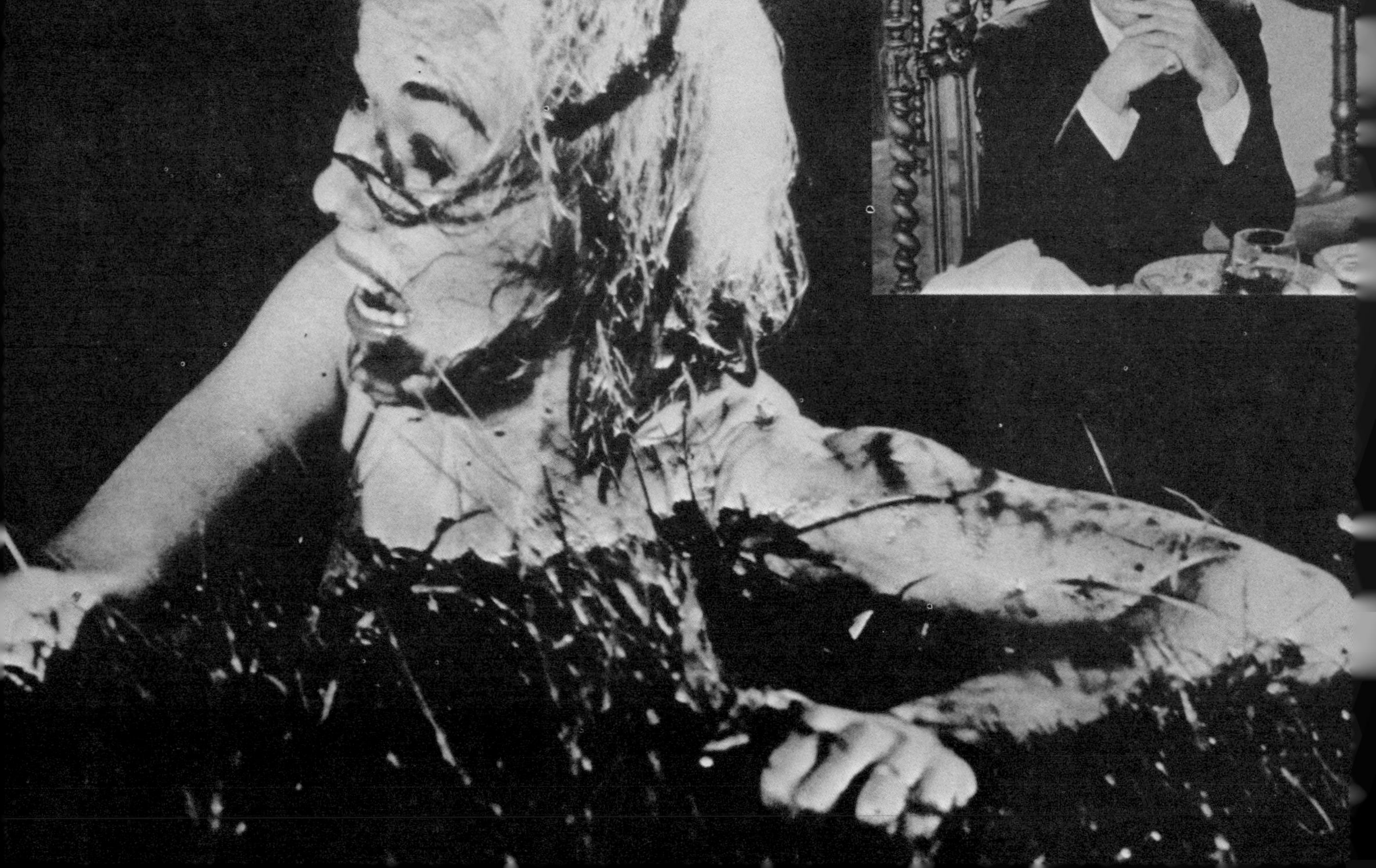

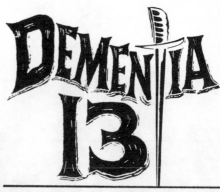

PIT STOP

Pit Stop was a very low-budget black-and-white film written and directed by Jack Hill. It was actually a rather well made picture. It was notable also because of Ellen Burstyn, who, under the name of Ellen McRae, played her first lead in the film and was very good. It was clear that she knew what she was doing. She was a great actress and an intelligent actress, and you could tell it.—CORMAN

MOVING VIOLATION

Moving Violation was a picture my wife Julie produced for Twentieth Century Fox. I was executive producer. The picture turned out very well because it was an attempt to deal with certain social values within the context of an entertainment film. It had to do with pervasive corruption in an oil town, involving collusion between the oil company and local government. It becomes a chase, so we have the entertainment value of the chase and at the same time the question as to the legitimacy of certain aspects of life today. —CORMAN

"BEACH BALL"

Beach Ball was directed by Lenny Weinrib, and I was executive producer. It was the first picture to star The Supremes. I had checked with some disc jockeys and record stores and asked who was the newest hot singing group, and they said The Supremes, so I hired them. They contributed immensely to the success of the film.—CORMAN

QUEEN OF BLOOD

Queen of Blood was actually one of a series of Russian science-fiction pictures that I bought to utilize the excellent special effects. Curtis Harrington wrote and directed it and shot the American sequences, which we cut into the Russian science-fiction sequences.—CORMAN

TARGETS

This was the first film directed by Peter Bogdanovich. Peter had worked as my assistant on The Wild Angels and wanted badly to direct. I had a commitment with Boris Karloff and said I would back Peter if he came up with an idea I liked which would give a good part to Boris. Peter gave me full treatments on each idea, and I kept turning them down. The treatments got shorter and shorter as Peter became more discouraged. In fact, Targets was an idea he simply told me, no doubt too pessimistic by this time to develop it into a treatment. I liked the idea, and he made the picture after writing the script himself.—CORMAN

"REMARKABLE! TERRIFYING AND THRILLING!"

–JUDITH CRIST, New York Magazine

"I just killed my wife
and my mother.
I know they'll get me.
But before that
many more will die..."

DEVILS ANGELS

Devils Angels had a story very similar to The Wild Angels, which at the time was the biggest success AIP had ever had. They wanted a follow-up picture immediately, and I was working on something else, so I produced it and Danny Haller directed it.—CORMAN

THE WILD RACERS

The Wild Racers was written by Chuck Griffith, directed by Danny Haller, and produced by Joel Rapp. I functioned as executive producer, just sort of setting it up. I had made a successful picture a couple of years earlier called The Young Racers, which followed Grand Prix racing around Europe.—CORMAN

IN PATHÉCOLOR
STARRING
'FABIAN'
MIMSY
FARMER
Produced by JOEL RAPP · Directed by DAN HALLER · Written by PAUL RAPP
AN AMERICAN INTERNATIONAL RELEASE
© 1968 American International Pictures

the Dunwich HORROR

The Dunwich Horror was from a Lovecraft short story. I produced it, Danny Haller directed. We shot it on location in northern California, a very beautiful place in Mendocino on the northern California coast.—CORMAN

BOXCAR BERTHA

This was the first feature film directed by Martin Scorsese. I had seen an experimental film he made while at New York University and signed him to direct Boxcar Bertha on the basis of it. The juxtaposition of a big-city point of view as shown through the character of Barry Primus and the country point of view through the characters played by David Carradine and Barbara Hershey (left) is interesting. This contrast was initially planned and written into the script by Bill Corrington and myself but was amplified with perceptiveness by Scorsese.—CORMAN

Roger really let me do what I wanted within the time schedule and the condition that every fifteen pages there had to be some nudity in the script. I drew out (on storyboards) every shot. Once Roger saw that I had the shots drawn out, he looked at me and said, "All right. I don't have to see any more." And I made the movie.—MARTIN SCORSESE, director

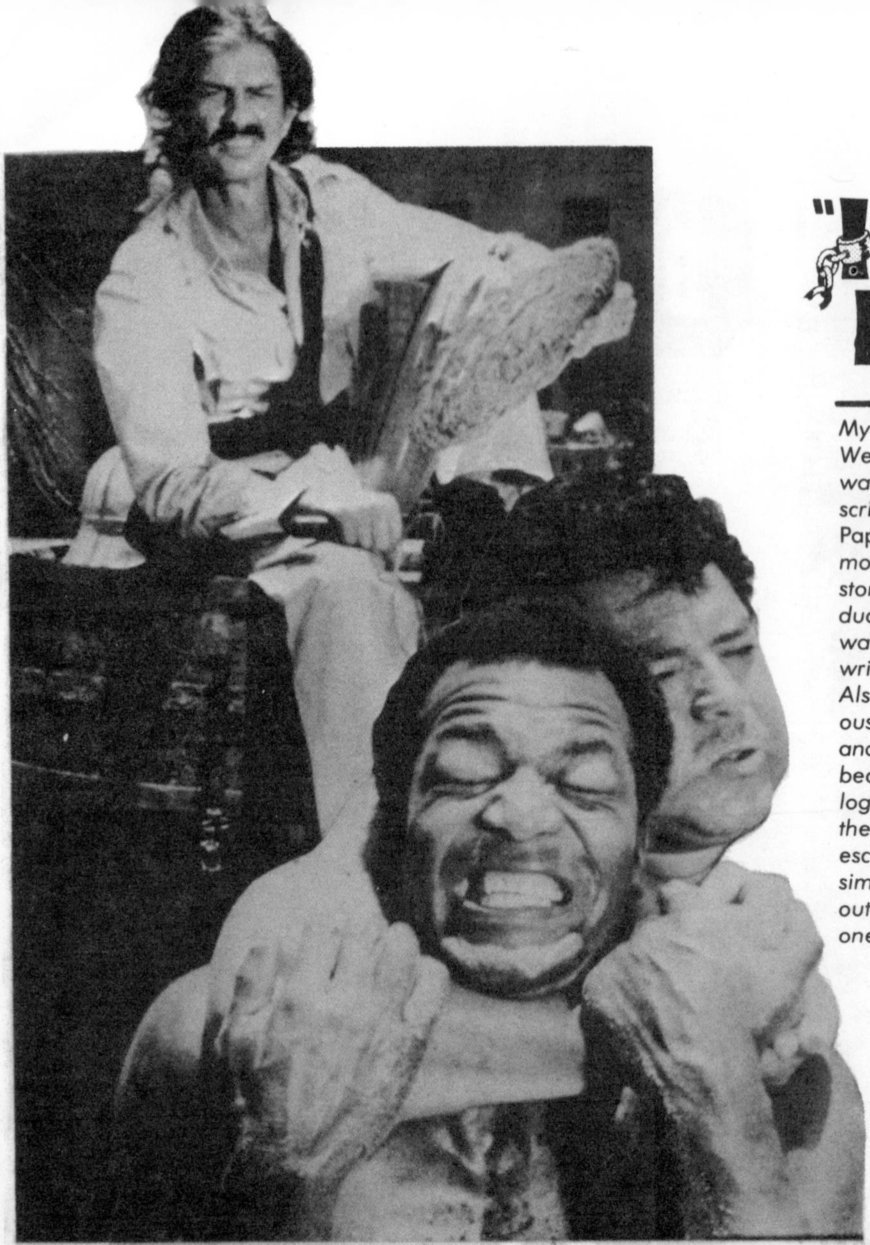

"I ESCAPED FROM DEVIL'S ISLAND"

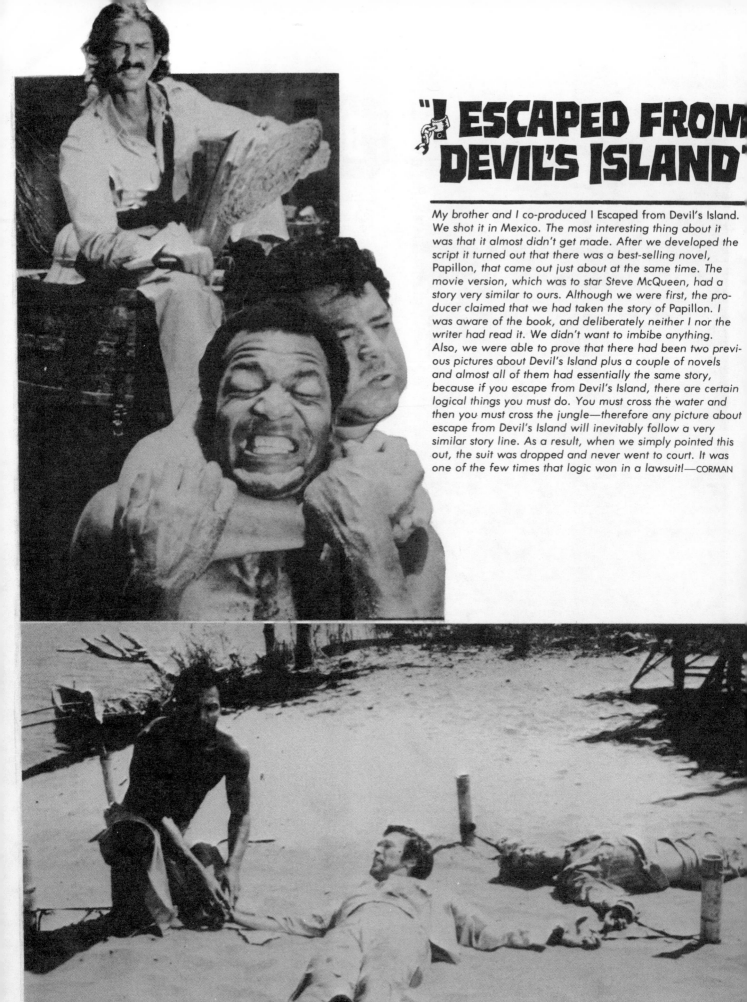

My brother and I co-produced I Escaped from Devil's Island. We shot it in Mexico. The most interesting thing about it was that it almost didn't get made. After we developed the script it turned out that there was a best-selling novel, Papillon, that came out just about at the same time. The movie version, which was to star Steve McQueen, had a story very similar to ours. Although we were first, the producer claimed that we had taken the story of Papillon. I was aware of the book, and deliberately neither I nor the writer had read it. We didn't want to imbibe anything. Also, we were able to prove that there had been two previous pictures about Devil's Island plus a couple of novels and almost all of them had essentially the same story, because if you escape from Devil's Island, there are certain logical things you must do. You must cross the water and then you must cross the jungle—therefore any picture about escape from Devil's Island will inevitably follow a very similar story line. As a result, when we simply pointed this out, the suit was dropped and never went to court. It was one of the few times that logic won in a lawsuit!—CORMAN

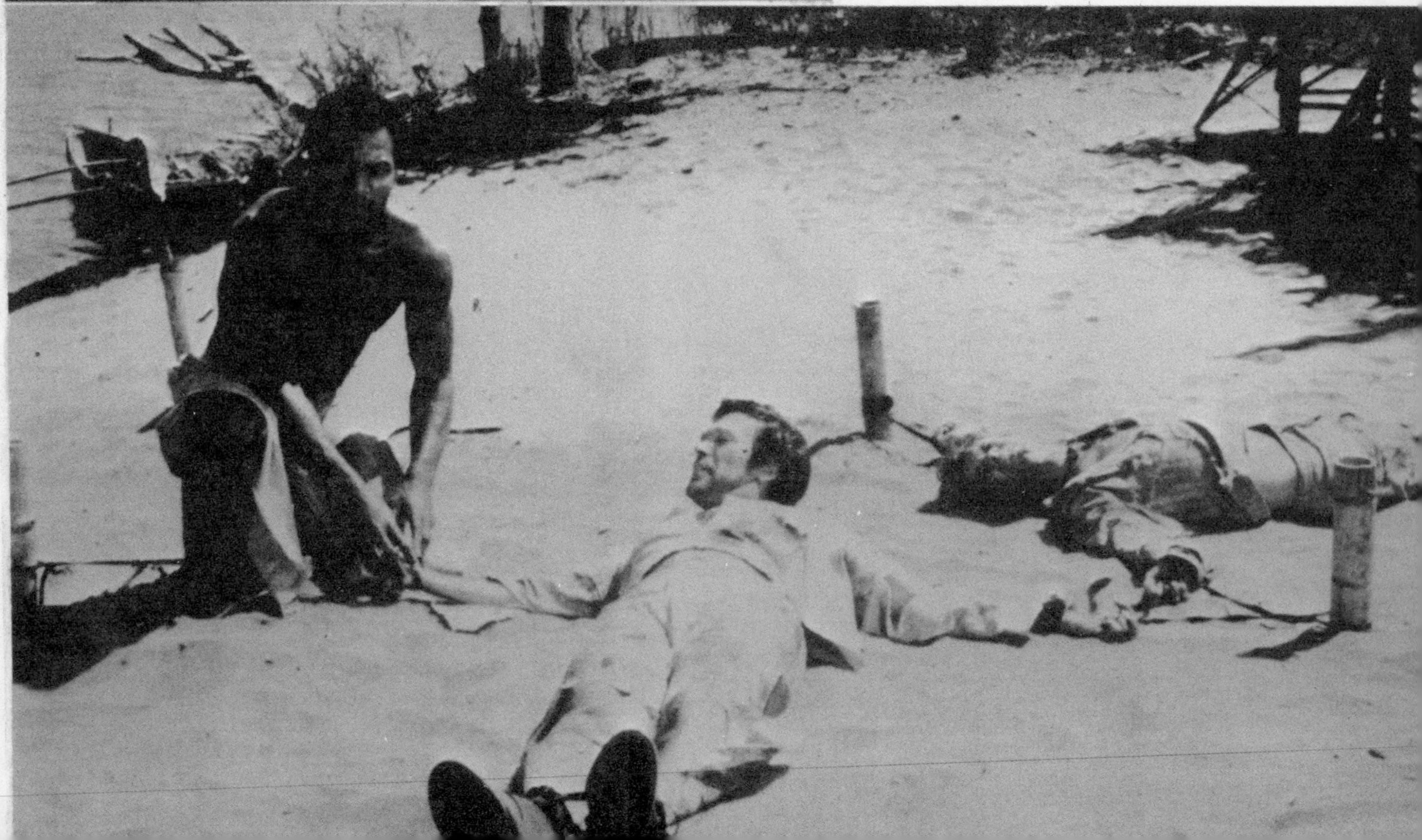

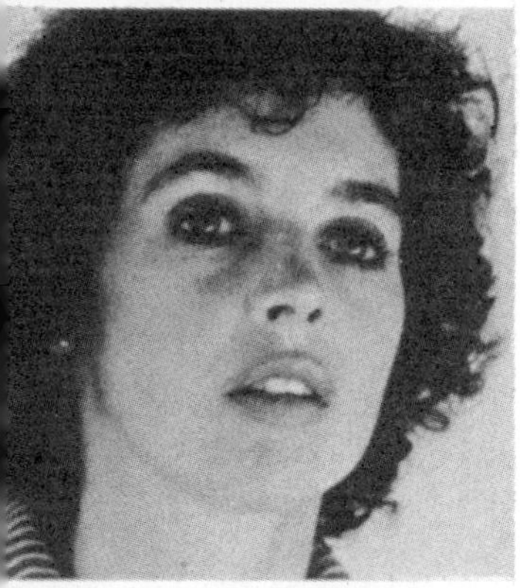

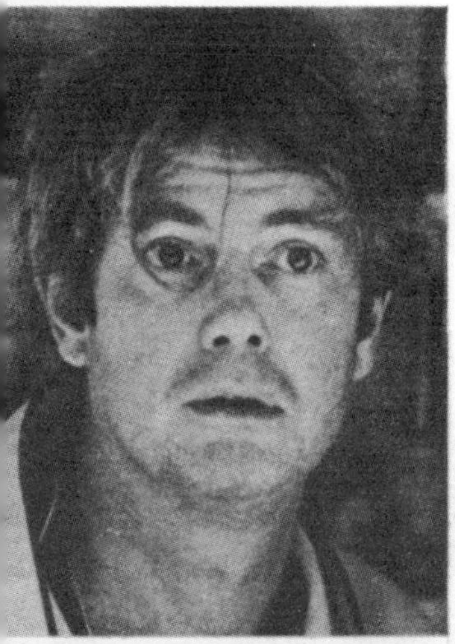

BORN TO KILL

Born to Kill is the last picture I made that lost money. In this decade, in the 1970s, it's the only picture I have produced that has lost money. I don't know if it was the fault of the picture or the subject matter. I read a novel called Cock Fighter, about cockfighting in the American South, and liked it very much. I thought it was a true picture of a certain segment of southern society, and I thought it was an interesting background film. Monte Hellman directed it and made it into a good picture, but possibly a little quieter than I had originally envisioned. The film opened under the title Cock Fighter and did not do well. I changed the title to Born to Kill, thinking that maybe cockfighting was holding it back. It did a little bit better, but it has not been a great success. Eventually it will probably get its money back with television syndication sale. It will never go network, because cockfighting is too rough for the networks, and even with syndication we will have to cut a lot of it out.—CORMAN

The
Big Money Sport
That's
Dirty-Violent
and
Outside the Law!

FIGHTING MAD

Fighting Mad was another in the series of pictures I did for Fox. It was an attempt, once more, to follow a style that you're probably familiar with now—an action picture with a certain social comment. It dealt with the destruction of farmland for strip mining and the efforts of one farmer, Peter Fonda, to protect his land. Jonathan Demme, whose career is rapidly rising, directed it. I think he is a very fine young director.—CORMAN

PETER FONDA is FIGHTING MAD
PRODUCED BY ROGER CORMAN · WRITTEN AND DIRECTED BY JONATHAN DEMME
R RESTRICTED
COLOR BY DELUXE®
20th CENTURY FOX

CAPONE

Starred Ben Gazzara, Harry Guardino, John Cassavetes, and Susan Blakely. Sylvester "Sly" Stallone played Frank "The Enforcer" Nitti, Al Capone's treacherous lieutenant, a role that finally showcased his talent and power as an actor. "Al was a big guy," said Ben Gazzara, who played the iron-hearted, death-dealing kingpin of Chicago's machine-gun gangs. "My wife told me I was too small for the part. Lemme tell you, that was all I was waiting to hear! I gained twenty pounds to play that part! Al loved his food, you know. It was wonderful—I ate spaghetti every day," he gleamed, "and I never had any guilt!"

Capone was the first in a series of pictures—low-budget pictures, by studio standards—that I did for Twentieth Century Fox. They wanted a series of films budgeted at about a million dollars—which was high for me but low for them—to fill out their distribution schedule. They made me a very nice offer. This was when New World was just starting, and I said yes and we agreed. They said they wanted to start right away and did I have any ideas, and I said, "Well, I made The St. Valentine's Day Massacre a number of years ago, which did well, and one possibility to get this started would be to do Capone." They agreed immediately—it was one of the fastest things. I made up the idea during the meeting! They agreed, and we went ahead and produced the picture on that basis. Steve Carver directed the film and did a good job. Gazzara was very good as Capone.—CORMAN

THUNDER AND LIGHTNING

Thunder and Lightning, *Moving Violation,* and *Fighting Mad were all released by Fox, as was* Capone. *The budget of each of these pictures was just under a million dollars—large for us, although for a major this represented a low budget. These films were all made after New World Pictures was fairly well established, and gave us a chance to perfect our action-picture expertise with a little more time and money to work with.*—CORMAN, actor

This film starred Kate Jackson, one of TV's *Charlie's Angels*, before she attained her heavenly affiliation.

FILMS PRODUCED AND DISTRIBUTED BY ROGER CORMAN

NEW WORLD PICTURES
(Produced and Distributed)

THE STUDENT NURSES

This was one of New World's first productions. It successfully established the pattern for a number of pictures to follow. In this genre the overt commercial appeal consisted of R-rated nudity with pretty girls, but the stories centered on the problems and conflicts of young women attempting independence and challenging authority in their careers and personal lives. The Student Nurses was directed by Stephanie Rothman. New World Pictures may be unique in that we employed two women directors, who each made two features for New World, in the earliest years of the company.—CORMAN

"What I do with my body is my business!"

"All you interns are alike — you all have one track minds!"

"I hope you all get kicked out of this lousy profession!"

They're learning fast.

COLOR

STARRING ELAINE GIFTOS • KAREN CARLSON • BRIONI FARRELL
BARBARA LEIGH • RENI SANTONI • RICHARD RUST • LAWRENCE CASEY AS JIM

R RESTRICTED Under 17 requires accompanying Parent or Adult Guardian

SCREENPLAY BY DON SPENCER • STORY BY CHARLES S. SWARTZ & STEPHANIE ROTHMAN • PRODUCED BY CHARLES S. SWARTZ
EXECUTIVE PRODUCER ROGER CORMAN • PRODUCED AND DIRECTED BY STEPHANIE ROTHMAN • A NEW WORLD PICTURES RELEASE

THEY LIVE HARD...THEY LOVE HARD...

"ANGELS DIE HARD!"

Angels Die Hard was the first film New World Pictures made and released. I wanted a proven genre picture to get the company going. I felt I understood the elements of this genre, having initiated the "biker" cycle with The Wild Angels, and at the time there was still a market for this type of picture.—CORMAN

Angels Die Hard, billed as "Chopper outlaws riding their hot throbbing machines to a brutal climax of violence, their battle cry 'Kill the Pigs,' " was independently financed through John Meier and myself. In 1970, the era of motorcycle choppers, this Hell's Angels classic was written and directed by Richard Compton, starred William Smith and Tom Baker.

We were only able to raise sixty-five thousand dollars for this production, which we knew was inadequate, so Roger's new company guaranteed the post-production budget. Amazingly, Angels Die Hard, which only cost one hundred and seventeen thousand dollars, did a gross film rental in excess of seven hundred thousand dollars and an estimated box-office take of over two million dollars! Within the first year after release our investors were repaid and realized a forty-six percent return on their money.—PAUL NOBERT, producer

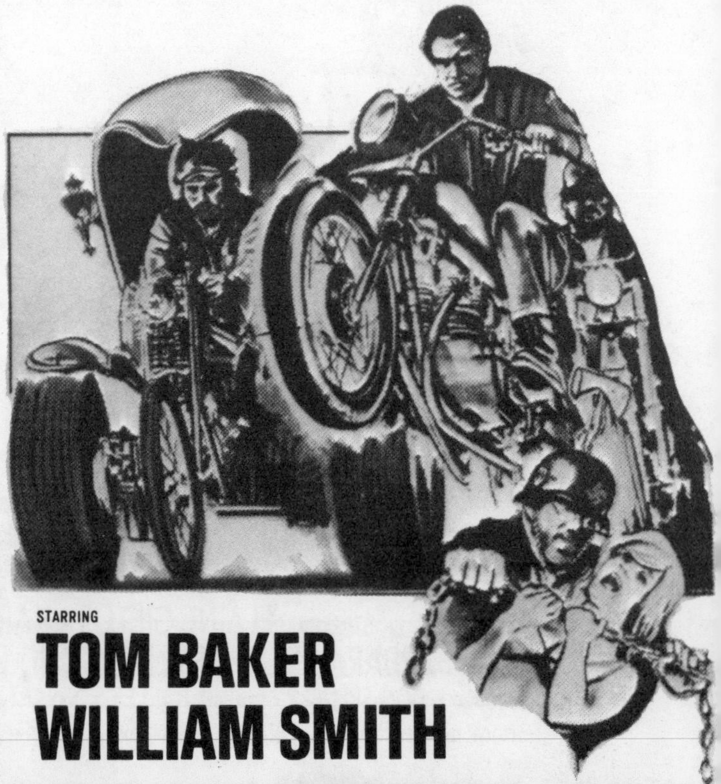

BIG DOLL HOUSE

The Big Doll House *was written by Jack Hill and was our* **gre***atest early success in the first year of New World. It cost about a hundred and fifty thousand dollars and took in about three million dollars in film rentals. The box-office gross was about nine or ten million dollars.* The Big Doll House *led to a sequel,* The Big Bird Cage.—CORMAN

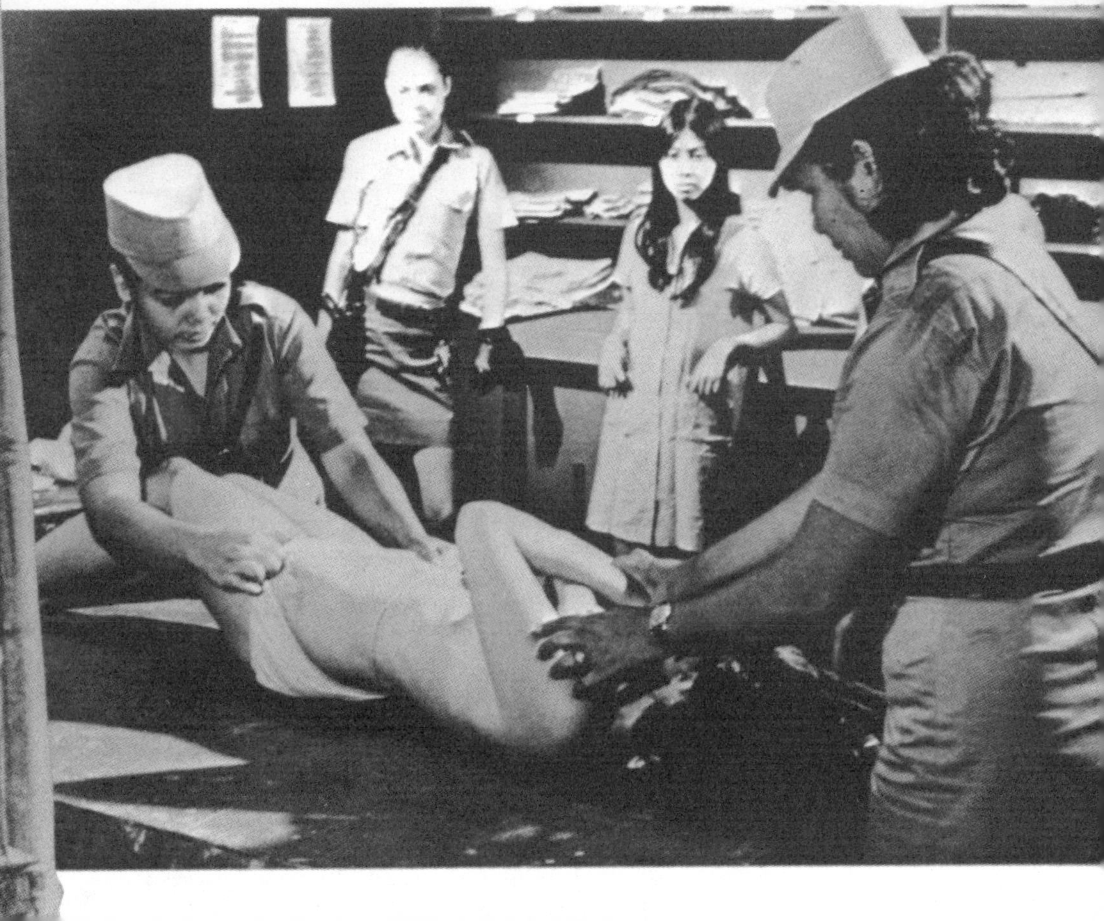

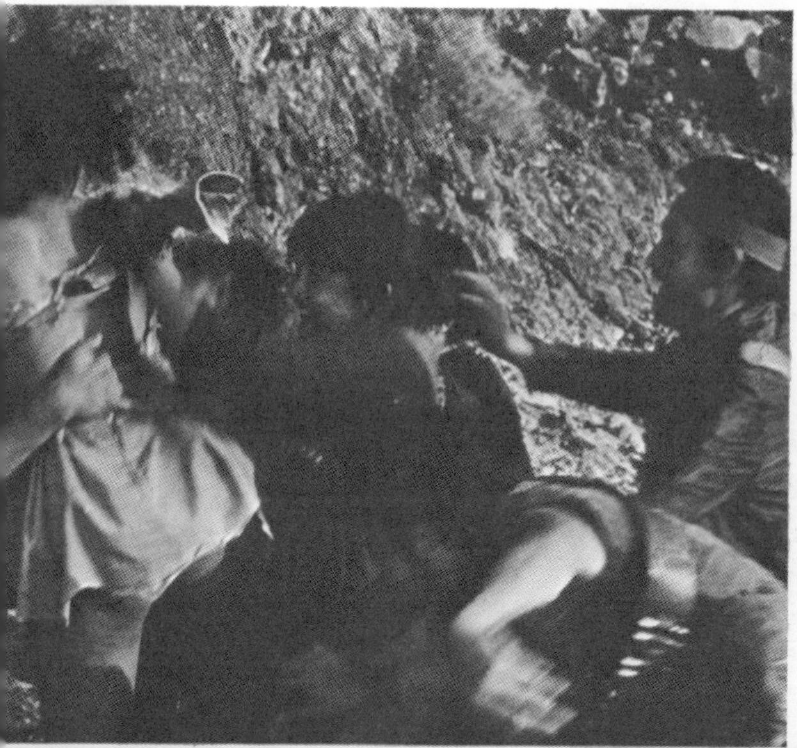

WOMEN in CAGES

Women in Cages was made as a follow-up to The Big Doll House, the first in our "women in prison" series. Usually a follow-up picture does less business than the first, but in this case we did even better with the second. With regard to both the "women in prison" and the nurses and teachers series, I think it is noteworthy that no one else at the time was making action pictures with female leads. In all the stories we tried to make the women genuinely the protagonists in that they initiated the action.—CORMAN

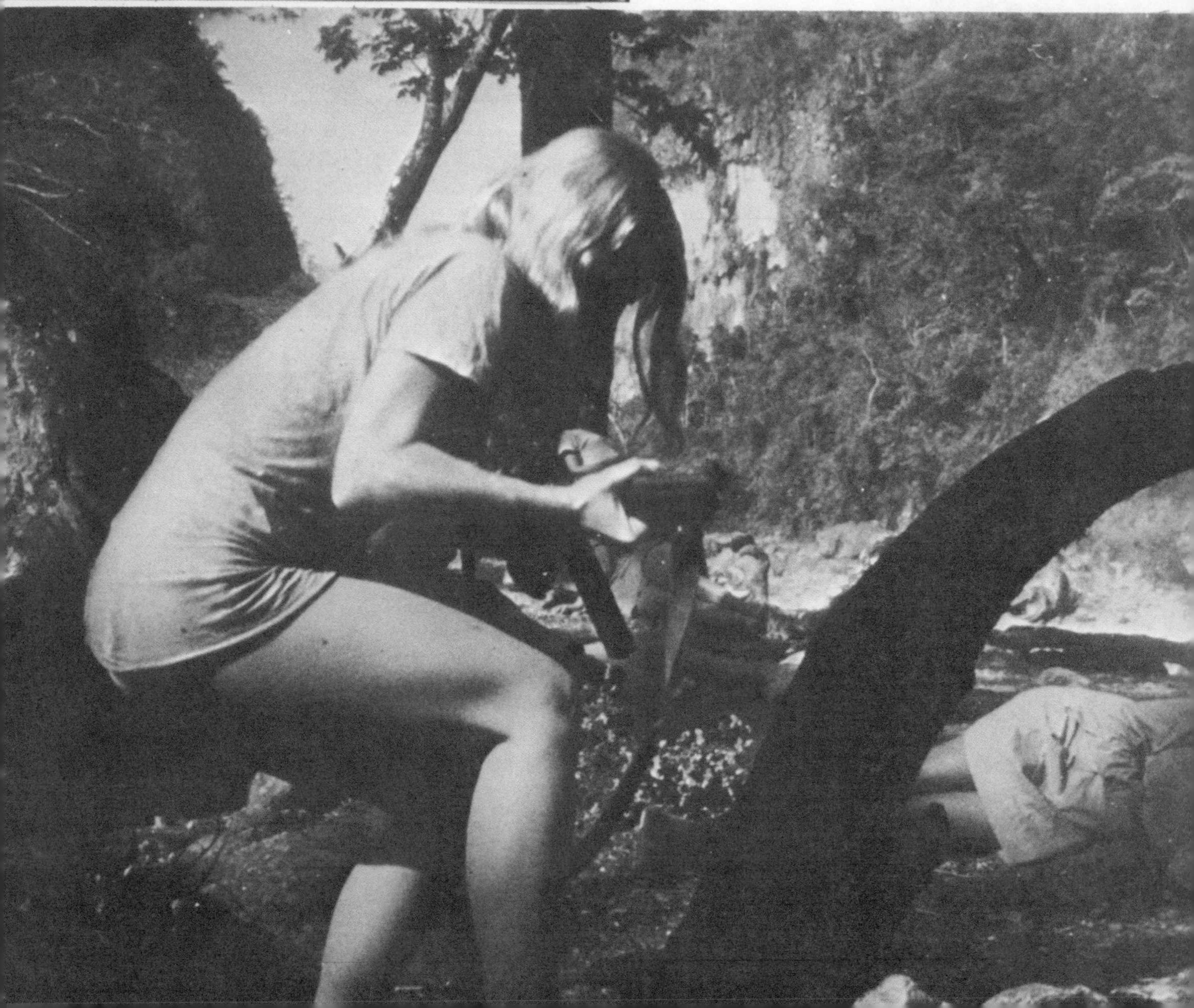

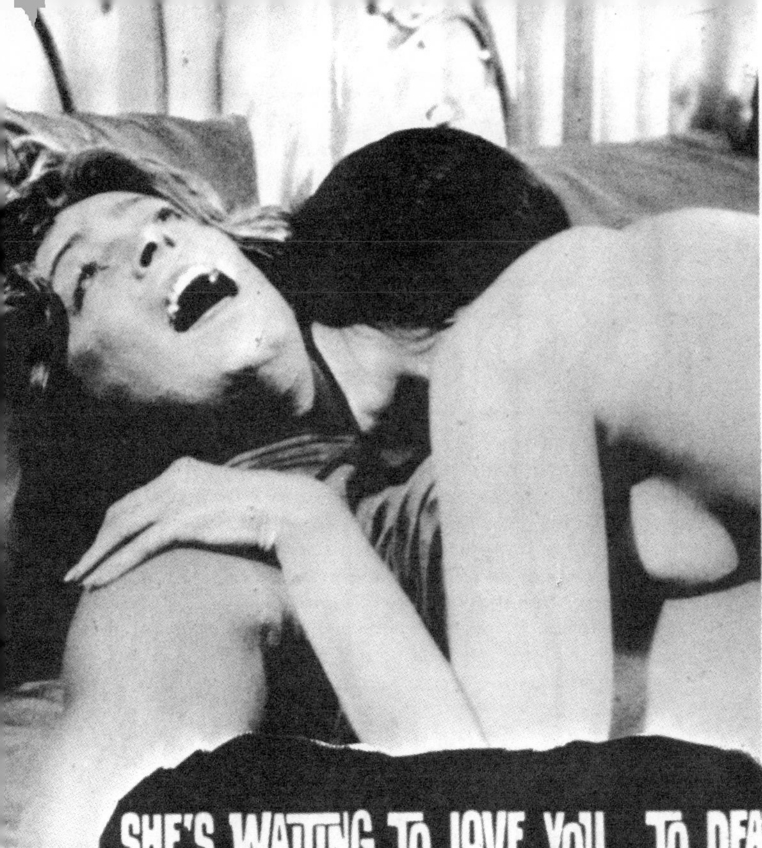

THE VELVET VAMPIRE

The Velvet Vampire was *Stephanie Rothman's second feature for New World. Her first was* The Student Nurses, *one of the company's first productions, which successfully established the genre of pictures whose overt commercial appeal consisted of R-rated nudity with pretty girls, but whose stories centered on the problems and conflicts of young women attempting independence in their careers and personal lives. New World may be unique in that we employed two women directors in the earliest years of the company.* —CORMAN

SHE'S WAITING TO LOVE YOU...TO DEATH
Climax after climax of terror and desire...
where the living change places with the dead.
IN METROCOLOR
THE VELVET VAMPIRE
STARRING
Michael Blodgett · Sherry Miles and Celeste Yarnall
A NEW WORLD PICTURES RELEASE
WRITTEN BY
Maurice Jules & Charles S. Swartz & Stephanie Rothman
PRODUCED BY
Charles S. Swartz
DIRECTED BY
Stephanie Rothman

SCREAM OF THE DEMON LOVER

Scream of the Demon Lover *was an Italian picture that I bought. We had made a picture called* The Velvet Vampire *which did not turn out as well as I had expected, and I felt that it could not stand alone as a top feature. I needed a second feature to go with it—a kind of co-feature. So I called a friend of mine in Rome and asked him to find an Italian horror film that had been dubbed into English and that I could buy for no more than twenty-five thousand dollars. He found one, and I bought it over the phone without ever seeing it, on the recommendation of this friend. It was a playable, decent film, and the best of the films available in Rome at that time. Francis Kimbrough, my story editor, was the one who actually came up with the title* Scream of the Demon Lover. *We put that on it and played it together with* The Velvet Vampire *as a double feature, and it did fairly well.*—CORMAN

COLOR
Hot fire consumes his body...
Burning passion consumes his soul!

Honestly doctor, I was only giving him a massage!
Heartbeat slow.. I have just the remedy for that.
I'm improving my technique in nurse/patient relations.

PRIVATE DUTY NURSES

Private Duty Nurses was the second in our string of nurse pictures. The first one was The Student Nurses. The title came about this way. The Student Nurses was a great success, and it really surprised us all how well it did. We knew we were going to do a sequel, and we were casting about for a title when we got a letter from a group called the Private Duty Nurses Association saying that The Student Nurses was not a truthful statement of how nurses function and that they wished to protest. My sales manager got the letter and brought it to me and said, "What are we going to do about this one?" I said, "They have given us the title for the sequel—Private Duty Nurses. It's a great title." So we made Private Duty Nurses!—CORMAN

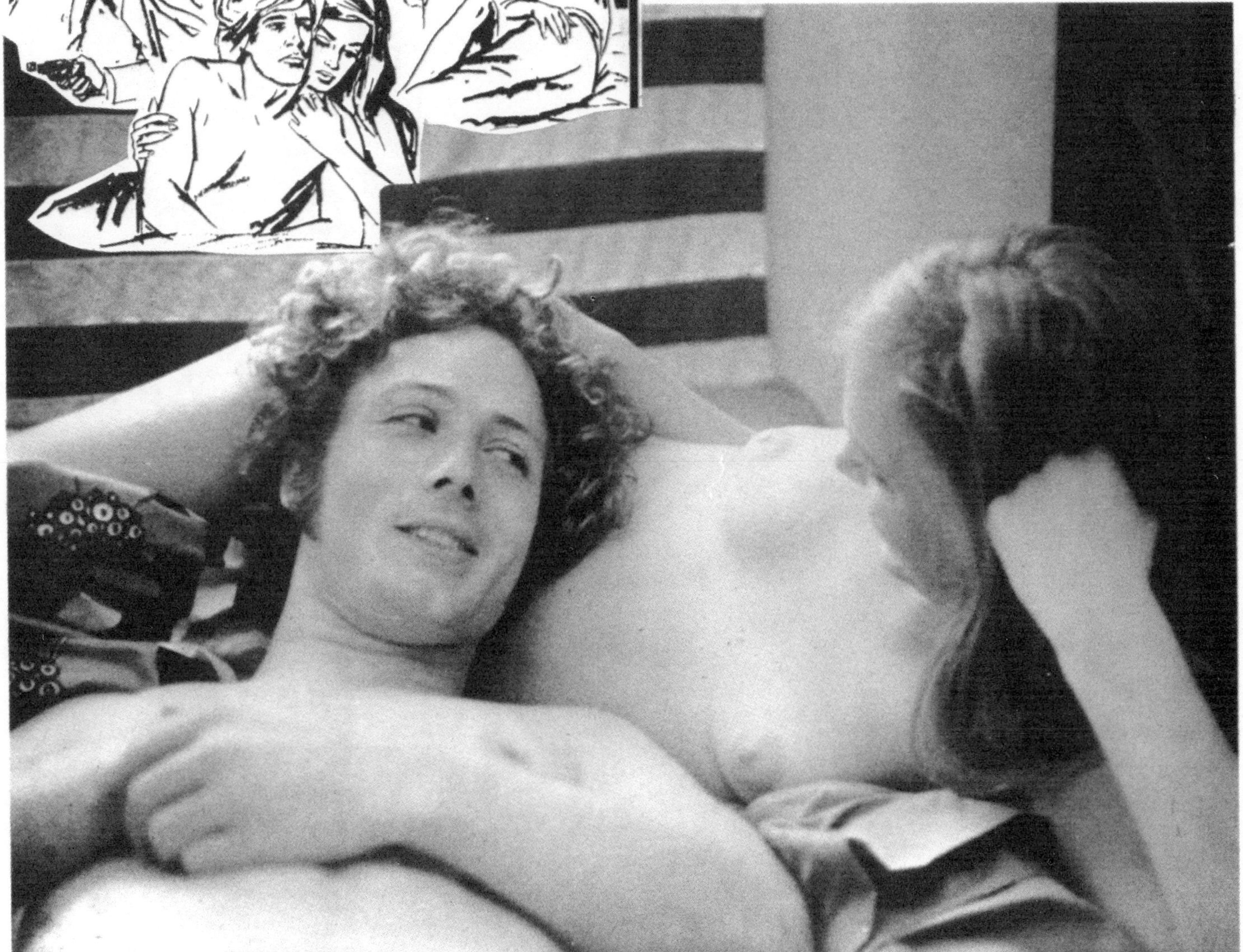

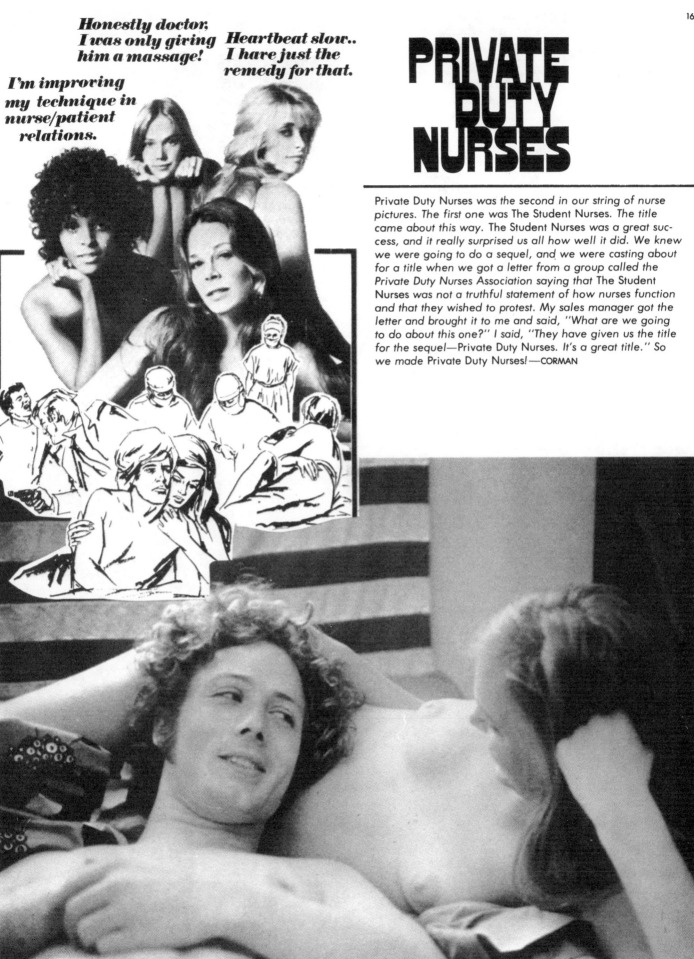

SHE TOOK ON THE WHOLE GANG!
A howling hellcat
humping a hot steel hog
on a roaring rampage
of revenge.
IN COLOR

bury me an angel

Bury Me an Angel was the only Hell's Angels picture, to my knowledge, that was directed by a woman. Barbara Peeters was the director, and it was her first feature film. She did quite a good job. It was the story of a girl whose brother is killed by the Hell's Angels, and she takes off after them on a trip of vengeance. The film was notable because Barbara got a really beautiful girl to play the lead who was really striking on the motorcycle. We used her in the ads, in the trailers, and on TV dates. Her name is Dixie Peabody.

—CORMAN

The Big Bird Cage

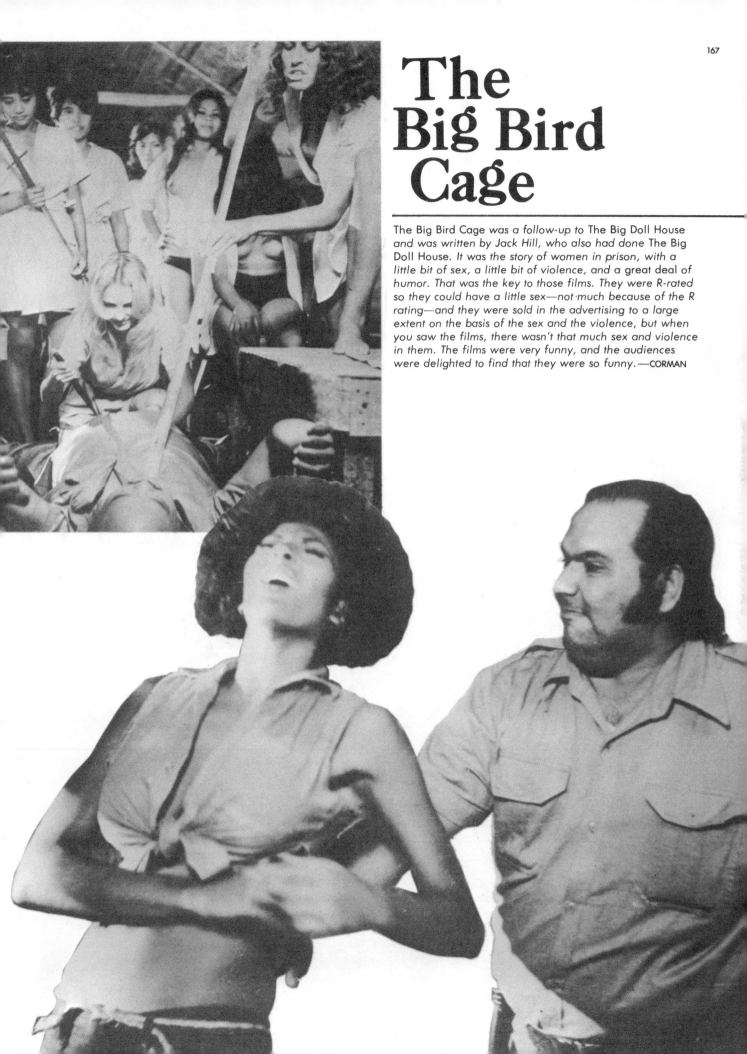

The Big Bird Cage was a follow-up to The Big Doll House and was written by Jack Hill, who also had done The Big Doll House. It was the story of women in prison, with a little bit of sex, a little bit of violence, and a great deal of humor. That was the key to those films. They were R-rated so they could have a little sex—not much because of the R rating—and they were sold in the advertising to a large extent on the basis of the sex and the violence, but when you saw the films, there wasn't that much sex and violence in them. The films were very funny, and the audiences were delighted to find that they were so funny.—CORMAN

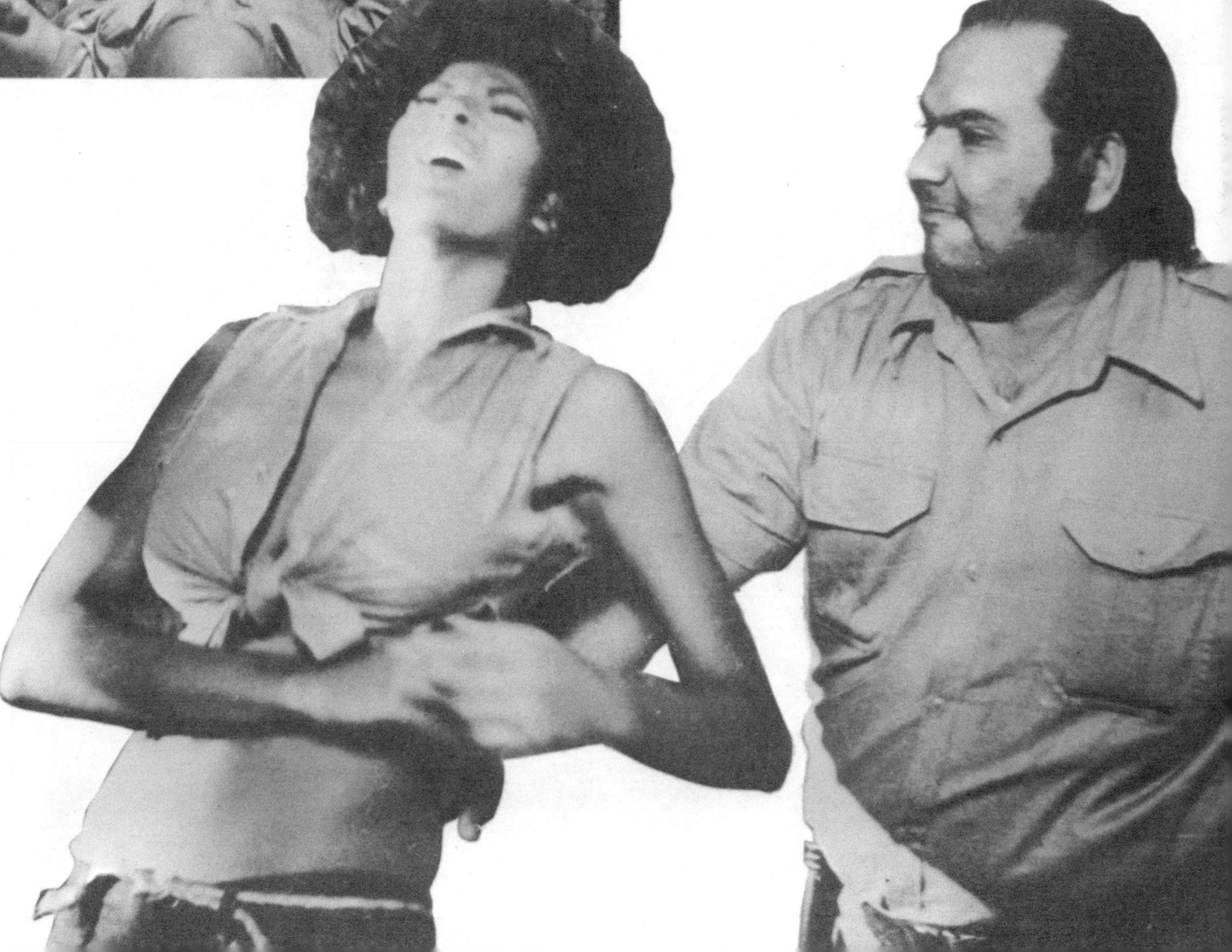

The CREMATORS

The Cremators was not a picture we made; it was a picture we acquired for distribution. It was a very low-budget science-fiction picture—one of the lowest, to my knowledge. The film was made completely in color by Harry Essex for about forty thousand dollars, which is something like a record in today's market and with today's prices in the 1970s.—CORMAN

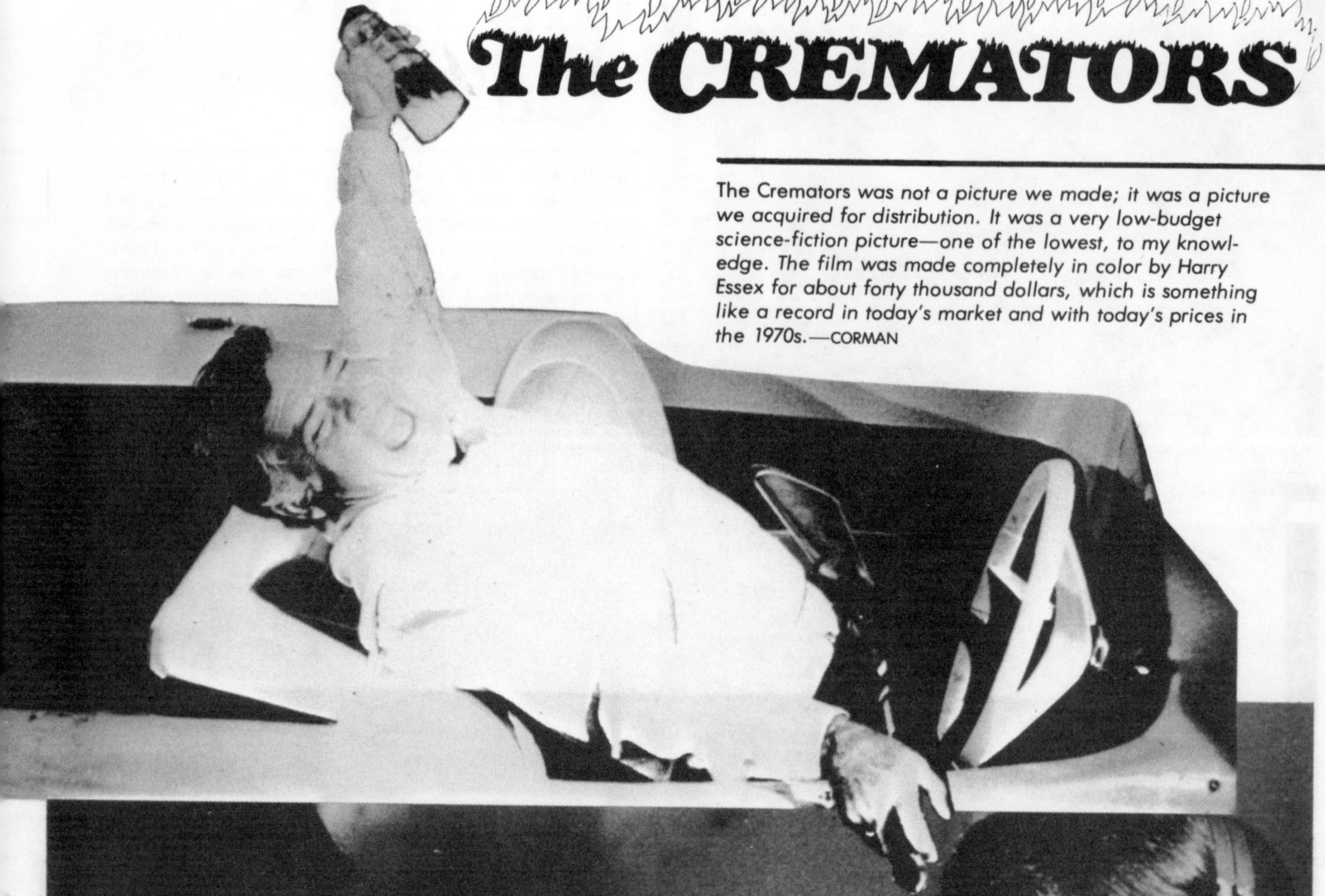

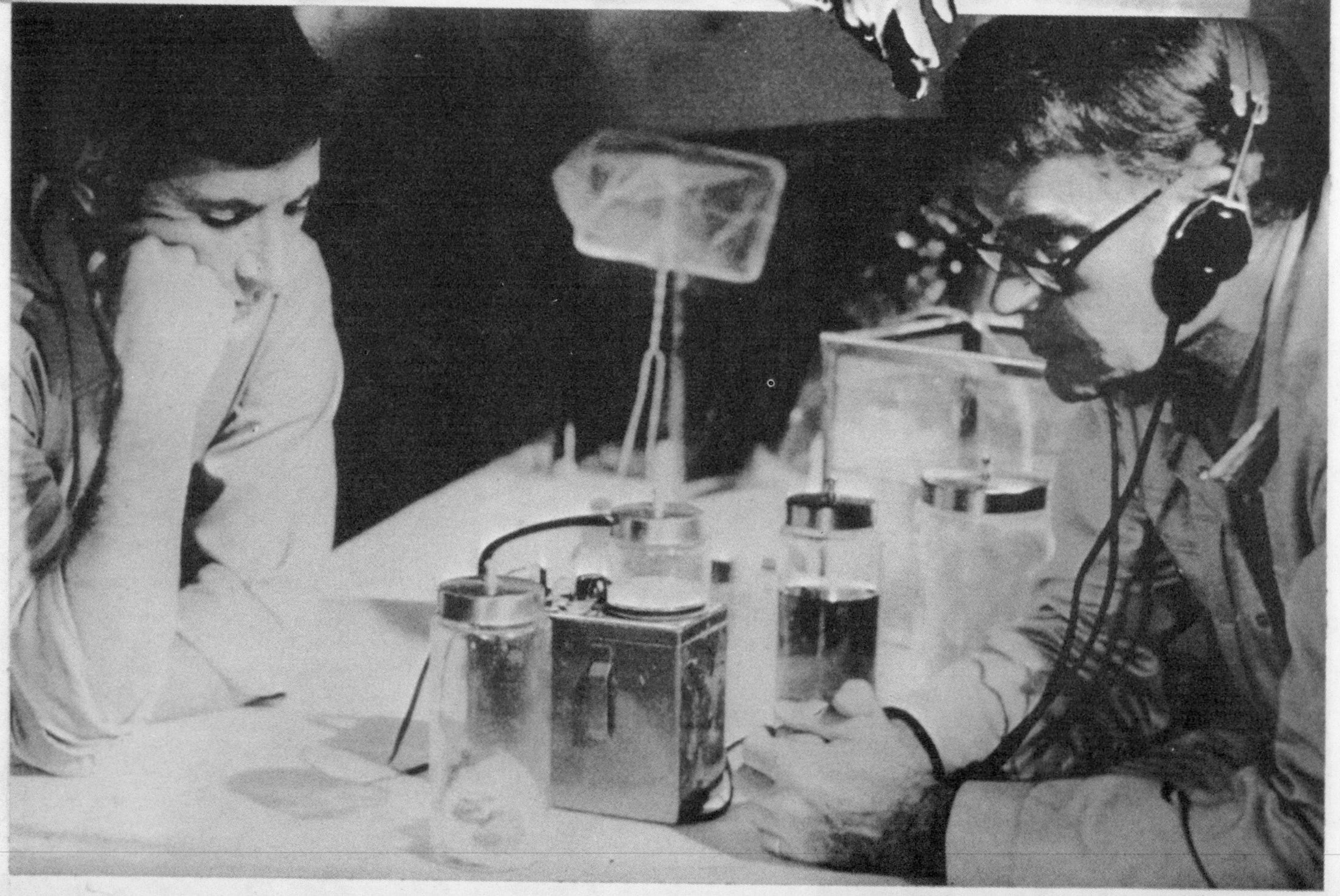

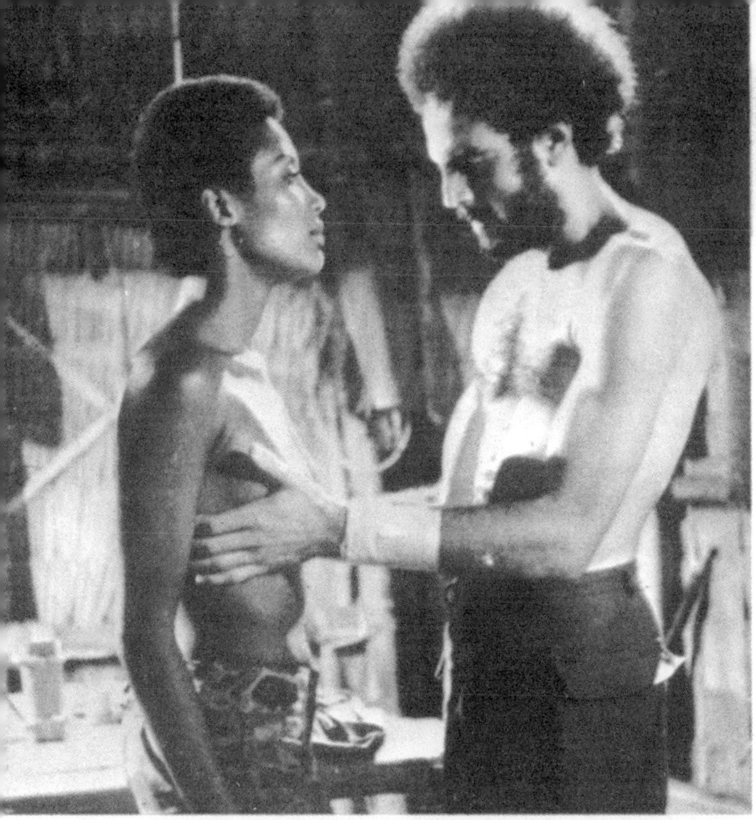

THE HOT BOX

The Hot Box was another one of our Philippine films starring women. Again it was a Jonathan Demme-Joe Viola picture. Once more they took a commercial format, tried to get a little more thought into it than most, and succeeded. It had to do with some American nurses in the Philippines who were captured by revolutionary forces who needed medical attention. It dealt with the straight American girls' dawning awareness of what was really going on in different parts of the world.—CORMAN

the WOMAN HUNT

Woman Hunt was another one of the Philippine films, but it was not made by New World. It was made by a group from Tulsa, Oklahoma, that had been associated with us as investors in some films.—CORMAN

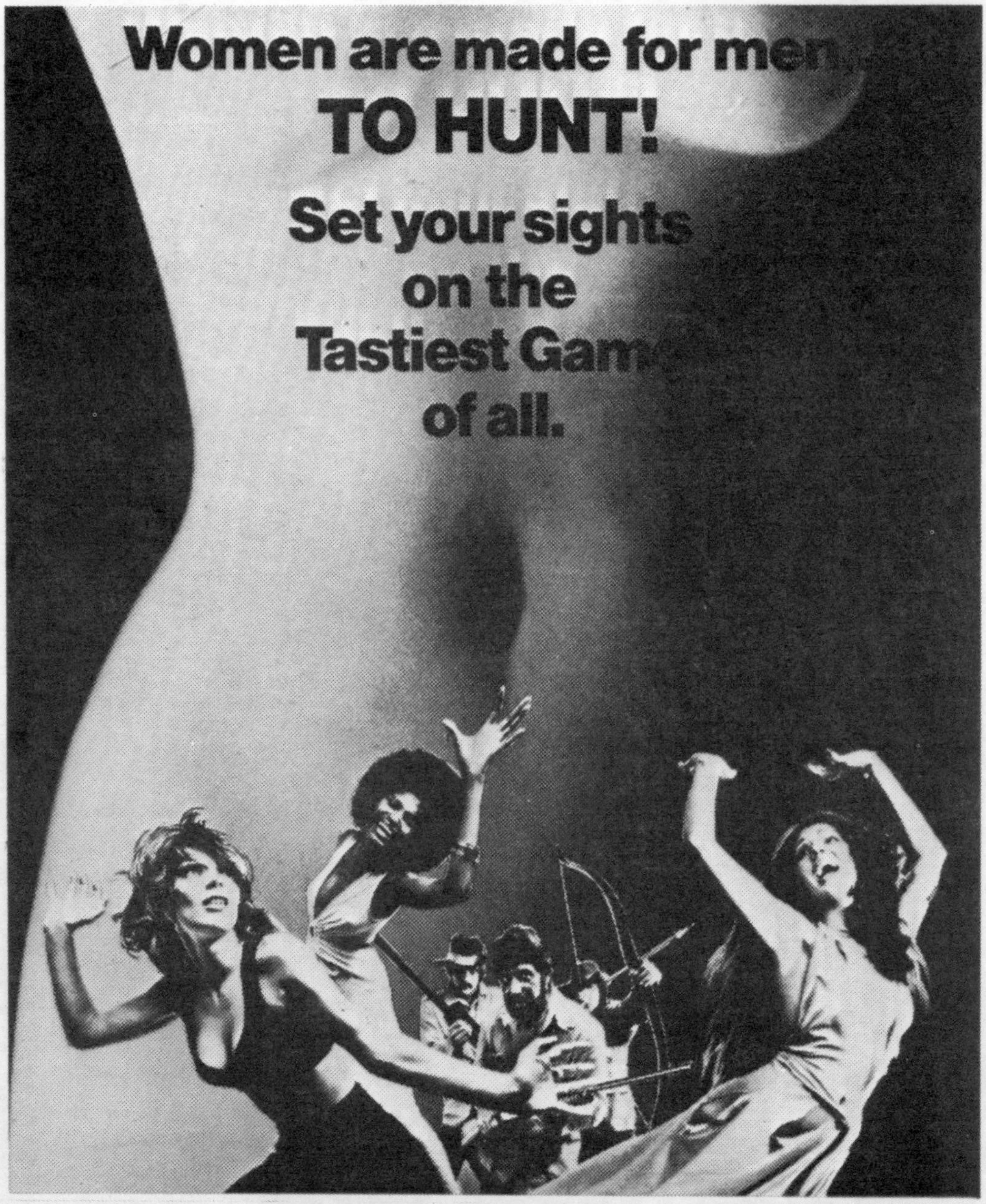

Women are made for men
TO HUNT!
Set your sights
on the
Tastiest Gam
of all.

Starring JOHN ASHLEY · PAT WOODELL · LAURIE ROSE
CHARLENE JONES · LISA TODD · SID HAIG
Produced by JOHN ASHLEY and EDDIE ROMERO · Directed by EDDIE ROMERO
A FOUR ASSOCIATES, LTD. PRODUCTION · A NEW WORLD PICTURES RELEASE
METROCOLOR

R

The Final Comedown

The Final Comedown was a very unusual film made at the height of the craze—and it was a craze—for black films for a couple of years. It was made by Oscar Williams, who was from Jamaica and was a student at the American Film Institute. He was able to make it almost totally on grants from the American Film Institute and various black organizations in Los Angeles, supplemented by a small amount of money from me. The film was not as successful as it might have been, because it was intensely political. It was a film of violence and of crime, but the political overtones were so heavy that they somewhat obscured the action. Although it was well made, it suffered for that reason. Oscar said when it was all finished, "Well, everyone has to make a film like this; now I'll make some commercial films." He did make some commercial films and had a fairly successful career. The Final Comedown starred Billy Dee Williams in, I think, his first film, before Billy Dee became a major star.—CORMAN

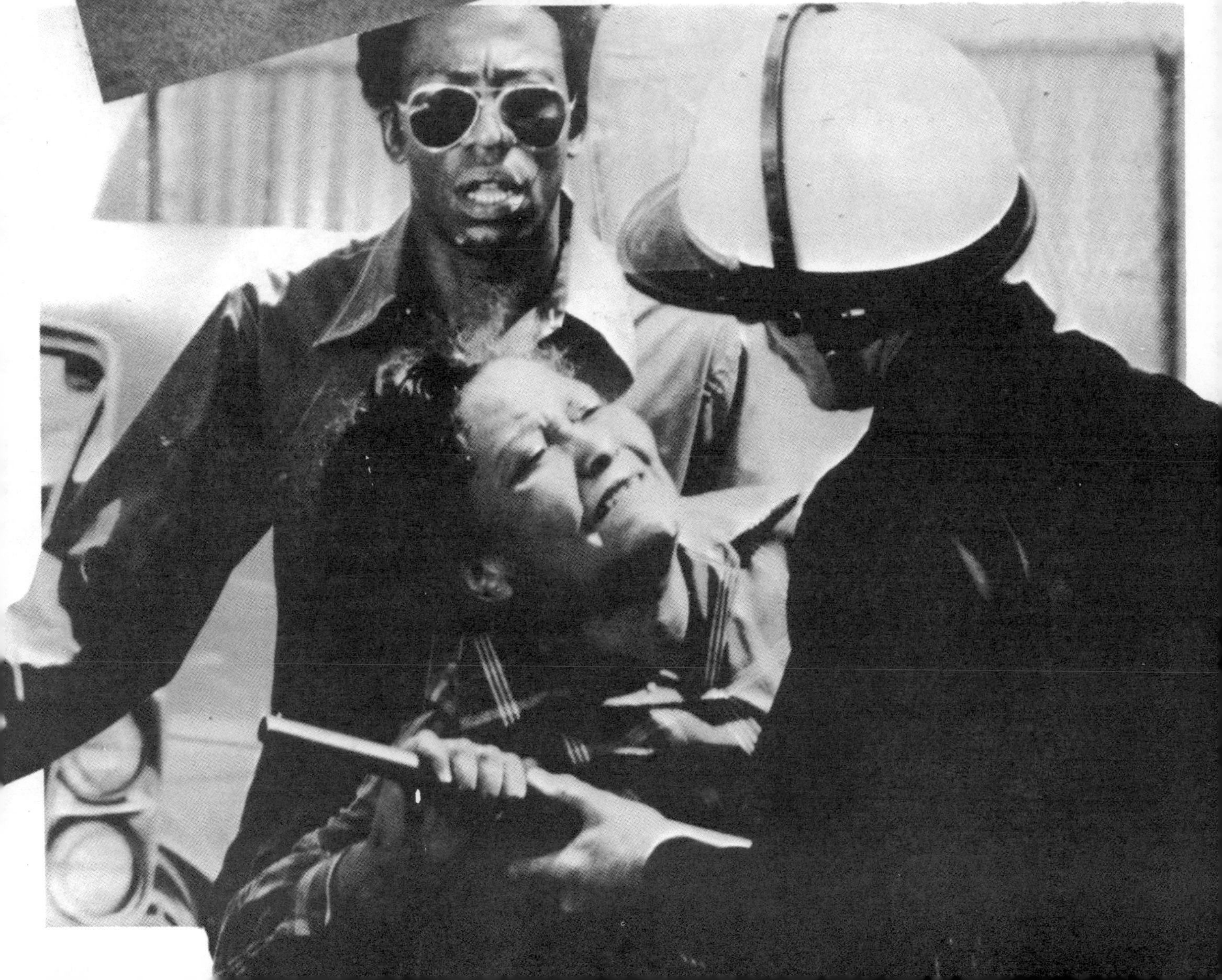

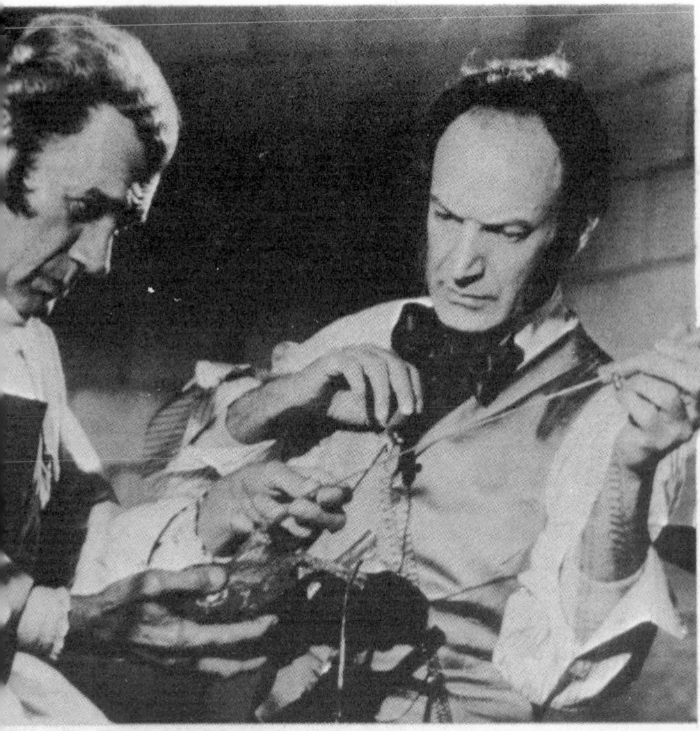

Lady Frankenstein

Lady Frankenstein was another picture I picked up sight unseen. It was produced and directed in Rome by Mel Welles, an old associate of mine. He had all of his financing except for a very small amount. While traveling through Los Angeles he mentioned that if he could just get a little more money from the United States to add to what he had, he could make the picture. I said I would put up that small amount of money in return for the United States distribution. This was a very interesting picture because it was a retelling of the Frankenstein story by Dr. Frankenstein's daughter. —CORMAN

NIGHT OF THE COBRA WOMAN

Night of the Cobra Woman was another of the horror films we did in the Philippines. It had a very interesting premise but was not as successful as some of the others. I think there was a very simple reason. In a horror or science-fiction film you can start with as outlandish a premise as you want, providing you are then logical in the treatment of the premise. I think the writer violated the laws of logic several times within the film. We were doing a number of scenes spontaneously at that time, and in my final meeting with him before going to Manila I pointed this out to him and said that upon his arrival on location he must have this straightened out, that he must solve these problems logically, but he did not. The film, although it was as well produced, directed, and acted as any of the other low-budget horror films, did not do as well, and I always believed it was because of that break in the logical chain. No matter how low-budget the film is, if you do good work you can make a good film. —CORMAN

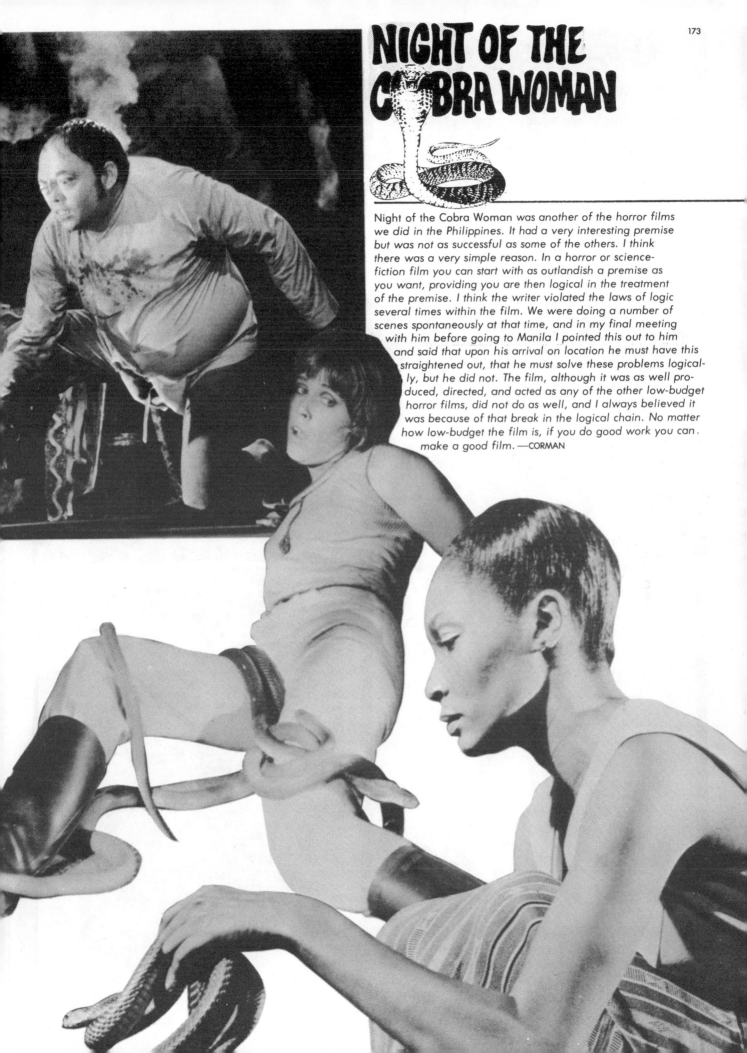

Sweet Kill

Sweet Kill was a suspense-horror film produced by Tamara Asseyev, who had been my assistant. It was her first job as a producer, and she did a very nice job. It was directed by Curtis Hanson, and this was his first job as a director. They have both gone on to the beginnings of what appear to be very good careers. Tamara is partnered with Alex Rose, another one of my assistants who is a woman. The two of them are now a producing team under contract at Universal.
—CORMAN

Angels, Hard As They Come

Angels, Hard As They Come was the first film made by the team of Jonathan Demme and Joe Viola, who went on to make several films for us. Jonathan is doing a large-budget film for United Artists at the moment. This was an interesting film because it was a motorcycle picture with a little more philosophical theme behind it. It dealt with the nature of guilt, which is something you don't normally deal with in that kind of film. I thought the film did a good job of it. —CORMAN

Night Call Nurses

It was very interesting working for Roger because the first meeting I had with him was very short. I think it lasted about ten minutes, and he basically laid out the requirements of the genre. Exploitation of male sexual fantasy, a comedic subplot, action and violence, and a slightly-to-the-left-of-center social subplot. And these were the four elements that were required in the nurses pictures. Then frontal nudity from the waist up, total nudity from behind, no pubic hair, and get the title in the film somewhere and go to work. That was essentially it.—JONATHAN KAPLAN, director of *Night Call Nurses* and *Student Teachers*

"Who says all men are created equal?"
"Your trouble is you're ashamed of your body!"

It's always harder at night.

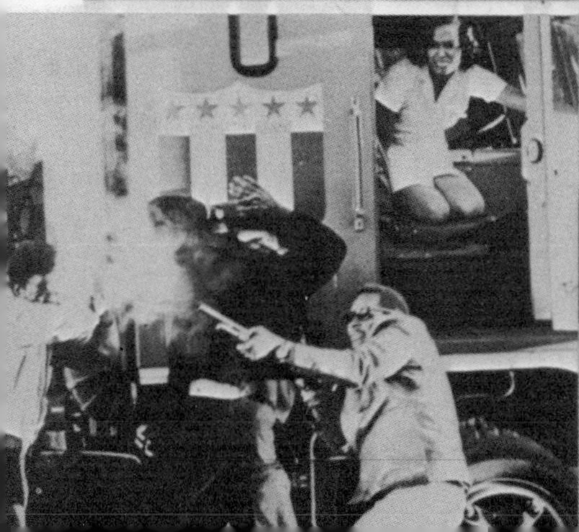

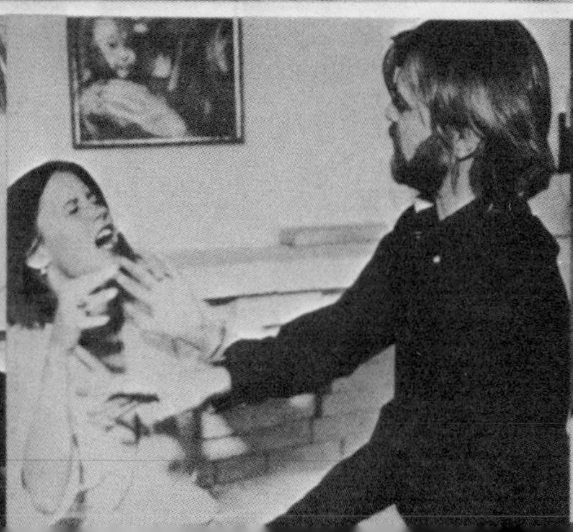

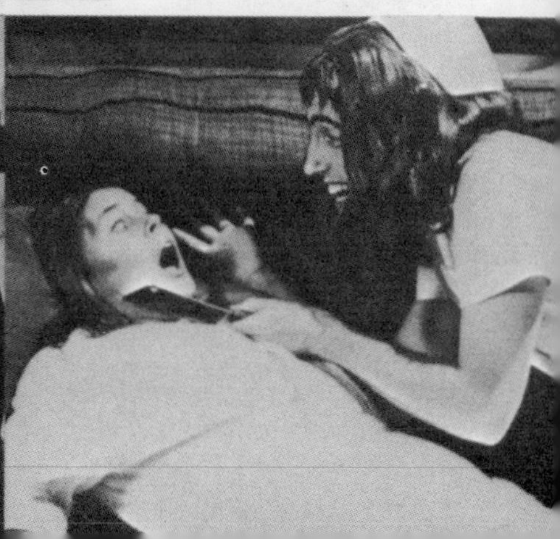

THE ARENA

The Arena was one of the few co-productions we did in Europe. It was the story of women and gladiators, based loosely on the Spartacus story. Again it was an attempt to make an R-rated film with some sex, some violence, some humor, and a political theme. The theme here was simply freedom with a women's-lib viewpoint. The film was quite successful, particularly because by this time two of the girls we had been working with, who were really very beautiful—a white girl, Margaret Markoff, and a black girl, Pam Grier—were beginning to be well known and were emerging somewhat as stars of this kind of film. —CORMAN

SEE WILD WOMEN FIGHT TO THE DEATH!
BLACK SLAVE VS WHITE SLAVE

SAVAGE!

HEAR THE SUPER SOUL SOUNDTRACK!

Savage was one of the black films we made in Manila. We didn't make as many black films as most of the other independents. This is interesting, because when a cycle starts—particularly in the low-budget field—the independents jump on that cycle, and they always overdo it. Although I am one of the most liberal and sympathetic to the black cause, I made only a few films on black subjects, largely for economic reasons. I felt it was foolish in the long run to be directing your films to only ten percent of the population of the United States and even less a percentage in the overseas market. We probably missed out on a few dollars on one or two films, but in the long run we were absolutely right, because the others that jumped in made money on their first one or two films but then got burned very quickly. Savage was a very politically oriented action film. It was a revolutionary film much as The Final Comedown was, but it was more successful because we kept the revolutionary concept in the background—the radical political beliefs—and concentrated on the straight action. The film had a great deal of action, which is one of the reasons we were able to shoot in the Philippines. You can really get the Philippine army to stage your battle sequences, and you can get really magnificent war sequences there in a low-budget film that you can't get in any other part of the world that I know of.—CORMAN

METROCOLOR
Men call him SAVAGE...
Women call him all the time.

THE BIG BUST-OUT

The Big Bust-Out was a really funny project. We had been making these women-in-prison films in the Philippines, and they'd been immensely successful. The Big Doll House had played Italy and done very well, and in the Rome film industry, as soon as a film comes from anywhere and does well, you can be sure that in a matter of weeks someone will be shooting a follow-up. As soon as The Big Doll House did well, The Big Bust-Out was made, and since I have friends living in Rome, I heard from them that this film existed. Now, my former sales manager and I are very good friends, so this is really a story of motion picture distribution. He had left to start his own company, and we were very friendly—as a matter of fact, I have recommended many producers to him. Anyway, he had heard of this Italian picture, and he knew how much money we had made, so he wanted this picture. He got on a plane to Rome before anybody could make the deal. I knew he had left. So while he was in the air, I bought the film by phone and telexed the money from Bank of America here to Bank of America in Rome and told my friend, "Get a letter of agreement; there's no time for a contract. Get a letter of sale; give him the down payment with a statement that the sale will come later." By the time my former sales manager landed in Rome, the film had been sold to me—to his surprtse. It was not a very good film, and we made a little profit with it.—CORMAN

Soft skin bursting through hard prison walls!
TECHNICOLOR

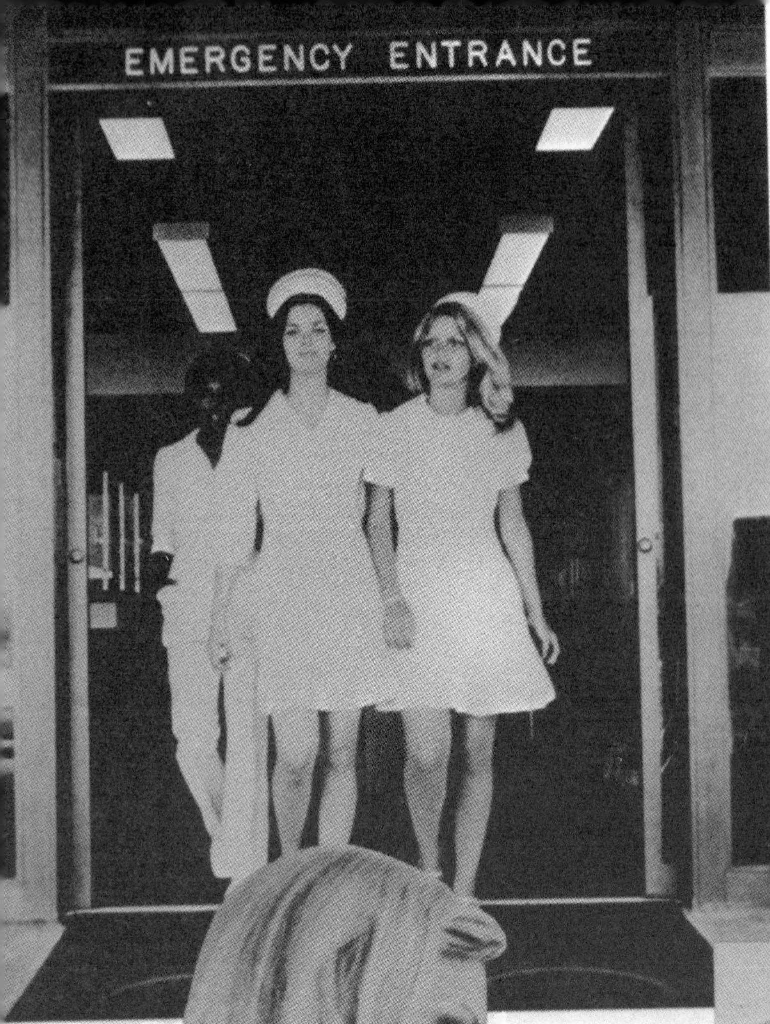

THE YOUNG NURSES

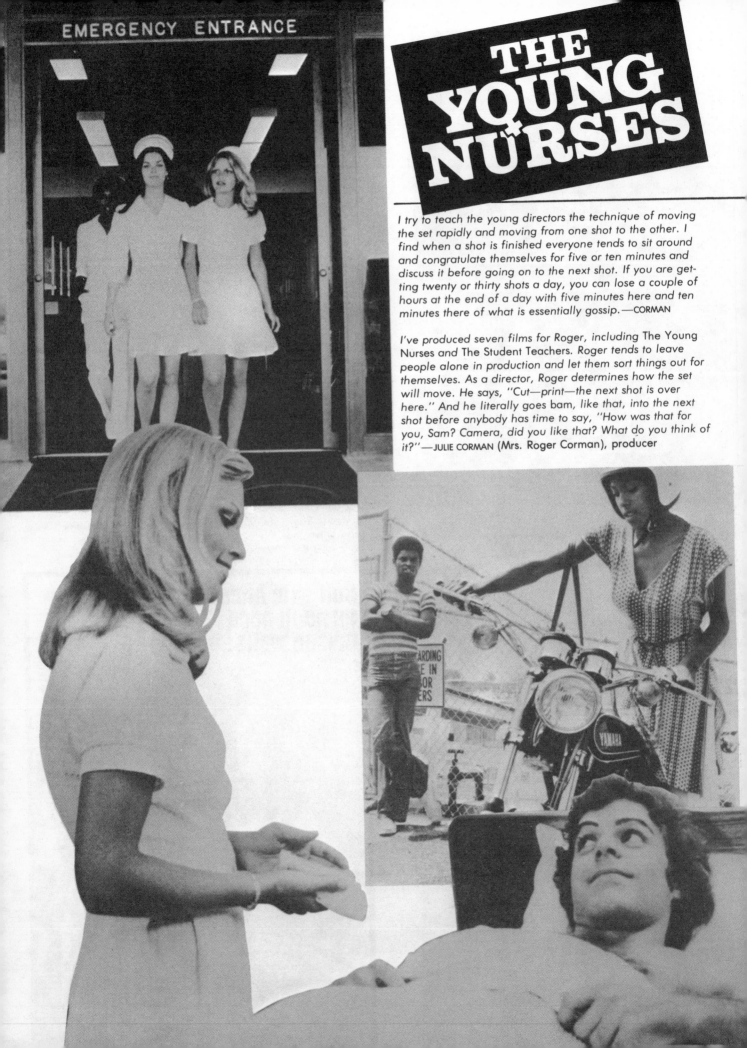

I try to teach the young directors the technique of moving the set rapidly and moving from one shot to the other. I find when a shot is finished everyone tends to sit around and congratulate themselves for five or ten minutes and discuss it before going on to the next shot. If you are getting twenty or thirty shots a day, you can lose a couple of hours at the end of a day with five minutes here and ten minutes there of what is essentially gossip.—CORMAN

I've produced seven films for Roger, including The Young Nurses and The Student Teachers. Roger tends to leave people alone in production and let them sort things out for themselves. As a director, Roger determines how the set will move. He says, "Cut—print—the next shot is over here." And he literally goes bam, like that, into the next shot before anybody has time to say, "How was that for you, Sam? Camera, did you like that? What do you think of it?"—JULIE CORMAN (Mrs. Roger Corman), producer

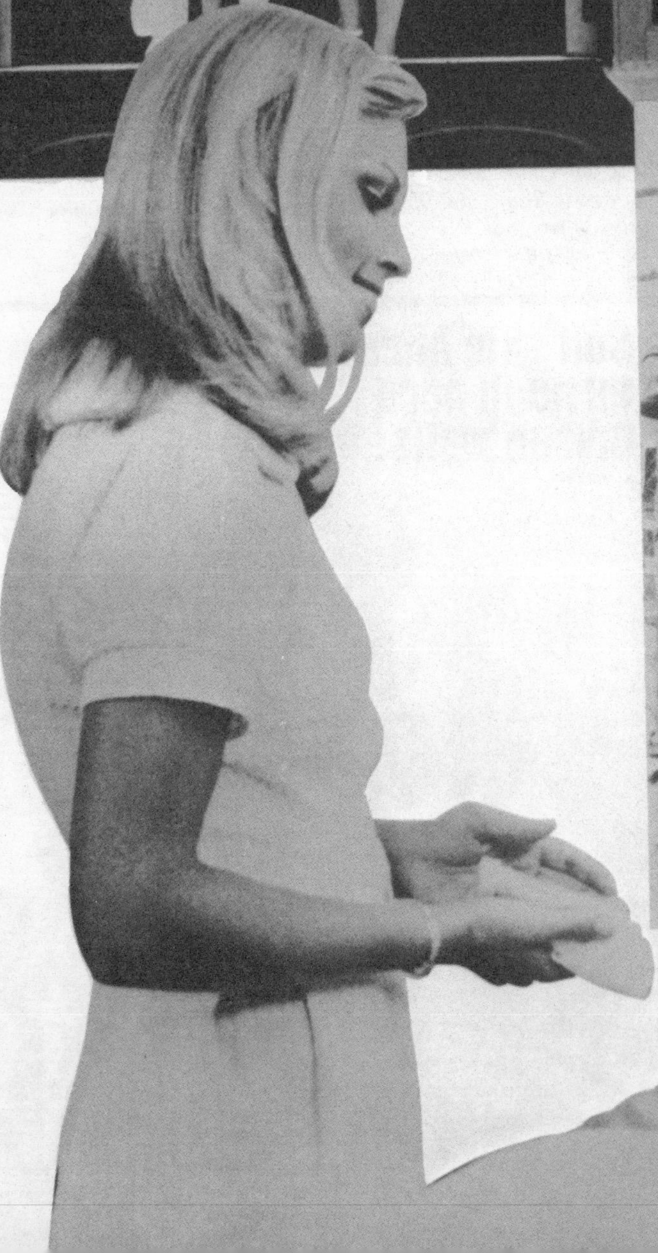

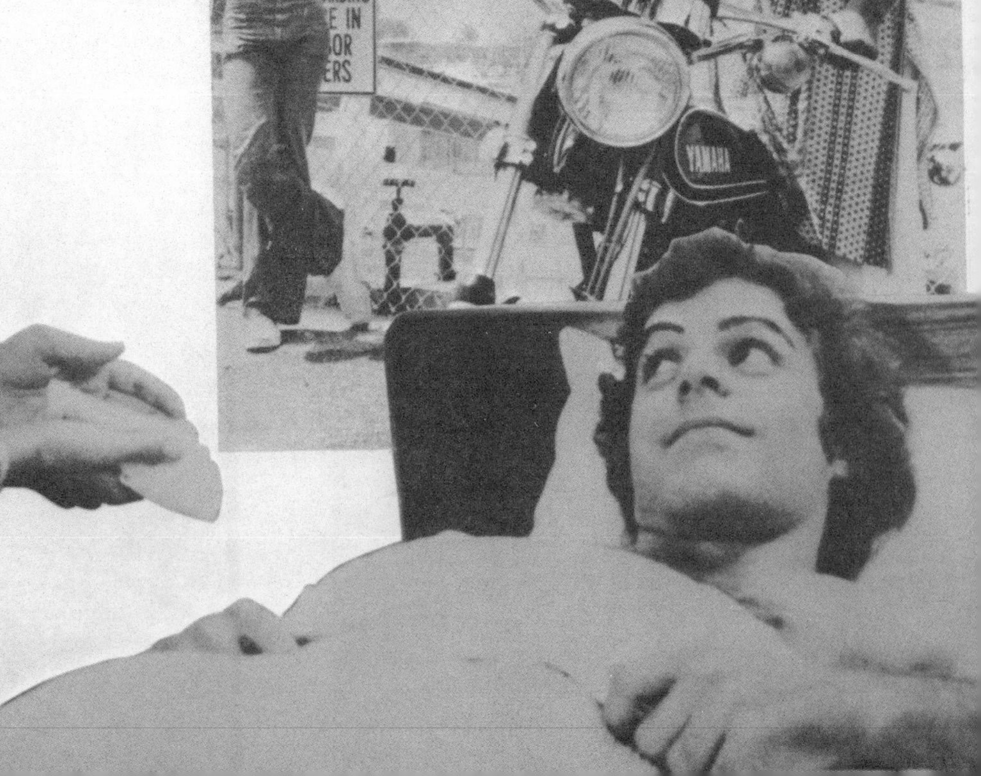

"I teach sex-ed my way!"
"I can't resist the student body!"
"What I do after school is my business!"
"I give very private lessons!"
SEX-ED LAB

THE STUDENT TEACHERS

The Student Teachers was produced by Julie and directed by Jonathan Kaplan. I thought it was one of the best of that series, and it was one of the most successful. I think it proves that if a film is made a little bit better than other films in the genre, it will do better. Most people do not think that; they think you take any low-budget film with a title and they'll all do about the same. We have found that even if you're in a one-week multiple run, you may open equal to everyone else, say on a Wednesday, but by Friday the better film will already be a little bit up and the weaker film a little bit down. Word of mouth works within twenty-four to forty-eight hours.—CORMAN

THIS AIRLINE SERVES THREE WILD DISHES
TAKE YOUR CHOICE
"I'm Toby, fly me as far as you want."
"I'm Sherry, buy a ticket and I come free!"
"I'm Andrea, my foreign lay-overs are very stimulating."
METROCOLOR
SEE STEWARDESSES BATTLE KUNG FU KILLERS!
Fly Me
STARRING PAT ANDERSON • LENORE KASDORF • LYLLAH TORENA • NAOMI STEVENS
KUNG FU sequences by DAVID CHOW DIRECTED BY CIRIO SANTIAGO
A NEW WORLD PICTURES RELEASE

Fly Me

Fly Me was a rather successful film with a little bit of sex, a little bit of action and humor—again playing that same combination. We had done a number of nurses films, and we decided to branch out. This time we treated stewardesses—again with that combination and with a somewhat pro-women's-lib viewpoint, so that though the films sold rather blatantly in their advertising, when the audiences came to see them, they actually saw a better film. We more or less originated this concept and were copied quite a bit. However, the people who copied us never achieved the theatrical success we did, and I think one reason why was that they copied the overt things and failed to copy the thematic material. Because ours were pro-women's-lib and really presented women as the leads and not as the second leads, we did very well. We might occasionally get a letter from a nurses' organization, but we got more letters from women's organizations saying they had seen these films and were really surprised at how good and how pro-women's-lib they were. We've even been written up in a number of women's magazines on these films. —CORMAN

SEVEN BLOWS OF THE DRAGON

Seven Blows of the Dragon was a Chinese picture originally called *The Water Margin*, made by Run Run Shaw in Hong Kong. As the Kung Fu craze started to hit, I simply bought the film from Run Run Shaw. One of the most significant things about that film was our poster. It was a beautiful poster, and the artist signed the original artwork. This is not usually done, but he was very proud of it.—CORMAN

THE HARDER THEY COME

The Harder They Come is a very interesting film. It was a Reggae film done in Jamaica, written and directed by Perry Henzell, and on a very low budget. It won awards at a couple of the regional film festivals. We liked the film very much and took it for distribution but did not have a great deal of success with it originally, although it got very good reviews. However, we stayed with it and eventually started playing it in New York as a midnight picture on Friday and Saturday nights. It ran that way for a whole year. We followed that pattern around the country, and after two years it became something of a cult film and ultimately was commercially successful. Again, I'm very proud to be able to handle a very good but difficult film by finding good but different ways of releasing it and turning it into a success.
—CORMAN

STACEY!

Stacey! was a film New World Pictures distributed—it was produced and directed by Andy Sidaris. He was a director for ABC television on college football games, and he used some of these sports camera-techniques in the automobile chase sequences, especially in the final chase scenes. These sequences were very well done. —CORMAN

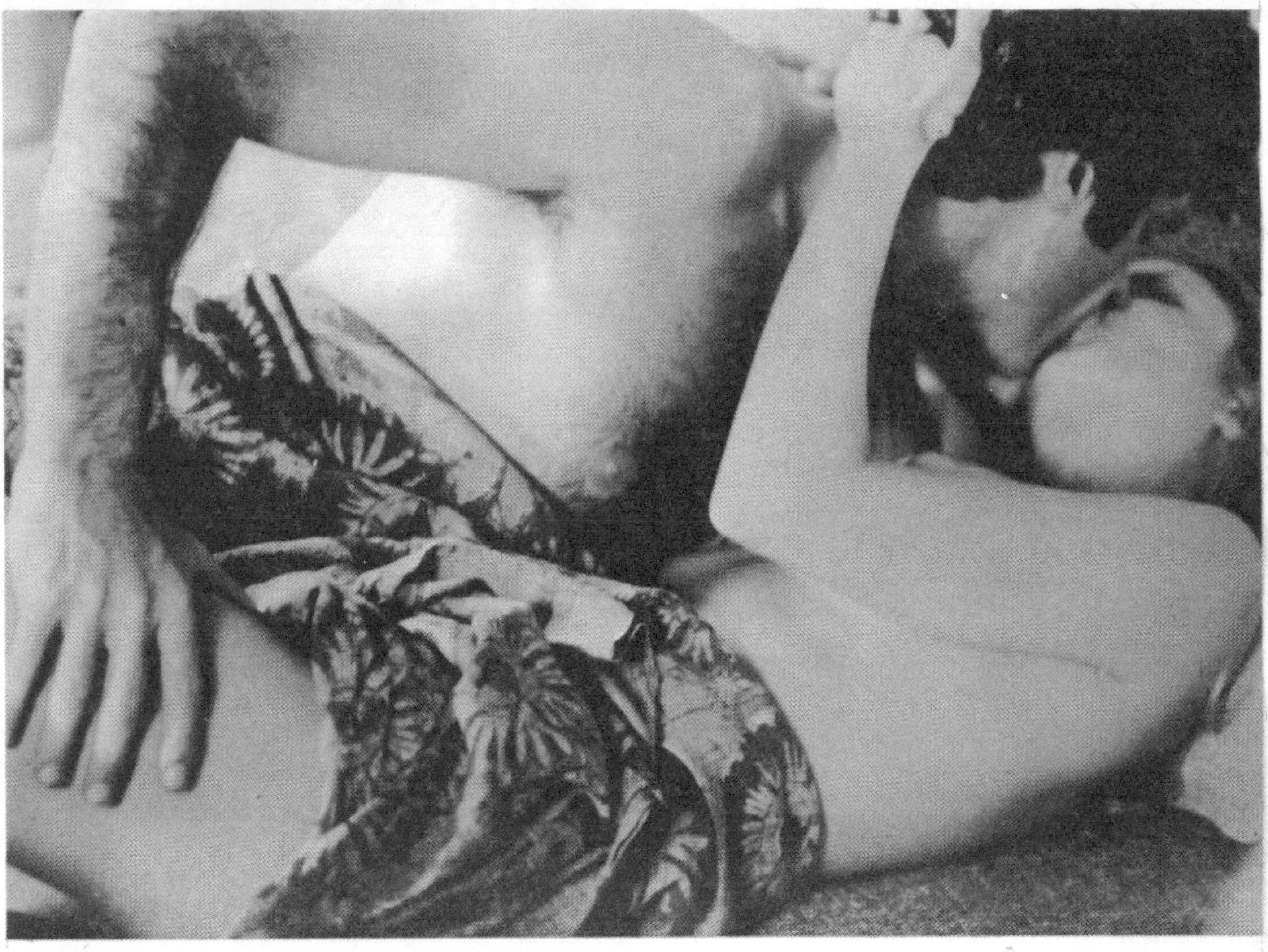

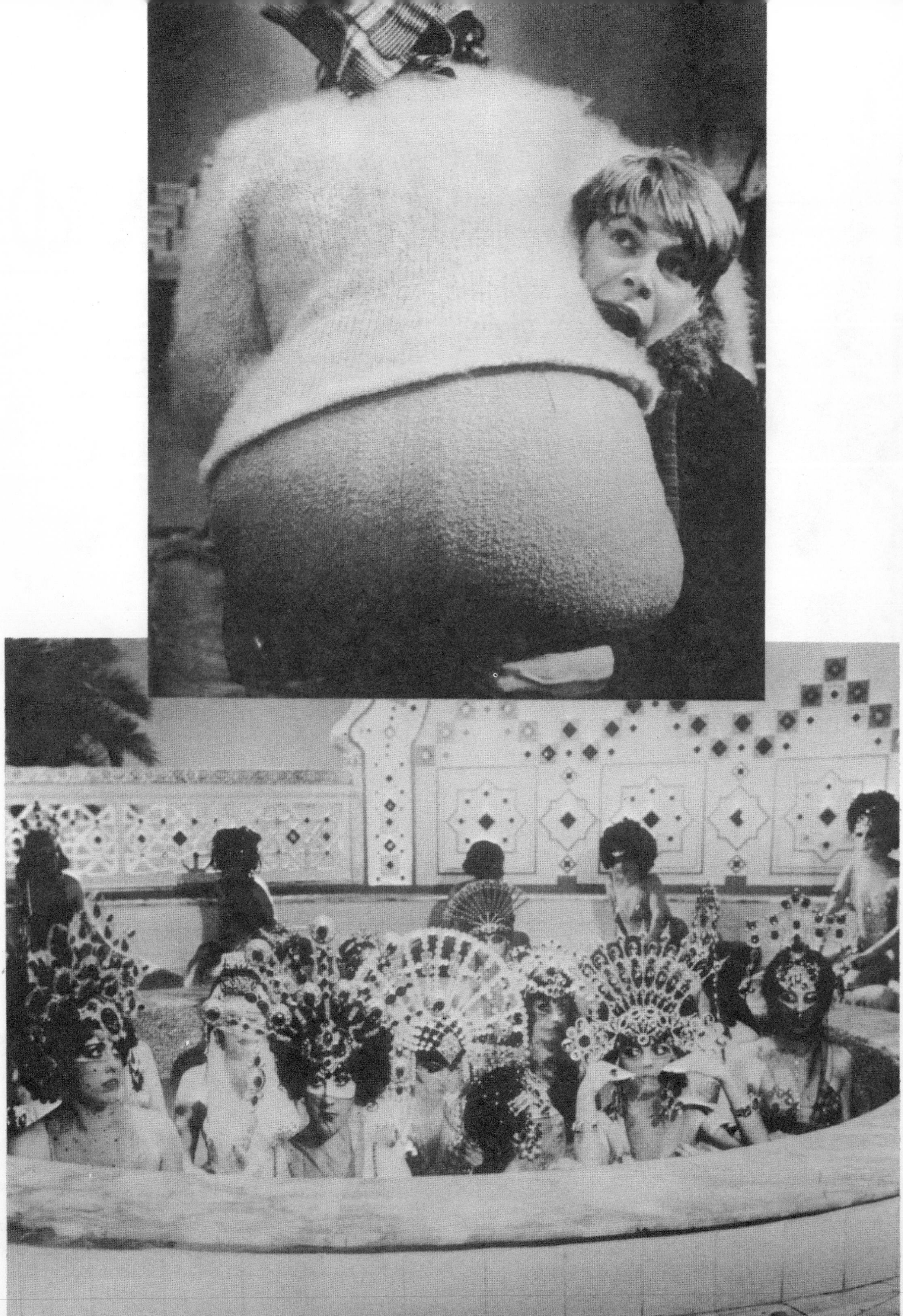

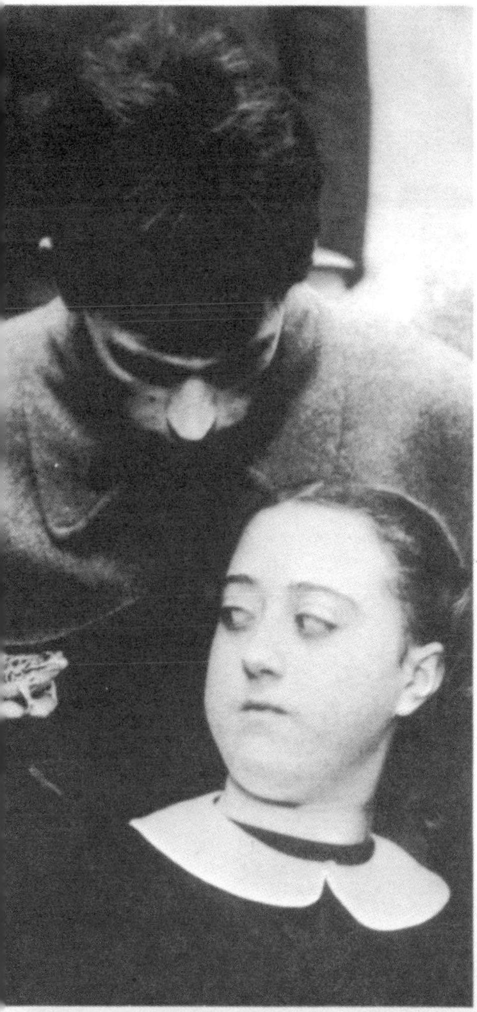

ROGER CORMAN presents

FELLINI'S AMARCORD

Amarcord is one of the finest films we ever distributed. I consider it to be one of the two or three best films Fellini has ever made. It was nominated for three Academy Awards and won for Best Foreign Film. It was just a good experience all around and a pleasure working with Fellini, who was extremely cooperative. He came to New York and made publicity appearances for us. He worked with us in a very friendly way. Again with the film we got a great deal of commercial success as well as critical acclaim. And that, together with Cries and Whispers, is the biggest commercial success we've ever had in the art-film realm.—CORMAN

BIG BAD MAMA

Angie Dickinson played a high-spirited widow with two nubile, uninhibited teenage daughters in the small dust-bowl town of Paradise, Texas, in this film set in 1932. William Shatner, a Corman favorite who starred in the controversial Corman film *The Intruder*, also starred in this film.

Unabashedly an exploitation picture with all the sex and violence an "R" rating can sustain, Big Bad Mama is nonetheless pretty good entertainment, lowdown and rambunctious, thanks to Angie Dickinson, William Shatner and Tom Skerritt, and above all, Steve Carver's admirable and resourceful direction.—KEVIN THOMAS, the *Los Angeles Times*, Oct. 16, 1974

LAST DAYS OF MAN ON EARTH

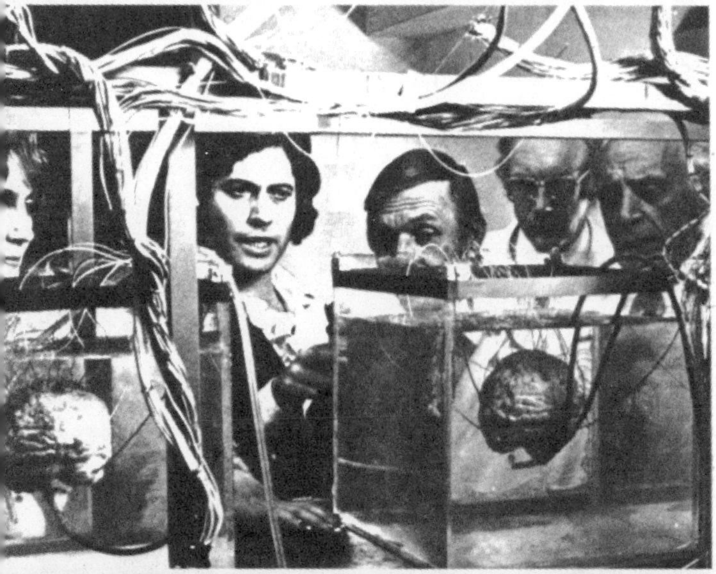

Written and directed by Robert Fuest, The Last Days of Man on Earth is beyond doubt one of the strangest ideas to ever hit the screen. It's got world catastrophe, an Ultimate Computer working out an immortality project, a dedicated lady scientist with an unusual goal, running gun battles with needle-guns, and even a house that's ingeniously rigged up with scientific traps.—MONSTERSCOPE MAGAZINE

THE FUTURE IS CANCELLED!
THE FUTURE IS CANCELLED!
THE FUTURE IS CANCELLED!

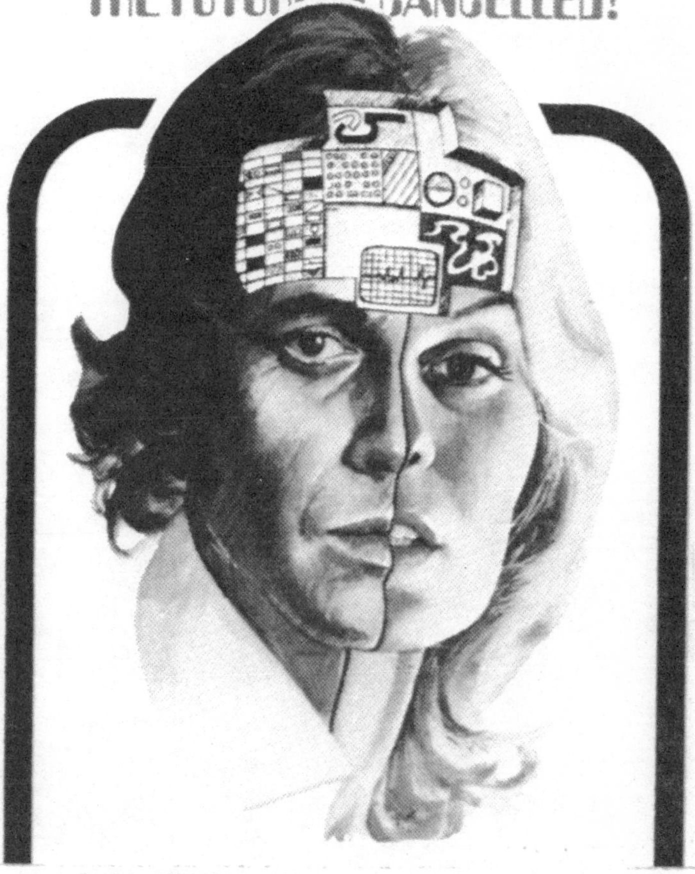

JON FINCH · JENNY RUNACRE · STERLING HAYDEN · PATRICK MAGEE
HUGH GRIFFITH
from the novel by MICHAEL MOORCOCK
designed, written and directed by ROBERT FUEST · an ANGLO-EMI film / distributed by NEW WORLD PICTURES
TECHNICOLOR
R RESTRICTED

FANTASTIC PLANET

Fantastic Planet is a film I am really proud of. I think it's just a beautifully made film. It won a special grand prize at the Cannes Film Festival, and I bought it at the festival from the producers. We opened it in New York in an art house, and it got brilliant reviews. The film was a major success, and I really consider it to be one of the finest films we've ever distributed. It's one thing for us to take an art film from Fellini or Truffaut and do well with it, but it's another to take an art film not from a famous director, and in particular from an animated director, and do well with it. It is a much more difficult challenge, and I'm particularly proud that the film was so successful. I think it bears repeating that it's to New World's credit that they picked up that film with no advance credentials other than the special grand prize at the Cannes Film Festival. It was a complete success both critically and commercially. I have nothing but good things to say about the film. —CORMAN

candy stripe nurses

Candy Stripe Nurses was one of the last of the nurse pictures. It played more for comedy than any of the previous nurse pictures. As I've stated before, we had a certain formula that worked, and one of the nurse pictures had a very strong political statement and theme. In this one the key fact of the political statement and theme is still there, but we made it less important and played it for the humor. The film was quite successful. As with all of that genre, we never lost money. This film was produced by my wife, Julie.—CORMAN

Playing doctor was never like this!
Keep abreast of the medical world
STARRING
CANDICE RIALSON • ROBIN MATTSON • MARIA ROJO • KIMBERLY HYDE
WRITTEN and DIRECTED by ALLAN HOLLEB
METROCOLOR
A NEW WORLD PICTURE

WOMEN'S PRISON U.S.A–RAPE, RIOT & REVENGE!
WHITE HOT DESIRES MELTING COLD PRISON STEEL!

CAGED HEAT!

Caged Heat was a picture that we didn't make but that we put some money into. It was made by Sam Geffman and directed by Jonathan Demme, who has made several pictures with us. It was a women's prison picture, but this time set in the United States because we felt we had done enough in that market, all in the Philippines, and Sam wanted to make an American film to follow the ones we had done in the Philippines. It was a well-made film and a successful film, again with a political statement and theme behind it.—CORMAN

SWEET SWEET-BACK

This film was produced, directed, written and edited by Melvin van Peebles, who also starred in it and wrote the musical score. With elements of sex and violence woven into a wild plot, *Sweet Sweetback* was a controversial treatment of the everyday oppression of blacks by the police and society at large. It did quite well at the box office.

TNT *Jackson*

TNT Jackson was a film made in the Philippines directed by Sirio Santiago. It was a straight action Kung Fu picture with Jeannie Bell, a very beautiful black girl, in the lead. It was highly successful.—CORMAN

The Romantic Englishwoman

The Romantic Englishwoman *was written by Tom Stoppard and directed by Joe Losey; it starred Michael Caine, Helmut Berger, and Glenda Jackson. It was a very well made film that we were very happy to distribute. It fell somewhere between a commercial film and an art film, and as such it was a little difficult to sell. Nevertheless, we achieved moderate success with the film and were very pleased.*
—CORMAN

The Romantic Englishwoman *is a sophisticated comedy of love and manners starring two-time Academy Award winner Glenda Jackson, Michael Caine, and Helmut Berger. The San Francisco Chronicle called it "a sardonic comedy finely edged with literate, astringent humor . . . a beautifully made, stunningly mounted work." Directed by the internationally famed Joseph Losey and co-scripted by Tom Stoppard (*Rosencrantz and Guildenstern Are Dead*),* The Romantic Englishwoman *is a film event for critics and moviegoers alike.*—NEW WORLD PICTURES

DEATH RACE 2000

Death Race 2000 was a science-fiction film with satiric overtones. It was a sly and entertaining comment on violence in our society. I believe in making films which work on two levels: entertainment on the surface, but with some comment or serious point of view on the subtextual level. So Death Race 2000 was a picture full of wild action and humor on the surface, with an implicit comment on the escalation of violence in our society.—CORMAN

If you've ever looked at Roger's pictures, you probably noticed that even the most depraved ones have a certain moral viewpoint—a political viewpoint, if you will, or a social attitude.—DAVID CARRADINE, actor

Roger called me and asked if I'd direct Death Race 2000, which I did. I also worked on the script. It was rather chaotic working for Roger then. There were times when Roger preferred not to communicate with me directly on this film. It was cancelled several times. There was somewhat of a disagreement on the comedy-violence mixture. I wanted more comedy and less gore. He wanted more gore and less comedy. However, in the compromise the film was successful. The MPAA made us take out some of the gore, and Roger compromised and left in some of the gags.—PAUL BARTEL, director

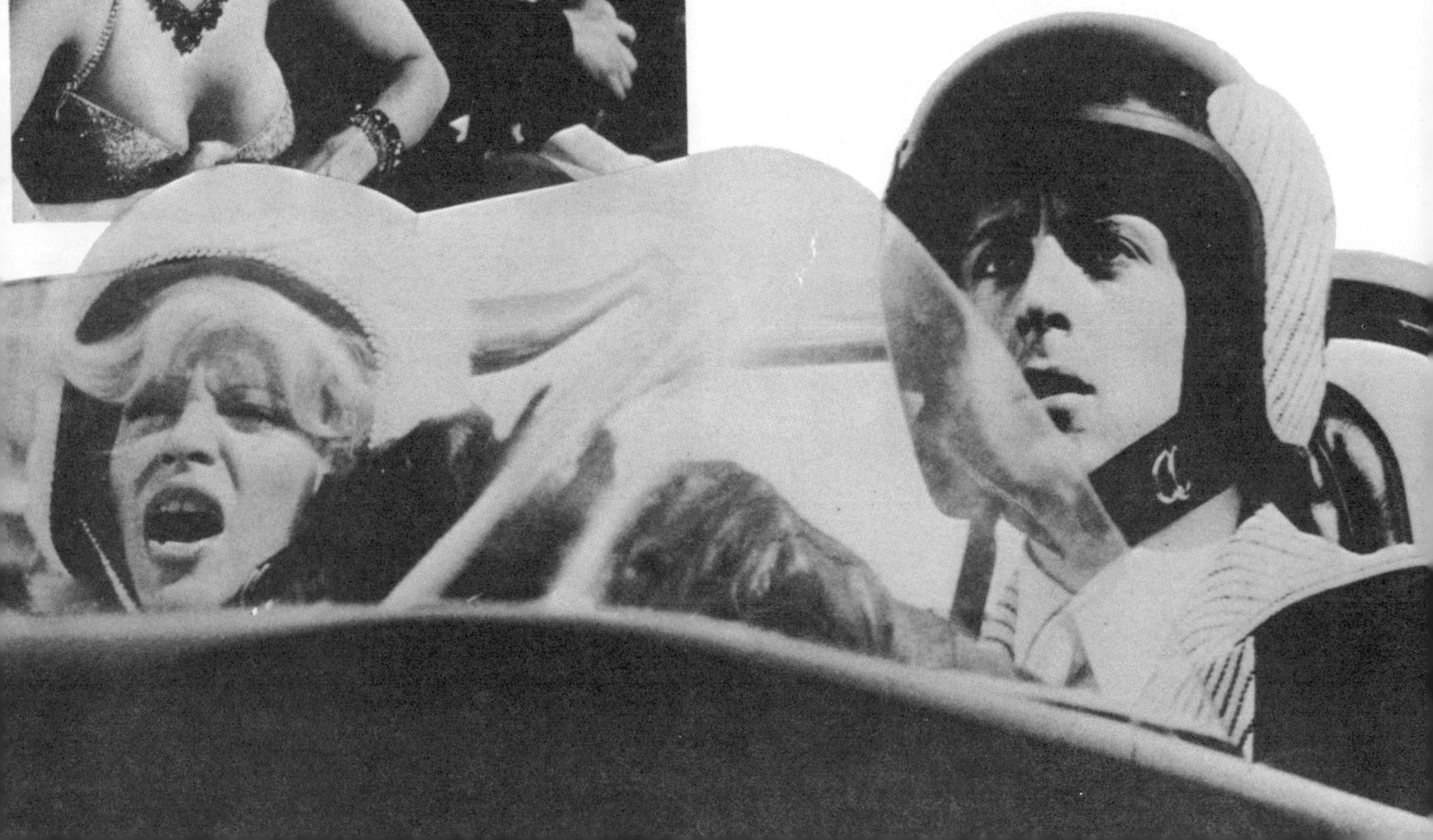

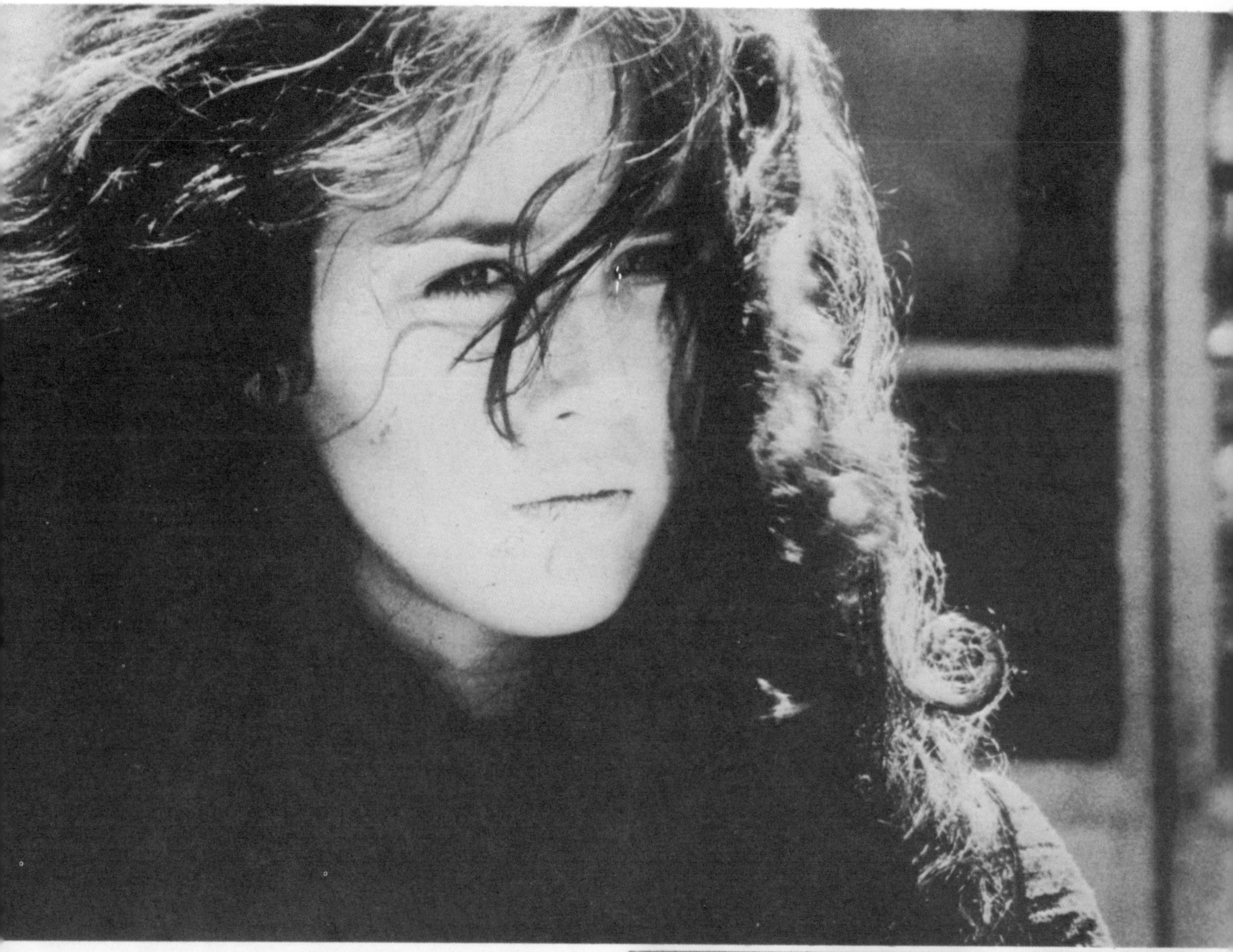

THE STORY OF ADELE H.

Francois Truffaut's *The Story of Adele H.* was the universally acknowledged hit of the New York Film Festival. Vincent Canby of the *New York Times* acclaimed it to be "profoundly beautiful," and the *New York Daily News* noted that it was "a tender, exquisitely romantic film, eagerly embraced by one and all. . . . Truffaut compassionately relates the bittersweet true story of Adele Hugo, daughter of French poet Victor Hugo, and her unrequited but unrelenting love for a rakish British lieutenant that began in the early 1860s and lasted till her death in an asylum." The film stars Isabelle Adjani, the beautiful, extraordinarily talented star of the Comédie Française.

With this picture I continued my plan to release the works of the finest directors. This was the first Francois Truffaut film I acquired for release in the U.S. The result was mutually satisfactory, and we then released Truffaut's subsequent film, Small Change.—CORMAN

In a Free Society Love Can Still be a Crime

THE LOST HONOR OF KATHARINA BLUM

The Lost Honor of Katharina Blum was an extremely well made German art film that played successfully in the New York Film Festival. We bought it from the distributor. It got very good critical notice around the country but was not quite as successful as some of our other art films, which proves again that in the art-film field generally, the director's name is a drawing card. That's one of the reasons I liked Fantastic Planet—because it was not directed by a famous director. Katharina Blum was directed by the husband-and-wife filmmaking team of Volker Schlondorff and Margarethe von Trotta. They shoot in an extremely naturalistic style with a very heavy political significance. I think they're very good, and with each film they get better. I consider them to be an important talent, and I think it's just a matter of time before they're really recognized.
—CORMAN

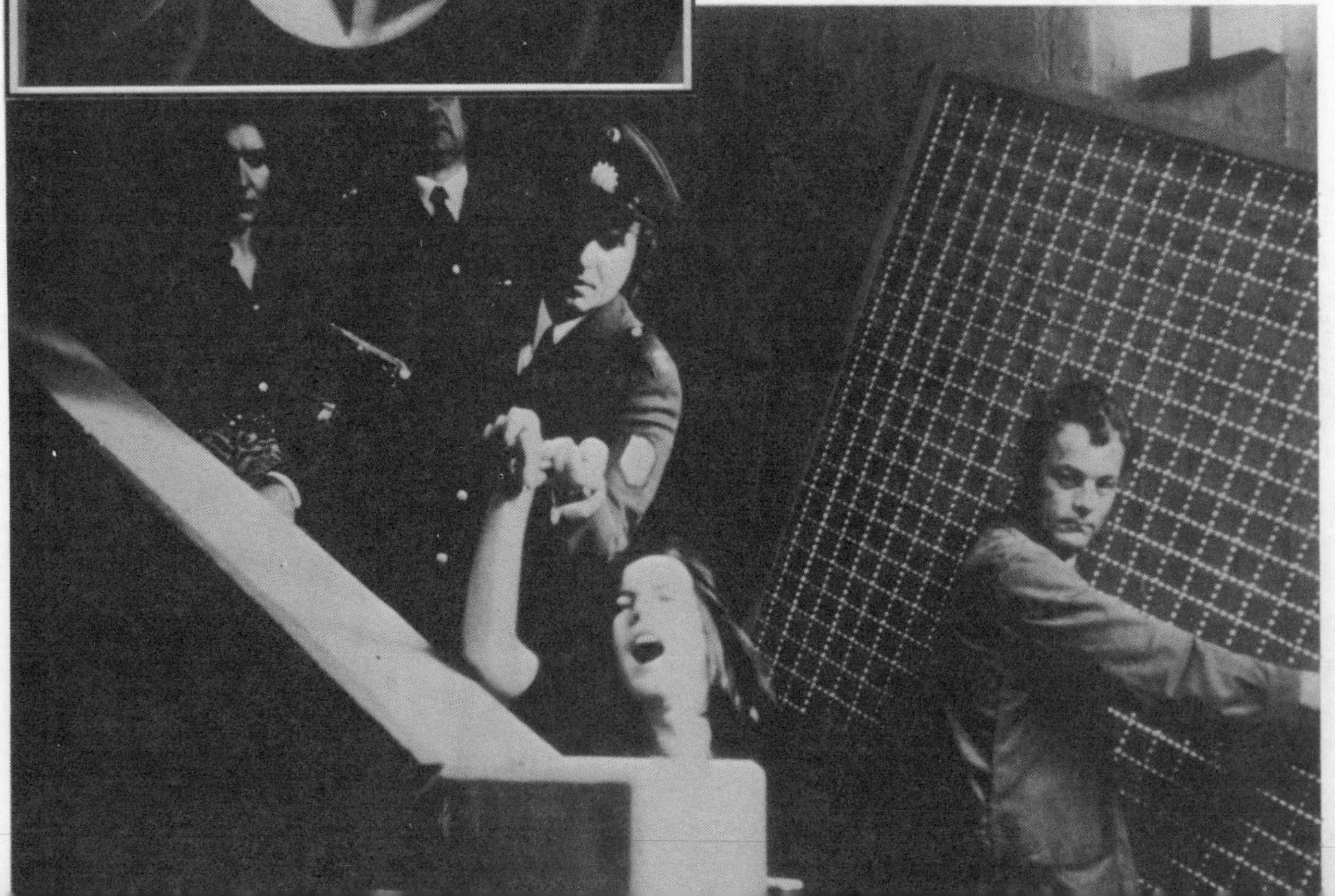

BETTER MOVE YOUR BUTT... WHEN THIS LADY STRUTS!
PG PARENTAL GUIDANCE SUGGESTED
SOME MATERIAL MAY NOT BE SUITABLE FOR PRE-TEENAGERS
DARKTOWN STRUTTERS
STARRING
TRINA PARKS · ROGER E. MOSLEY · SHIRLEY WASHINGTON · BETTYE SWEET · STAN SHAW
THE DRAMATICS
Written by George Armitage — Directed by William Witney · A New World Pictures Release — Metrocolor

DARKTOWN STRUTTERS

Darktown Strutters was a film my brother Gene had made for a company in Tennessee without a release, and when it was finished he brought it to us for release. It was the story of a black women's gang, but done as a comedy—it was truly a black comedy. In this film, the comedy was the most important element, whereas in most films of this type, we kept the comedy as the secondary element—CORMAN

COVER GIRL MODELS

Cover Girl Models again dealt with the story of women, only this time we switched to models. This was one of the last pictures we did in the Philippines. We found the prices rising very heavily, and one of the reasons for shooting there was that it was economically suited to low-budget filming—partially the exotic locales and partially economics. But as the prices rose, we retreated to the United States. —CORMAN

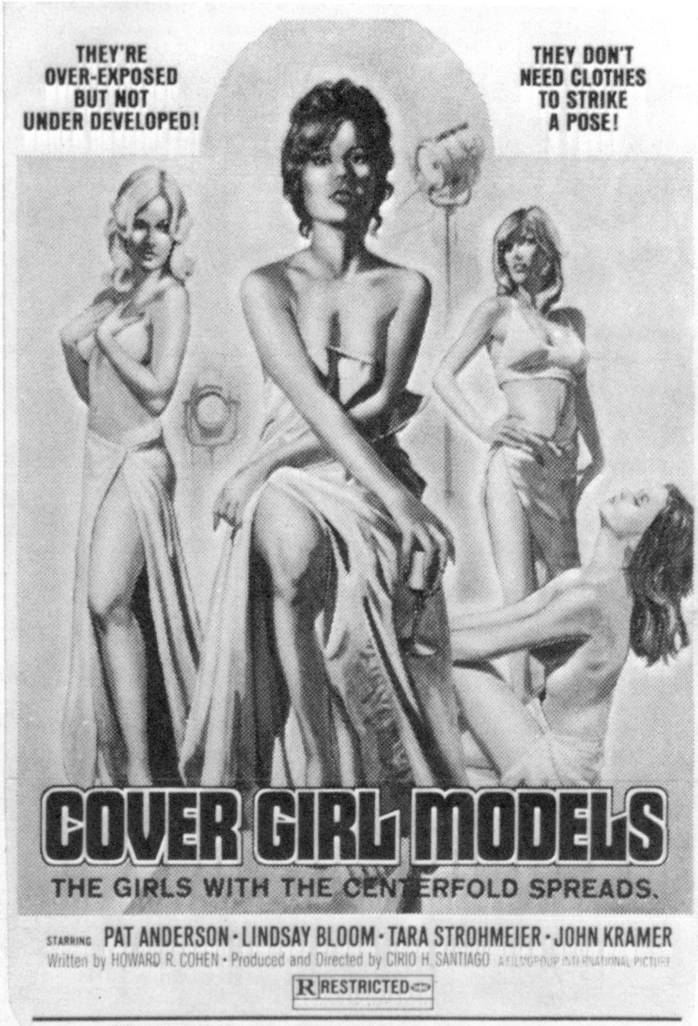

THEY'RE OVER-EXPOSED BUT NOT UNDER DEVELOPED!
THEY DON'T NEED CLOTHES TO STRIKE A POSE!
COVER GIRL MODELS
THE GIRLS WITH THE CENTERFOLD SPREADS.
STARRING PAT ANDERSON · LINDSAY BLOOM · TARA STROHMEIER · JOHN KRAMER
Written by HOWARD R. COHEN · Produced and Directed by CIRIO H. SANTIAGO
R RESTRICTED

CRAZY MAMA

This was director Jonathan Demme's second feature for New World Pictures, the first being Caged Heat. He is the most recent of the directors who got their start at New World to break through into major studio directing assignments.—CORMAN

TIDALWAVE

I took this terrible Japanese disaster picture, and I threw out everything but the good special effects the Japanese do so well. Then I got an American star, Lorne Greene, and I shot some additional footage with him. I made him an American delegate to the UN so that whenever the action got too complicated and you couldn't follow what was happening with this monster tidal wave killing all these people, we cut to Lorne at the UN and he made a speech that explained what was going on . . . quite ingenious, I think.

—CORMAN

STREET GIRLS

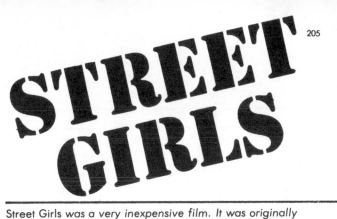

Street Girls was a very inexpensive film. It was originally shot in 16 mm. for about fifty thousand dollars at the University of Oregon. It was produced by Jeff Begun and directed by Mike Miller, and it dealt with the street life of the people hanging around the university but not actually in the university—just as groups hang around Berkeley and some of the other major universities. It was quite well made on an extremely low budget with a small cast and crew. The picture itself was reasonably successful, but I took it as part of an arrangement to bring Jeff and Mike into the company, because I thought they were a talented team. They went on to make their second picture—their first for New World—Jackson County Jail. It was a major critical and commercial success. Jackson County Jail was named on several of the ten-best-pictures-of-the-year lists, including the New York Times.—CORMAN

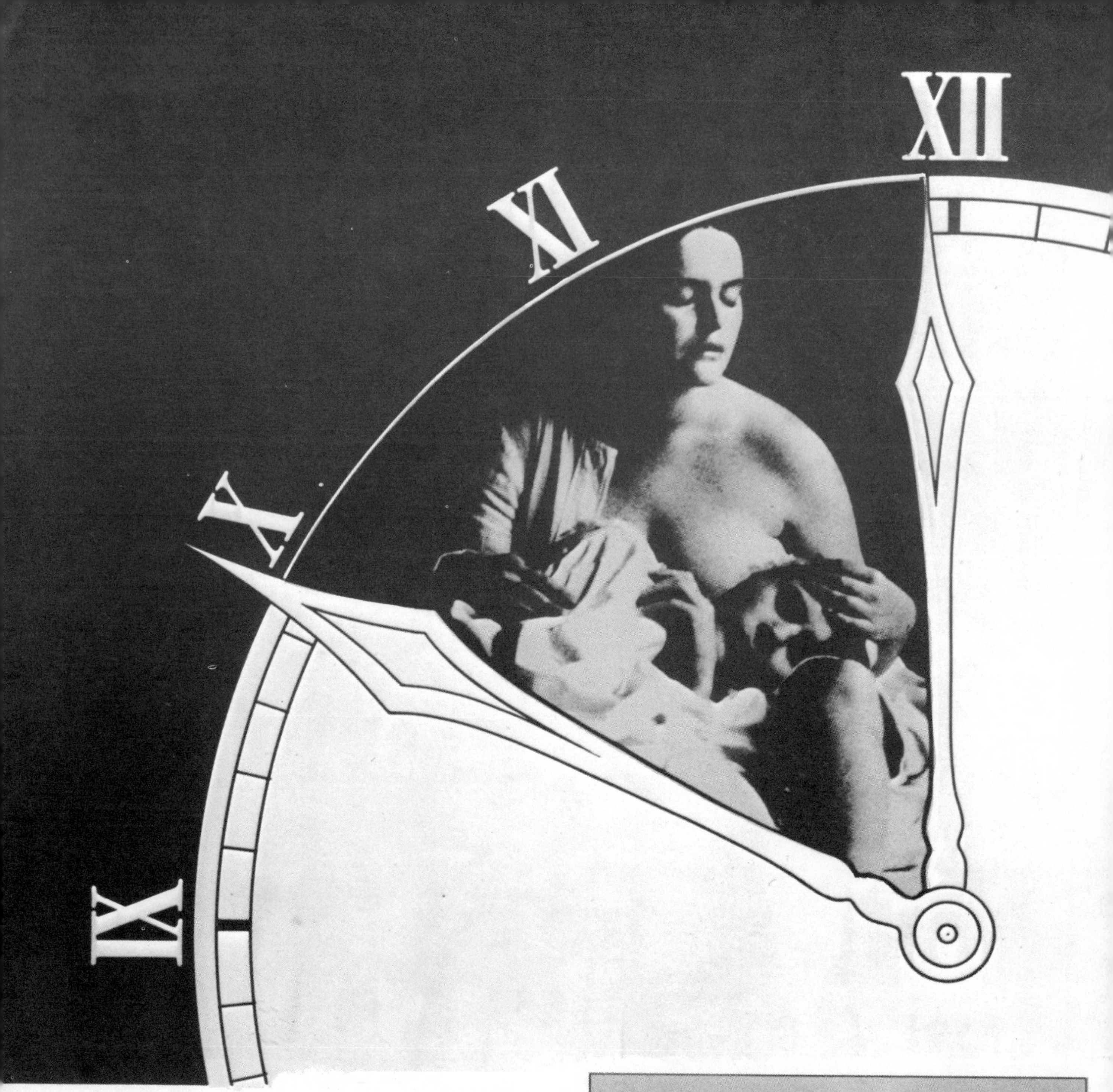
XII
XI
X
IX

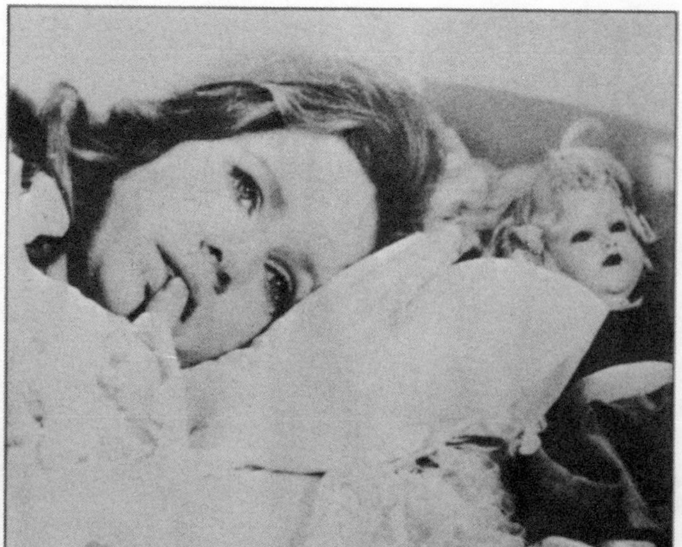

CRIES AND WHISPERS

Cries and Whispers was the first art film I acquired for release in America after I founded New World Pictures as a distribution company. Following some success and a secure foundation with the marketing of commercially oriented American-made films, I wanted to establish the company in the art-film field. I had always admired that kind of filmmaking and felt that the films made by some of the directors whose work I followed with great personal interest had not been distributed well in this country. I felt I could make a contribution in handling such a film as Cries and Whispers. *I take a personal pleasure in distributing this kind of film, and the company put a great deal of effort into it.* Cries and Whispers *became the biggest-grossing Ingmar Bergman film in U.S. history.*—CORMAN

To everyone's surprise, in 1973 Roger Corman came up with Bergman's *Cries and Whispers* after Bergman had become disenchanted with the financial returns from his previous American distributors. This film not only won the Best Foreign Film Oscar for that year, but also enriched both Bergman and New World Pictures by about a million dollars each.

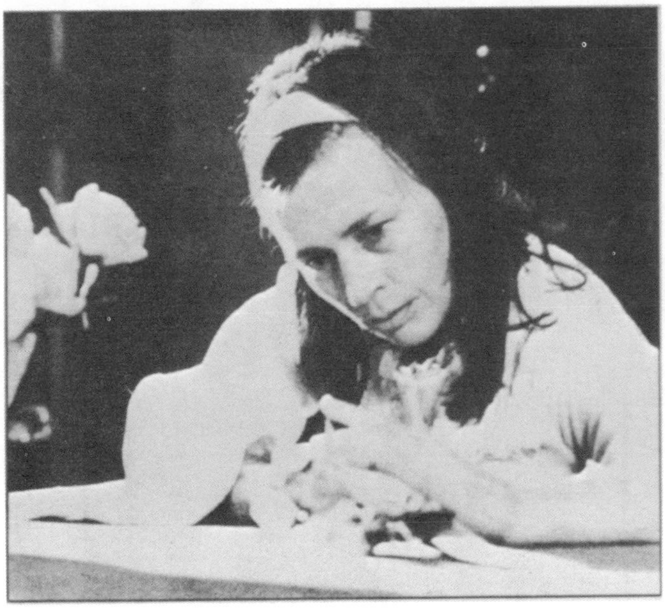

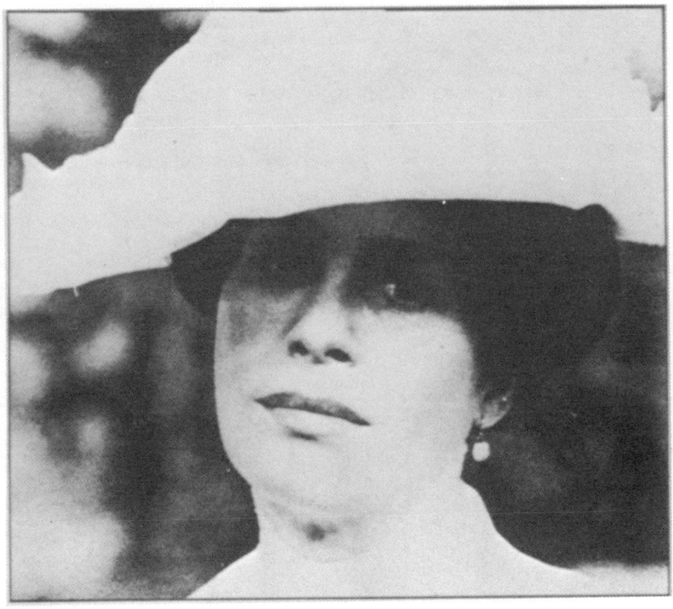

SUMMER SCHOOL TEACHERS

Summer School Teachers was a very nice film directed by Barbara Peeters and produced by my wife. I think the ones of that genre produced by my wife were particularly successful because she dealt with the problems of the girls so sympathetically and, I think, a little more honestly, or at least insightfully, than a man might. In the hands of Barbara Peeters, who is a writer-director, it became probably the strongest women's-lib statement of all the pictures we've made. It was also very successful, and I think the strong women's-lib statement helped it.—CORMAN

They Teach Things You Never Learned in School!

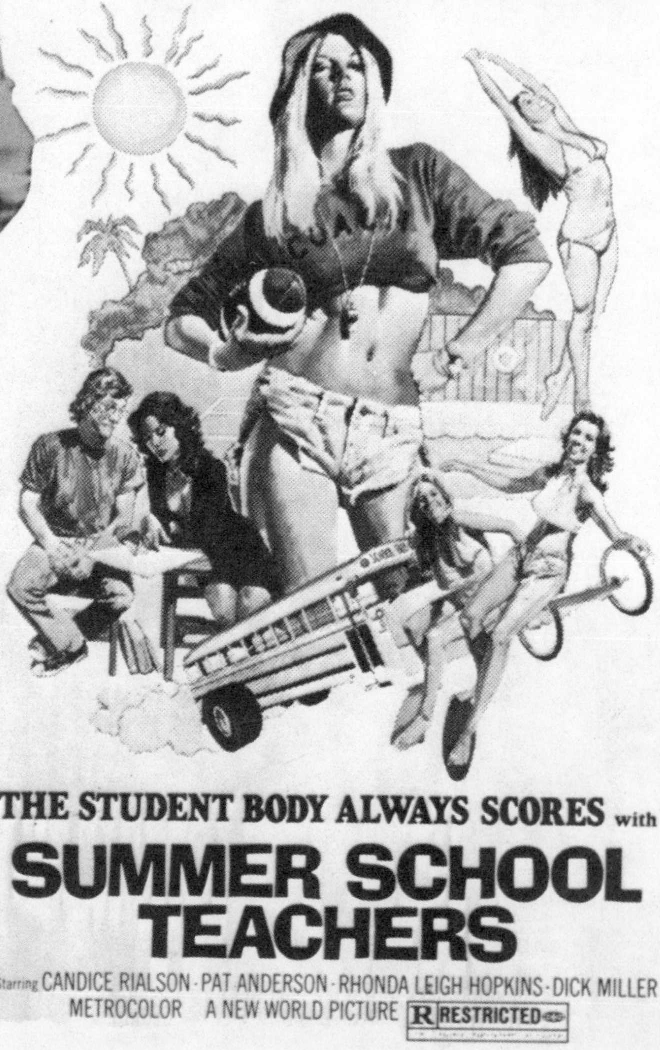

THE STUDENT BODY ALWAYS SCORES with

SUMMER SCHOOL TEACHERS

Starring CANDICE RIALSON · PAT ANDERSON · RHONDA LEIGH HOPKINS · DICK MILLER

METROCOLOR A NEW WORLD PICTURE R RESTRICTED

DIRTY DUCK

Dirty Duck was not a film we made. It was a film we acquired, and it was made by Chuck Swensen, an animator who had worked for Murakami-Wolf. It was an animated comedy that I thought was rather interesting, and it was modestly successful. Some of the animation was very nice, and he mixed live action and animation in some of the sequences—it was almost an experimental film in its techniques.—CORMAN

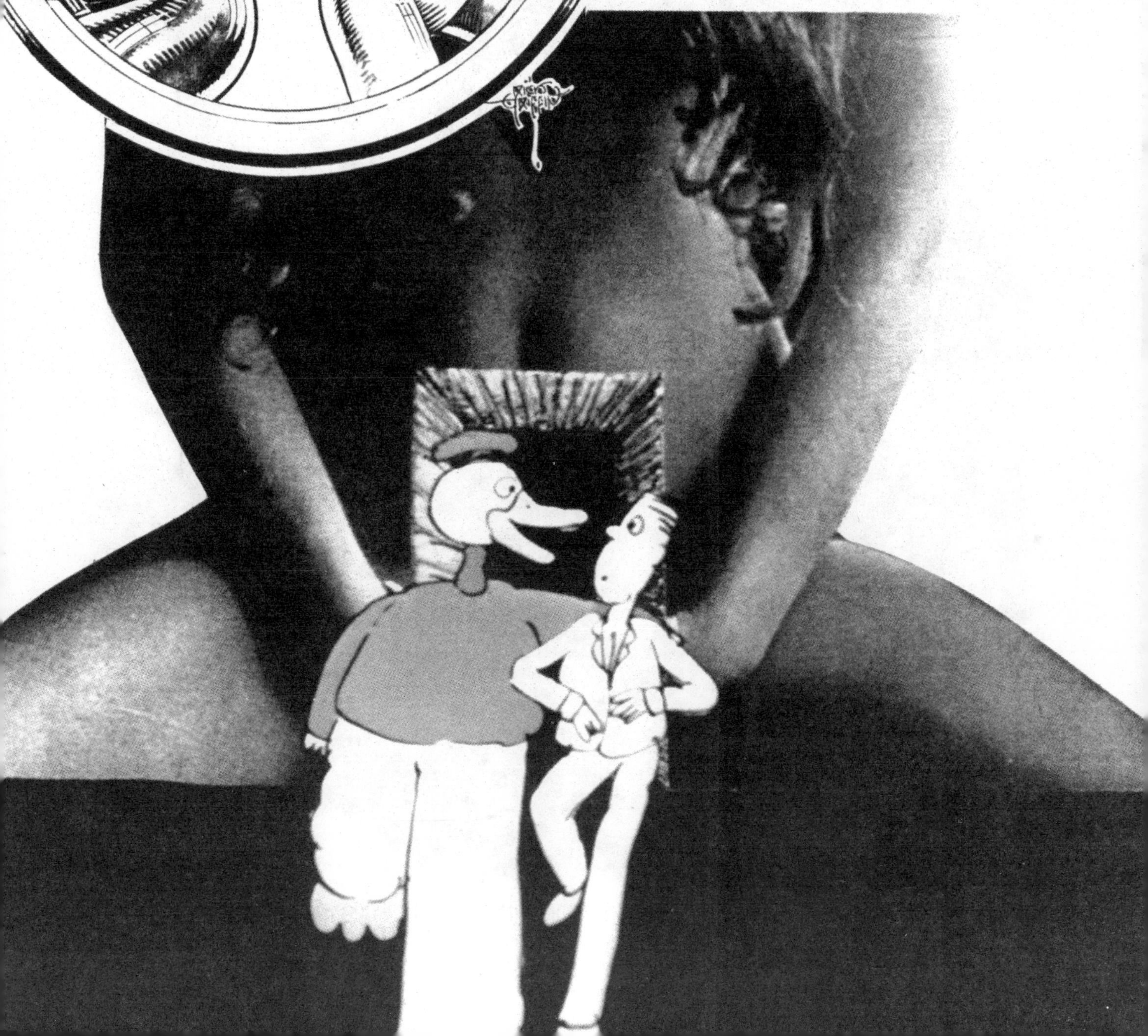

HOLLYWOOD BOULEVARD

It tells the story of some young people, actresses and crew, and their adventures making what looks suspiciously like a parody of a New World picture—or maybe five New World pictures. The budget was the lowest of any New World picture—which must be the reason I let them get away with this.—CORMAN

Hollywood Boulevard was billed as "the *Ben-Hur* of Exploitation Movies" and called "our homage to 'B' movies" by Jon Davison, the director.

CANNONBALL

The main thing is, Roger gave me movie stardom—and when no one else was willing to do it. Paul Bartel, the director of Cannonball, told me once that he stood and watched Roger's eyes turn from blue to black and then back to blue again. Somehow I can believe that, ya' know, because there is something supernatural about Roger. I mean, there really is. An ordinary human being can't change the color of his eyes, and one wants to think that Roger can, because somehow it explains the phenomenon of Roger.—DAVID CARRADINE, actor

NASHVILLE GIRL

Nashville Girl was a film made by Peer Oppenheimer in Tennessee, and it tells of the rise of a country-western singer. It was a very nicely made film, and we were very pleased with it. It was extremely successful in the South, as we had predicted, and moderately successful outside of the South. Surprisingly enough, it did fairly well in some European countries, which we had not anticipated.
It was directed by Gus Trikonis, who I think is one of the best of the young directors we have worked with.—CORMAN

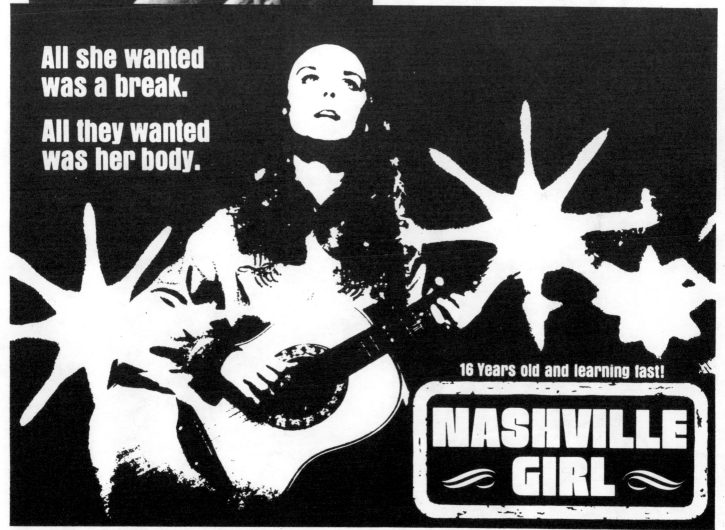

All she wanted
was a break.
All they wanted
was her body.
16 Years old and learning fast!
NASHVILLE
GIRL

NASHVILLE GIRL starring: MONICA GAYLE • GLENN CORBETT JOHNNY RODRIGUEZ
ROGER DAVIS • JESSE WHITE • Songs by Rory Bourke, Johnny Wilson, Gene Dobbins, Bob and John Wills
Directed by GUS TRIKONIS • Written and Produced by PEER J. OPPENHEIMER • An R. P. Service Co. Production
A NEW WORLD PICTURES RELEASE Metrocolor R RESTRICTED

LUMIERE

Jeanne Moreau said, "*Lumiere* [her first directorial effort] is about the life women lead when we are alone together." The framework is a story about four actresses—she plays one—and although their relationships with men and society are part of it, the focus is on their relations with each other, on the character and condition of women, and particularly on a quality that Miss Moreau calls intimacy. "I didn't do this as an activist or a feminist," said Moreau, "though I am for equality. But I thought it was necessary to show that intimacy that is only possible among women alone."

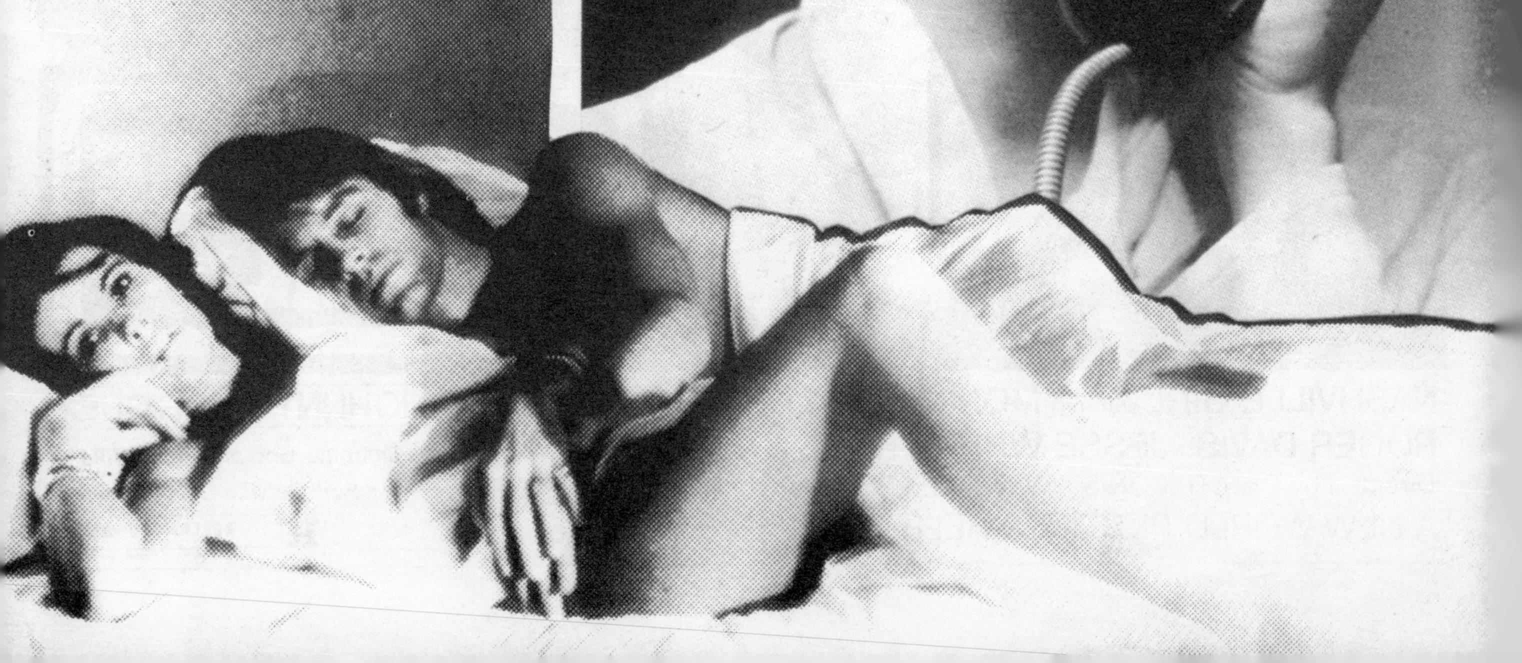

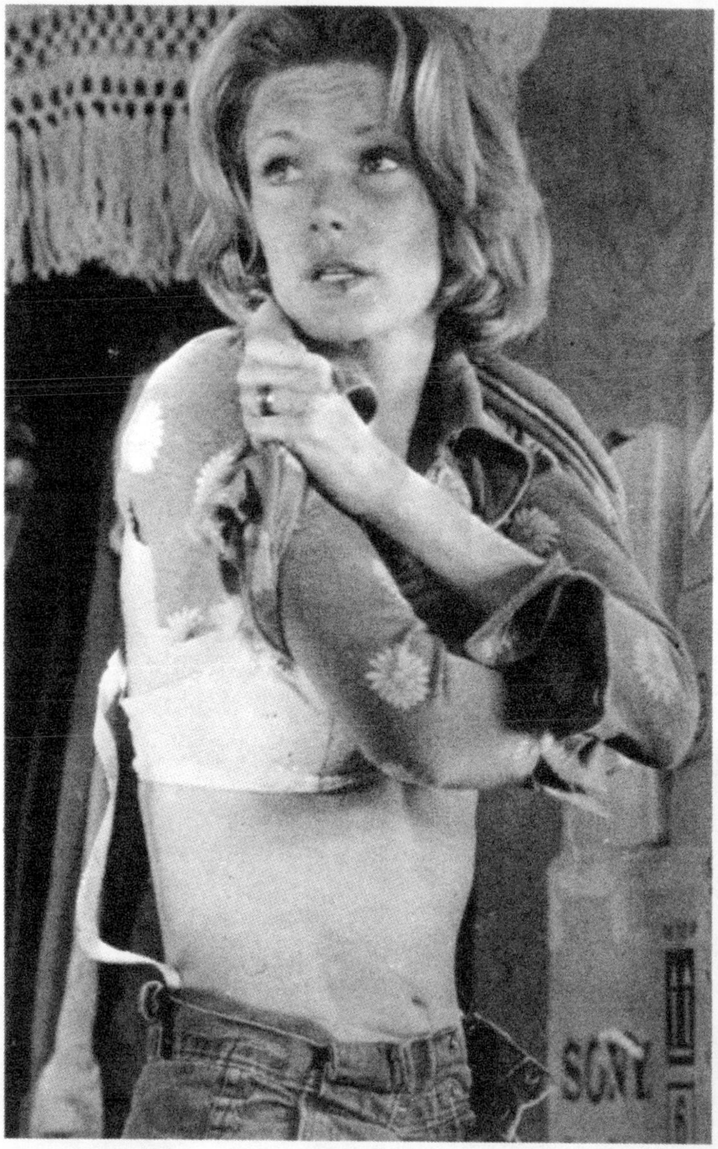

JACKSON COUNTY JAIL

Yvette Mimieux (left) and Tommy Lee Jones (below) starred in this film, which drew high praise from the New York critics. It shows a young urban career woman confronting the harsh realities of an America she never knew. Driving alone across country, she picks up a couple of teenage hitchhikers. They hold her up, steal her car and ID. Staggering into a roadside bar, she is booked by the local police for vagrancy and prostitution. In the small country jail, she is brutally raped by the night guard and kills him. She escapes with fellow prisoner Tommy Lee Jones. As fugitives they are pursued. He is shot to death and she is arrested to face a murder charge.—CORMAN

GOD TOLD ME TO

God Told Me To and Demon are the same picture. The title was changed when God Told Me To failed to draw audiences and, to some, gave a false impression of the nature of the picture. This picture is essentially a supernatural thriller in somewhat the same genre as The Omen. We acquired the picture for release.—CORMAN

DEMON!

Demon, written, directed, and produced by Larry Cohen, is a tale of eerie horror set in New York City. A siege of mass slayings terrorizes the city, and an intense young detective's investigation brings terrifying consequences when the mysteries of the past are revealed and the horrors of the future are foretold. Joining Tony Lo Bianco of French Connection fame is a distinguished cast including Sandy Dennis, Deborah Raffin, Sylvia Sidney, and Sam Levene.

—NEW WORLD PICTURES

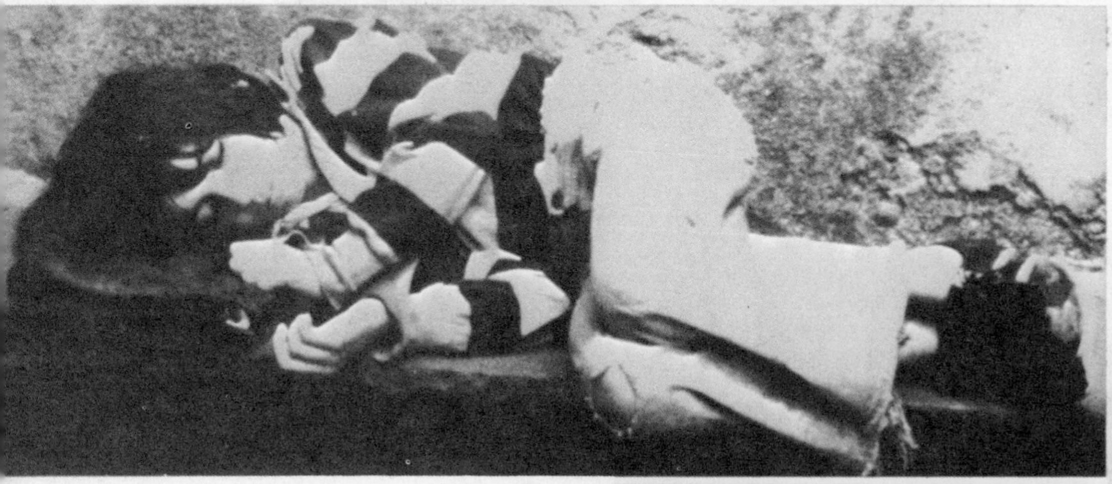

small change

Academy-Award-winning director Francois Truffaut directed this charming essay on a much-loved topic—childhood. Within the framework of a small French town, two hundred children participated in the making of *Small Change*, and it is truly a gentle portrait of the world that belongs to them.

The distribution of Small Change *was a continuation of my desire to bring recognition to the work of the finest directors, in this case Francois Truffaut.*—CORMAN

EAT MY DUST!

Corman sent me the script for Eat My Dust! while I was still a film student and a film buff. I liked Corman because he had initiated the careers of so many young people. He agreed to let me direct after Eat My Dust!, but the "givens" were that the film must be entitled Grand Theft Auto, the theme must be about young people on the run, and the film must be an action-comedy with car crashes. He also said that I must be in it. From these two films with Corman, I learned that he is a wizard technically and that he understands completely the making and editing of a film.
—RON HOWARD, director and actor

The wildest car chase ever filmed—see cars, trucks, boats, buildings destroyed!

The craziest driver in town steals
the fastest wheels in the state
and tears up Puckerbush County!

GRAND THEFT AUTO

As long as actors acknowledge what Roger needs from them, he is supportive. He is absolutely intuitive as to what will sell. He makes no bones about what he expects—he is a successful executive, and completely honest. Roger wanted Grand Theft Auto *to be the ultimate car-crash movie, but he pulled back on the money while we were in production. He is blatantly commercial, which gives him a certain courage to take chances on young people. He exploits everyone, and people leave only when they are no longer benefiting from the exploitation. His commercial sense always wins over the artistic.*—RON HOWARD, director and actor

THE GREAT TEXAS DYNAMITE CHASE

The Great Texas Dynamite Chase was a film about two girls from a small town in Texas who became bandits. It was quite successful, again because the action was treated with humor. Claudia Jennings was one of the leading ladies, and she was very good. She has been in several films for us. Both leading ladies were good, and the film was well made of its type. Michael Pressman, who was doing his first job as director, went on to do some major films.—CORMAN

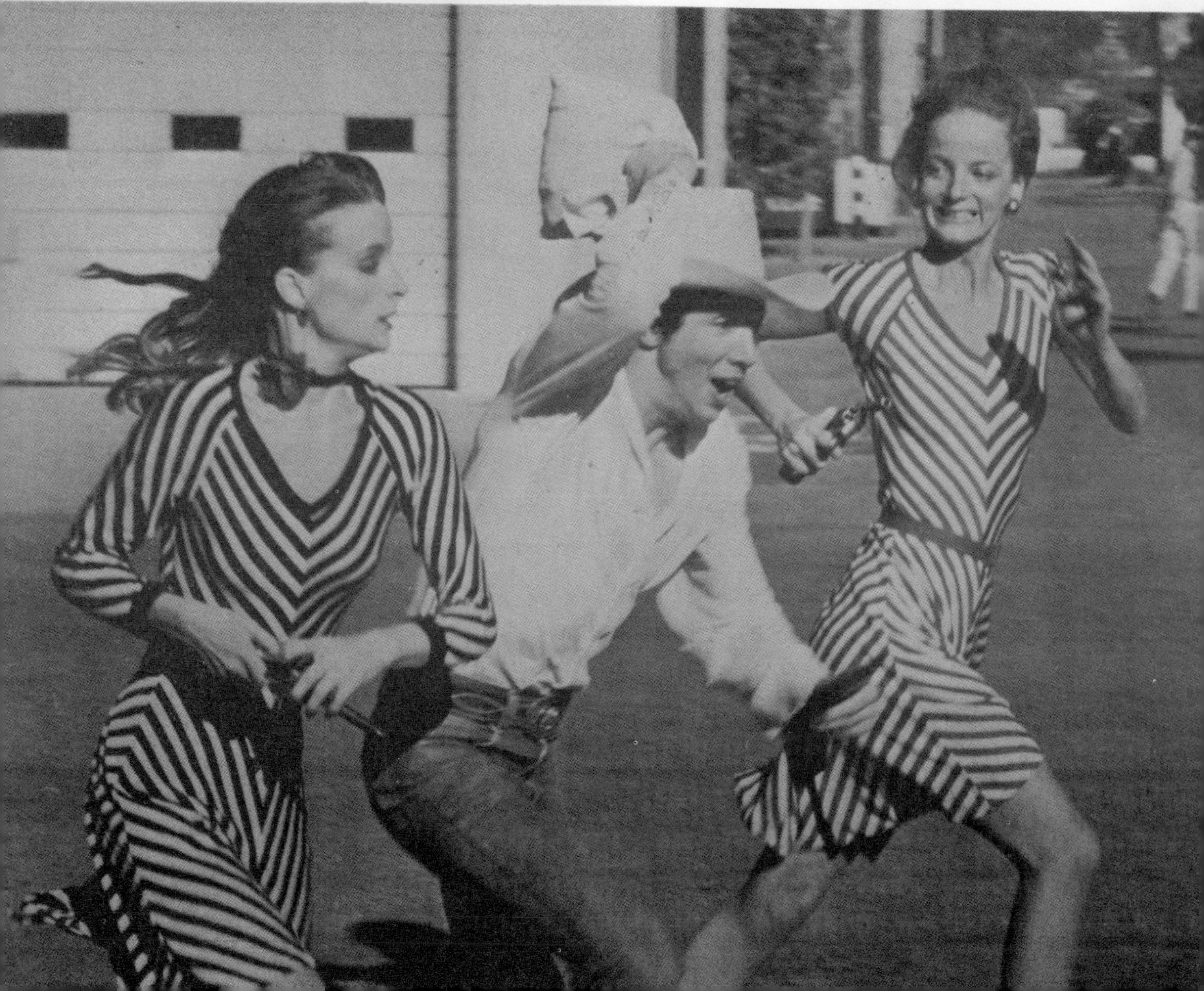

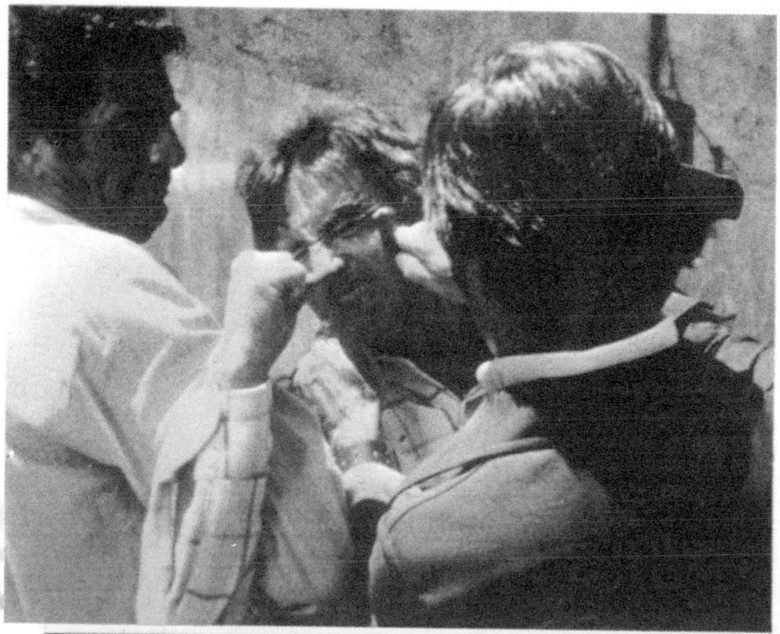

BLACK OAK CONSPIRACY

Black Oak Conspiracy was a film that starred Jesse Vint and was produced with money from Oklahoma, which was Jess's home state—he raised the money down there. It was moderately successful. It's distinguished most by Jesse's performance. He's very good in it, and I think he's one of the actors we've used several times who may go on to have a very important career.—CORMAN

CATASTROPHE

Catastrophe was a documentary of great catastrophes around the world. It was produced by Larry Savadove, and we acquired it for distribution. I remember specifically some really amazing scenes of a burning building in Rio and the crash of the Hindenburg.—CORMAN

Andy Warhol's BAD

Bad was an Andy Warhol film we acquired for distribution. It was a straighter commercial film than some of his earlier far-out pieces, and not as successful. I have a feeling that when the audience saw the name Andy Warhol they really wanted a more experimental-type film rather than a straighter commercial-type film. However, this was not really very straight. When you get right down to it, it was still a rather strange film, but it was a little closer to the normal commercial mode.—CORMAN

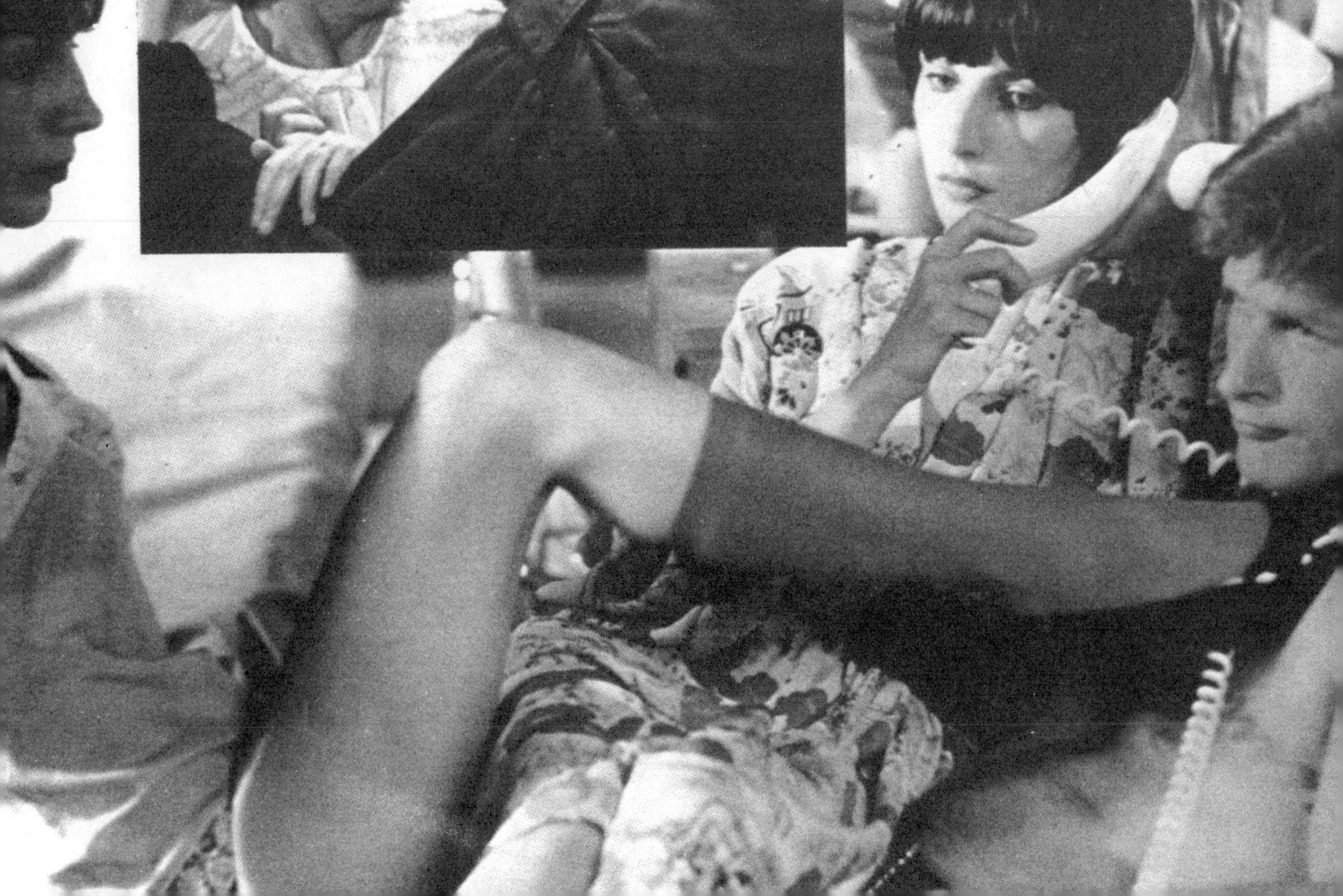

I Never Promised You a Rose Garden

Following the success of our more commercially oriented American-made pictures and European art films, this picture was my attempt to make an American film of somewhat more artistic significance. It was also the first film I have produced with a million-dollar budget. It was released in 1977, and the young girl was Kathleen Quinlan. It opened in Europe, has gotten excellent reviews, and has done extremely big business, so it has begun to help us overseas just as much as domestically. I believe that this film will be as important for the company as Cries and Whispers was previously. —CORMAN

MOONSHINE COUNTY EXPRESS

Moonshine County Express was a very successful genre picture that was produced by Ed Carlin, who worked for our company in a variety of ways. I liked it very much because it was an action picture played in the South that did not put down the southerners. It tended to be very honest. There's a tendency very often for people coming out of Hollywood and New York to consciously or unconsciously insult the sensibilities of the southerners, and I think Moonshine County Express was a success partially because it's a low-budget film that's quite well made and that presents a very fair viewpoint. —CORMAN

100 Proof Women
Runnin Shine Cross The County Line!
MOONSHINE COUNTY EXPRESS
THEY MAKE IT EVERY NIGHT.
starring JOHN SAXON · SUSAN HOWARD · WILLIAM CONRAD
MAUREEN McCORMICK · JEFF COREY · CLAUDIA JENNINGS
UNIVERSAL MAJESTIC, INC. and SUNSHINE ASSOCIATES present A DORO VLADO HRELJANOVIC and PAUL JOSEPH picture
"MOONSHINE COUNTY EXPRESS" Produced by ED CARLIN · Directed by GUS TRIKONIS
Screenplay by HUBERT SMITH and DANIEL ANSLEY
color by Movielab · A NEW WORLD PICTURES RELEASE
PG PARENTAL GUIDANCE SUGGESTED

DERSU UZALA

Dersu Uzala won an Academy Award in Hollywood for Best Foreign Film and the grand prize at the Moscow Film Festival in the same year. It's a beautifully made film—I think photographically it's one of the most beautiful films of our day. Then again, I was very proud of the film on the basis that it got both critical acclaim and commercial success. I can say it was a little bit long, and some people thought it was slightly slow. In every country in the world where it played it was cut by the distributors, except in France and the United States, and the greatest success it had was in France and the United States—which says something about making unauthorized cuts. We have occasionally made cuts in films, but we always make them with the cooperation of the producer and the director. We never cut somebody else's film.—CORMAN

Why did they call him MANIAC?
Because his plan was so monstrous that if it succeeded . . .
See for yourself why they called him . . .

MANIAC!

Assault on Paradise is the official title—we tried it once as Maniac, and it didn't work. This was a picture we picked up for distribution from some people outside of Phoenix, Arizona. It was a locally produced and financed film with some very good action sequences.—CORMAN

Starring
OLIVER REED · DEBORAH RAFFIN
STUART WHITMAN · JIM MITCHUM
JOHN IRELAND in "MANIAC" and PAUL KOSLO as VICTOR
Produced by JAMES V. HART Executive Producer PATRICK S. FERRELL Directed by RICHARD COMPTON
Screenplay by JOHN C. BRODERICK and RONALD SILKOSKY Music by DON ELLIS
PG

THE EVIL

An ancient horror slept beneath the elegant old mansion...

witness its awakening.

The Evil is another film produced by Ed Carlin, and it was very successful for us. It was a very good medium-budget horror film—genuinely frightening. It made people in the audience scream, and although we didn't produce it, we distributed it just as we distributed his other films, which were also successful. The Evil was directed by Gus Trikonis, the director of Nashville Girl and other pictures we distributed. I think, of Gus's films, this was the best that he directed.—CORMAN

A RANGOON PRODUCTION **"THE EVIL"**

STARRING **RICHARD CRENNA·JOANNA PETTET**

ANDREW PRINE AND **VICTOR BUONO** AS "THE EVIL"

EXECUTIVE PRODUCERS **PAUL A. JOSEPH / MALCOLM LEVINTHAL** PRODUCED BY **ED CARLIN**

DIRECTED BY **GUS TRIKONIS** SCREENPLAY BY **DONALD G. THOMPSON** R RESTRICTED Under 17 requires accompanying Parent or Adult Guardian

A New World Picture

THEATRE

a hero ain't nothin' but a sandwich

This picture won Best Film, Best Actor, and Best Actress awards at the Festival of the Americas. I wanted to release this film because it was intelligent and well made. It is not a "blaxploitation" film. There was a time when only lurid, action-oriented films were being made for black audiences. We now have the opportunity to present films of a better caliber which are intended primarily for black audiences but which have also the substance and quality to appeal to changing tastes in both black and white audiences.
—CORMAN

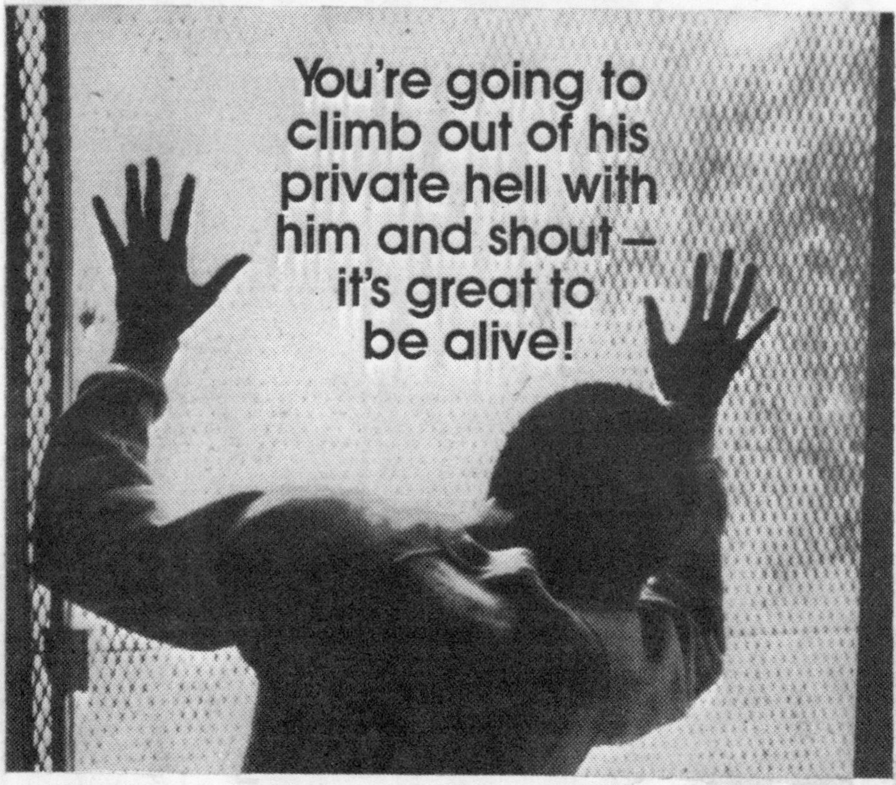

You're going to climb out of his private hell with him and shout— it's great to be alive!

RADNITZ/MATTEL PRODUCTIONS PRESENTS
"A HERO AIN'T NOTHIN' BUT A SANDWICH"
A ROBERT B. RADNITZ/RALPH NELSON FILM
starring **CICELY TYSON** and **PAUL WINFIELD**
introducing **LARRY SCOTT** also starring **DAVID GROH**
HAROLD SYLVESTER and **GLYNN TURMAN**
screenplay by ALICE CHILDRESS based on her novel
produced by ROBERT B. RADNITZ · directed by RALPH NELSON
ORIGINAL SOUND TRACK ALBUM ON COLUMBIA RECORDS & TAPES
MUSIC BY TOM McINTOSH, PERFORMED BY THE HUBERT LAWS GROUP
PAPERBACK FROM AVON BOOKS

PG PARENTAL GUIDANCE SUGGESTED
SOME MATERIAL MAY NOT BE SUITABLE FOR CHILDREN

A NEW WORLD PICTURE

A Little Night Music

A Little Night Music *is the most expensive picture New World has ever distributed. It cost over six million dollars and was a very lavish and beautifully produced picture. It was nominated for two Academy Awards—for art direction and music—and won one Academy Award.*—CORMAN

DEATHSPORT

We made this film as a result of the success of Death Race 2000. Deathsport stars David Carradine, and like Death Race 2000, it is a science-fiction action film with some implied social comment. It is less satirical in tone than Death Race 2000, since it is less a sly comment on the escalation of violence in our time than a speculation about the polarities of society in the future.—CORMAN

Roger is an enigma, a very contradictory kind of person. He is extremely hip and at the same time very square. He is a person who has vast understanding of the social inequities of the world, and yet he lives in a closed, rich community. Roger seems to be able to find a space of his own, however—right in between everyone else's space, or perhaps it includes everyone else's—I can't explain it. It's difficult. But ya' know, Roger is a genius, there's no doubt about it.
—DAVID CARRADINE, actor

AVALANCHE

Starring Rock Hudson and Mia Farrow, this film is the biggest New World production to date—the last film produced before this book went to press. Avalanche cost more than ten times the budget of the first film produced by New World, and we hope there is a corresponding increase in quality. It marks a turning point for the company, as we hope it is but the first of more productions which will be bigger in budget and scope. Currently shooting in Singapore, for example, is Saint Jack, based on the novel by Paul Theroux, directed by Peter Bogdanovich, and starring Ben Gazzara. Our plans for future productions include Robert E. Lee, Iwo Jima, Space Chronicles, and Volcano, all of which will be in the multimillion-dollar range.—CORMAN

FILMOGRAPHY

ROGER CORMAN

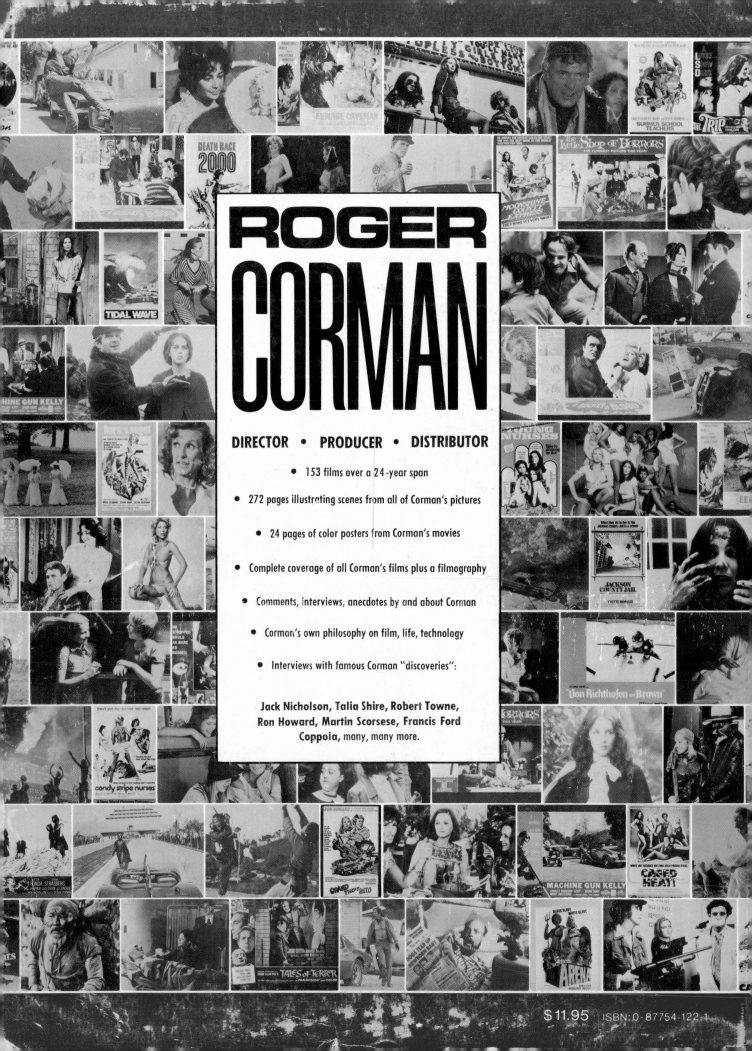

DIRECTOR • PRODUCER • DISTRIBUTOR

- 153 films over a 24-year span
- 272 pages illustrating scenes from all of Corman's pictures
- 24 pages of color posters from Corman's movies
- Complete coverage of all Corman's films plus a filmography
- Comments, interviews, anecdotes by and about Corman
- Corman's own philosophy on film, life, technology
- Interviews with famous Corman "discoveries":

Jack Nicholson, Talia Shire, Robert Towne, Ron Howard, Martin Scorsese, Francis Ford Coppola, many, many more.

$11.95 ISBN:0-87754-122-1